BRIAN CLOSE

BRIAN CLOSE

Cricket's Lionheart

ALAN HILL

Methuen

Published by Methuen 2003

10 9 8 7 6 5 4 3 2 1

First published in Great Britain in 2002 by
Methuen Publishing Ltd
215 Vauxhall Bridge Road, London SW1V 1EJ

Copyright © 2002 by Alan Hill
The right of Alan Hill to be identified as author of this work has been asserted by him in accordance
with the Copyright, Designs and Patents Act 1988

Methuen Publishing Ltd Reg. No. 3543167

A CIP catalogue record for this book
is available from the British Library

ISBN 0 413 77297 7

Typeset by SX Composing DTP, Rayleigh, Essex
Printed and bound in Great Britain by
Cox & Wyman Ltd, Reading, Berkshire

Contents

To Betty,
for scoring so well as a key member of the Yorkshire team.

Foreword

As a young boy in the 1970s, it was an immense privilege to be part of the Somerset team captained by Brian Close. He was a great leader and an exceptional man. Viv Richards would agree with me that Closey had a major influence on what happened to us in the cricket world. We will always be indebted to him. He taught us how to win gracefully and how to lose, not to enjoy the experience, but to accept it.

Closey is a man of dignity and a man of strength. He showed these qualities in abundance on the cricket field. He was one of the hardest, if not the hardest competitor I encountered during my playing career. There was the bulldog spirit of a patriot carrying his sporting flag for Queen and country. Physical pain he relished in Rambo style, as the hard man on the field. Anyone who saw him take the tremendous battering from Hall and Griffith in one of his finest hours, at Lord's in 1963, will testify to his courage.

Then you must look at him at the age of 45, defending heroically in his last Test innings against another West Indian team at Old Trafford in 1976. Closey faced one of the most awesome bowling packs that ever hit the cricketing scene. He took them on in a remarkable display of courage. If you cannot draw strength from playing with a guy like that, as we did in Somerset, then what can you do?

His former Yorkshire colleagues all said that they used to go out on to the field fully expecting to win. He galvanised us with this attitude in Somerset. Not the least of Closey's qualities as a captain was his ability to raise the standards of lesser players and make them play better. He told them what to do and they would go through a brick wall for him. Closey led from the front and expected the same level of commitment within his team. Everyone was expected to give it his best shot and no one was carried.

Somerset, known as the Dragons, scarcely measured up to this emblem until Brian Close turned up. The club was founded in 1875 and had won nothing over the following 104 years. Closey taught the team how to win and all the successes we enjoyed in one-day competitions from the late Seventies to the early Eighties were down to his instructions and the advice he gave us in the dressing room during his captaincy. He was the man who put us on the road and transformed a happy-go-lucky band, as Somerset was regarded, into the winning machine we became.

IAN BOTHAM
September 2002

Introduction

Behind the terse façade lies a sensitive and emotional man. Brian Close belies his septuagenarian status with a Peter Pan spirit. His enthusiasm is unquenched and bubbles forth in every sentence he utters. He has had, as one fellow Yorkshireman says, enough setbacks to 'sink the *Titanic*', and yet he has bounced back through all his trials to confound his critics.

Sporting prodigies carry the burden of high expectations. Close in his cricketing infancy was praised as a wondrous talent, gifted beyond measure. The buoyancy of the rough-hewn Yorkshire boy was crushed in an ill-starred tour of Australia in 1950–51. The failure to nurture an immature youth would deprive England of an all-rounder who could have vied with the greatest in the game. Fred Trueman, a friend from boyhood, laments the neglect of undiscerning elders in the corridors of authority. 'Brian was an extraordinary man with so much talent within one frame.' Trueman staunchly declares that this was stifled by lack of recognition. 'He was treated very badly by his country and, later, his county.'

All those, including myself as a teenager, who watched Close in his magnificent opening season testify to his thrilling command as a batsman. His power and supremacy at the crease provided onlookers with an early demonstration of the adventurous approach that always governed his cricket. Raymond Illingworth, another close friend and later an astute ally in Yorkshire's championship years in the 1960s, remembers the confidence of an imperious young giant. Close would groan with impatience as he waited for his turn to bat. 'Just let me get out there. I'll murder 'em.'

It took Close a long time to recover from his disappointments in

Australia. The courage faltered in the seasons of rejection by the England selectors. He seemed then, like Don Quixote, to be wielding his defiant lance unavailingly in a field of misfortune. The turning point in his crusade was his appointment as Yorkshire captain. This was always his true calling and the 'wise old owl', in the words of Bill Bowes, was immediately resplendent in his new role. Close's trials in the intervening years had given him insight into the man-management he had been denied as a boy. His legendary status as a hard and indomitable cricketer was then unfurled. It was dauntlessly expressed in his historic duel with the West Indians Wes Hall and Charlie Griffith, watched by a rapt audience at Lord's and on television.

Controversy unerringly shadowed Close throughout a roller-coaster career; he won acclaim for his tactical acumen and adventurous approach before being abruptly ousted after alleged time-wasting at Edgbaston in 1967. An even greater indignity administered after 22 years of loyal service was his sacking by Yorkshire three years later. Somerset could hardly believe their luck when Close joined them to groom and harness the talents of a band of aspiring boys, including Ian Botham and Viv Richards. It was a triumphant swan-song for the veteran which was sealed by his recall by England, at the age of 45, to withstand the ferocious assault of the West Indian pace brigade at Old Trafford in 1976.

For this book Rachel O'Connor, Norman Threapleton, Harry Dean, Jack Lees and Peter Ellis have provided fascinating glimpses of Close's dominance as a junior in Yorkshire League cricket. Bryan Stott, a fellow pupil at Aireborough Grammar School and later a county colleague, has recalled the mischief and audacity of Close in school escapades and how he marvelled at the exuberant strokeplay displayed by his partner in their batting alliances.

Ted Lester remembers the exceptional prowess that aroused hopes of a distinguished future in 1949. John Dewes and Doug Insole, two Cambridge opponents on Yorkshire's southern tour in that season, and Trevor Bailey have supplemented Lester's impressions with their own measured praise. Bailey was England's leading all-rounder in the 1950s and his involvement in cricket spans more than

50 years. He maintains that Close was the best young player of his time and unrivalled until Sachin Tendulkar, the present-day Indian stylist, displayed his own uncommon artistry.

I have been indebted to the reminiscences of the late Bill Bowes in charting Close's progress to high estate in Yorkshire. Other county confidants have included Bob Platt, Bob Appleyard, Ken Taylor, Don Wilson, Dickie Bird, Sidney Fielden and the late Ronnie Burnet. They all attest to the unselfishness, the competitive nature and the exciting flair that brought Close respect and admiration during Yorkshire's championship years. Close, in Taylor's view, exercised powers of motivation to rank with those of Bill Shankly, his football manager at Huddersfield. 'We used to go out on to the field with Brian fully expecting to win,' recalls Bryan Stott. 'We couldn't see any reason why we should lose a game.'

Brian Close paraded a physically imposing presence on the field. He crouched menacingly without protective headgear in his familiar short-leg position. Peter Walker, another superb fielder with Glamorgan, remembers how he, along with others, could be cowed into submission. 'Memories of the balding pate, the huge forehead and beetle eyebrows and two intense blue eyes staring at me when batting still make me sit up in bed with a start during a restless night.'

It is the valour of Close's cricket that instantly spools back the memories. David Allen was one of his batting partners in what is regarded as his finest hour against the West Indies at Lord's in 1963. Allen ranks Close's innings on that occasion as without parallel for courage. The body bruises he suffered in the bowling onslaught, gruesomely featured in a famous photograph in the sports pages the following morning, might have been the work of a demented tattooist.

Many England contemporaries have contributed to my store of memories of a fearless cricketer. Their illustrious ranks include Ted Dexter, Jim Parks, Tom Cartwright, the Rt. Rev. Lord Sheppard of Liverpool, Raman Subba Row, Donald Carr, Arthur Milton, Tom Graveney, John Murray and Frank Tyson. Alan Davidson, the former Australian all-rounder, was another of my allies during his visit to Sussex last summer. Geoffrey Howard, a long-time friend and supporter of my work, has also revisited his winter as the MCC manager on the 'A' tour of Pakistan in 1955–56. Close was among his charges, one of many young players destined to represent England at full international level. Howard remembers a multi-talented sportsman who hated to lose at any game. Close was always happiest as a winner, even in light-hearted games of tennis and soccer on the tour.

Ian Botham has kindly provided the foreword to this book. As one of Close's protégés in Somerset, he remembers Close's genuine enthusiasm for cricket. 'It rubbed off on all those playing alongside him. You couldn't help but get excited about the game.' Close was the father figure to a host of impressionable boys. His wise counsel would provide the stimulus for a time of unprecedented success in Somerset.

I must also gratefully acknowledge the courteous assistance of the British Newspaper Library staff at Colindale, London. Jeff Hancock, the Surrey CCC librarian, and Rob Boddie, the Sussex CCC librarian at Hove, were other allies. They have, as ever, been unstinting with their help, placing archive materials at my disposal. My thanks are once again due to Paul Dyson for his comprehensive statistical work and to Mick Pope in south Yorkshire for other researches. I have delved profitably into the reminiscences of fellow writers, notably Jim Kilburn, the Yorkshire historian, and Jim Swanton, Neville Cardus, Raymond Robertson-Glasgow, Gordon Ross, Peter West, Rex Alston, Alan Gibson, Mike Selvey and David Foot.

Capturing and recording the great sweep of a momentous career could not have been fulfilled without the support of my subject. I am deeply indebted to him and his charming wife, Vivien, for their keen interest in the project and their hospitality at their hilltop home in Baildon in Yorkshire. It is beyond doubt that Vivien, a strong personality in her own right, has helped to keep her husband afloat amid all the vicissitudes of a challenging life.

The long summers of a cricketing gladiator did seem unending and there was widespread disbelief when Close at last departed from the first-class game. An irresistible wit produced one of the best comic sallies in his salutation. Eric Morecambe said, 'You know the cricket season has arrived when you hear the sound of leather on Brian Close.'

ALAN HILL
LINDFIELD, SUSSEX
SEPTEMBER 2002

1

Arrival of a Wonder Boy

'At eighteen, Brian was the best straight driver I've ever seen. He used to pepper the rugby stand at Headingley – and that's a big hit.'

RAYMOND ILLINGWORTH

A winter of torment could not have been presaged in a conversation in Wharfedale in the summer of 1950. Bill Bowes, an illustrious member of Yorkshire's pre-war championship team, was the host and his guest was Freddie Brown, the newly-appointed MCC captain for the tour of Australia in the following winter. The discussion dwelt upon the emerging talents of a brilliant newcomer. After dinner one evening Brown said, 'Bill, I'm going to take Brian Close to Australia with me, if the Army will let him go. What do you think?'

Bowes at once expressed his serious misgivings about the choice, although he knew from experience that his companion had made up his mind. He did, however, try to warn Brown of the harm that could be done to the young recruit. 'I pleaded in vain for Freddie to reconsider his decision, saying he wasn't ready for it yet; it was rushing him and he hadn't enough experience.' Bowes, as a Yorkshire newspaper cricket correspondent, was to write later on the sad undermining of Close's confidence in Australia. His verdict then was of a 'tremendous ability spoilt by moments of extreme spontaneity, and of determination marred by rashness'.

It would be interesting to speculate on the course of a chequered career had Close not obtained deferment from National Service because of a football injury in 1949. He should have been called up in February on his eighteenth birthday and his entry into Yorkshire

– and international cricket – would have been delayed. As it was, the gods smiled on a supremely confident youth in a momentous summer. Close established three records. He became the youngest player, aged 18 years and 149 days, to represent England in a Test match. He was the youngest Yorkshireman to gain his county cap, which followed national recognition, and the youngest all-rounder to accomplish the double of 1000 runs and 100 wickets, and he was the only player ever to reach this milestone in his first season.

The previous record-holder was John Neville Crawford, who performed the double when he was 19 and also represented England at that age. His prodigious feats at Repton School had led to him making his debut for Surrey in August 1904 when he was 17. Earlier in that summer he had crowned his school accomplishments by averaging 85 with the bat and taking 51 wickets at 12 runs each. His contemporaries claimed that he was the best schoolboy player there had ever been. The bespectacled Crawford was a fearless all-rounder, wielding a punishing brand of straight hitting coupled with medium-pace off-spin, in the manner of his Yorkshire successor. In his first Test in Johannesburg the following winter he made his highest score for England and returned home to make 1000 runs and take 100 wickets in his first two full seasons for Surrey.

The overtures when Brian Close burst upon the cricket scene in 1949 were persuasive and a telling expression of his credentials. Jim Kilburn, the Yorkshire historian, wrote glowingly of the thrill of delight which the young Close raised in response to his 'powerful and confident left-handed batting, his easy right-arm action for his off-spin or swing bowling and agility in the field. He was handsome in all his athletic pursuits.'

The rapid emergence of Close deprived an old campaigner of a deserved swan-song with Yorkshire. Ellis Robinson, a key member of the pre-war championship side, had to surrender his off-spinning role and reluctantly moved to Somerset. Bill Bowes, in his postscript to the season in the *Yorkshire Evening News*, dwelt upon an even more significant development. He considered that Close's all-round abilities put him at the head of the queue as a successor to Frank

Smailes. 'Close can be relied upon to bowl six or seven good overs with the new ball, then revert to off-spin, and, with the bat, do everything that Frank ever did.'

Herbert Sutcliffe was an impressed observer at Fenners when Close and two other Yorkshire trialists, Fred Trueman and Frank Lowson, made their debuts against Cambridge University in May 1949. In the Cambridge ranks were four future England players: John Dewes, Hubert Doggart, John Warr and Doug Insole. Insole, as captain, remembers Close as 'physically hugely mature'. It was said at the time that Australian and South African sportsmen, unlike their English counterparts, matured earlier in the beneficial climate of their countries. Close, standing over six feet and weighing twelve and a half stone, disproved the theory. By his mid-teens, he towered above his peers and had almost completed his physical development. He was, as Insole recalls, 'a big lad and a very hard striker of the ball'.

Dewes reinforces the memory of an exciting and aggressive hitter. 'We had heard that Yorkshire were bringing three inexperienced boys down and thought we should beat them.' The Cambridge expectations were confounded in a surprising upset. Close and Trueman, the latter described without apparent irony in *Wisden* as a 'spin bowler', opened the Yorkshire attack. Both Trueman and Trevor Bailey now believe that Close should have sought to develop his promise as a fast-medium bowler. He was sharp and quick, with pronounced swing, and superior to many available in England at that time. 'Brian was a better seam bowler than he realised himself,' says Bailey.

Close and Trueman shared seven wickets in Yorkshire's victory by nine wickets over Cambridge. 'Both acquitted themselves commendably,' reported Jim Kilburn in the *Yorkshire Post*. 'Their quality was precisely according to less excitable expectations; there was enthusiasm, obvious natural talent and anyone who looks for much more in 18-year-olds in first-class company is approaching myopia.'

The celebrations of Yorkshire's young men were tempered when Oxford turned the tables over the visitors in the following match at the Parks. The captaincy of Clive Van Ryneveld prevailed in the university's win by 69 runs. Close, armed with his off-spin, took eight wickets in the match. Chesterton, Bartlett and Whitcombe provided the bowling counter. They were taut in their accuracy as Oxford recorded their first victory over Yorkshire since 1896.

At Oxford, Close batted for over an hour for 36 before he was beaten and bowled by Whitcombe. 'He should be a happy cricketer,' wrote Jim Kilburn. 'His little innings was an essential part of the day's play. It was an innings of struggle in difficult times and played with a cool head and a cheerful heart against the background of defeat.'

Of the other batsmen, Harry Halliday must have pleased Herbert Sutcliffe, his fellow Pudsey townsman, with a first-innings century at Fenners. But the batting focus of attention especially fell upon the third and eldest of the county recruits, 23-year-old Frank Lowson, who shared a match-winning partnership with Ted Lester against Cambridge. Earlier in the year, Lowson had resigned from his position as a clerk in a Bradford insurance office and pledged his future to cricket.

Lowson had been schooled in the fiercely competitive atmosphere of the Bradford League, joining Undercliffe at the age of 14. After service in the Royal Air Force in Gibraltar, he rejoined his home club and scored 800 runs in 1948 and a further 200 for the county colts eleven. The Bradford man, slightly built but endowed with deft strokeplay, was destined to play in only seven Tests against South Africa and India. He did, though, for a time arouse hopes of a distinguished future as an opening batsman. Leg problems, including surgery for varicose veins, deprived him of the rewards of his dedication. His batting was strongly reminiscent of his Yorkshire partner, Leonard Hutton. Indeed, he had so closely followed his example that he seemed like a clone of the master. There were times when his cover drive was so much a copy of Hutton's that people had to look twice to be certain who had hit it. It reflected, like a picture in a mirror, more than a little of the elegance daily paraded for his tuition.

On that Cambridge and Oxford tour in 1949 Lowson scored 78 and 66. In a remarkable first season, he confirmed the prophecy of Ernest Holdsworth, chairman of Yorkshire's cricket sub-committee:

'I have said Lowson would be a great player ever since he was sixteen and now he has proved my words.' Lowson placed the seal on his apprenticeship by scoring 1799 runs, the second highest aggregate in a debut season, which was only exceeded by Herbert Sutcliffe.

Ted Lester, a prolific scorer in his own right in 1949, was in at the beginning of the careers of Lowson, Trueman and Close. He keenly observed Close on his first appearances for the county. In a telling tribute, he states that his young colleague on the southern tour was superbly equipped in all departments of the game and the best 18-year-old cricketer he has ever seen. In an amusing aside, he remembers teasing the abstemious Close on his drinking habits. Lester advised that the accession to adult company would require something stronger than orange juice, the youngster's preferred drink.

Jim Kilburn offered a typically measured response to the exploits of Close on the universities' tour. 'Close has the makings of a batsman as clearly as he has the makings of a bowler. He has the grace and balance of a natural player of games. He bowled some splendidly vital and accurate overs. The native artistry was evident enough.' Yet many would go further. For them, Brian Close wore the cloak of majesty in his opening season. His cricket communicated the joy of a born entertainer to the watching throng. Raymond Illingworth, with whom he shared a Yorkshire apprenticeship, was to become a key ally in their mature years.

Illingworth, like others, was in awe of Close's batting mastery as a boy. 'At eighteen, Brian was the finest straight driver I've ever seen. He used to pepper the rugby stand at Headingley – and that's a big hit.' He remembers that the ferocity was just as unrelenting in the old Winter Shed practice quarters at Leeds. 'The lighting was not too good there,' he recalls. 'You had to keep awake as the ball came whistling back at you.' Arthur Mitchell, the pre-war batting stalwart and then county coach, wryly told his bowling pupils, 'You'd best bowl out of the net.'

Trevor Bailey was another eye-witness of the batting splendours unfurled by Close in the match against Essex at Headingley in 1949.

Close also took five wickets, including that of Bailey – caught in the leg trap by Hutton. But it was the audacity of his batting that captivated those privileged to observe him. Close was unbeaten on 88, with a hundred at his beckoning, when Yorkshire declared.

Peter Smith, the England leg-spinner, took six wickets but conceded 83 runs, six of them from a straight drive which sent the ball soaring on to the roof of the stand. Bailey, who demonstrated his own growing assurance with bat and ball at Leeds, remembers a magnificent all-round performance by Close. 'My own personal reaction today is that I'm glad that I didn't have to bowl to Brian while I was at school. We were all astonished by his big hitting at Headingley.'

Bailey voices the view that only Sachin Tendulkar can match Close in his youthful fervour. 'Until I saw Tendulkar play at Lord's forty years later, Close was the best young player of my time. Brian was also a lively fast-medium bowler and a superb fieldsman.'

At Headingley, against Essex, Close shared a seventh-wicket partnership of 128 runs in 90 minutes with Alec Coxon. 'Close enjoyed himself hugely,' wrote Jim Kilburn. 'He experienced one of those occasions when it seemed more difficult to miss the ball than hit it. From the first over he was playing full confident shots, hooking the long hops and driving the half-volleys as though he had been in all day. He watched the ball too and suffered no rush of blood merely because he had struck a fierce boundary or straight-driven Peter Smith into the stand.'

Kilburn expressed his pleasure in viewing a handsome batsman in every degree. Then, toning down his rhetoric, perhaps aware that his eulogy had exceeded its bounds, he impishly noted that Close 'was given much rubbish to dispatch'. He did, however, concede that 'firm cricket had helped to originate the rubbish.'

The temperatures in Yorkshire were in the upper eighties in the summer of 1949. Close's batting exploits also touched the heights. In less than two months he scored 571 runs and took 61 wickets. There was hurricane hitting against Surrey at Bradford. His innings of 50 (out of 63 in 35 minutes) included three sixes and eight fours. He was selected for the Players against the Gentlemen at Lord's, top-scoring with 65 in the first innings and sharing a stand of 56 with Godfrey Evans.

The Players won by four wickets and Close also impressed as a bowler, taking three wickets – those of the Oxford University and Indian all-rounder Abdul Kardar, Reg Simpson and Freddie Brown, his future England captain, caught by John Langridge at slip. This was the occasion when Close, innocent of the social niceties then prevailing in cricket, unwittingly breached the strictly applied etiquette. 'When I got to 50, the Gentlemen's wicket-keeper, Billy Griffith, said: "Well played, Brian," and I just replied: "Thank you, Billy." '

Ten days later, he was astonished to be told that Brian Sellers, the pre-war Yorkshire captain who was then a member of the county committee, wished to see him. Sellers sternly reprimanded Close for his effrontery. 'In future, when you address an amateur, you call him "Mister".' Bill Bowes, wiser in the ways of the world, offered counsel. 'I know what's happened,' he said. 'If you have to address an amateur, just say what you have to say. Don't say Mister, Sir or anything else.'

Tom Graveney, as another erring professional, relates a similar incident. David Sheppard had actually stayed with him during one match at Bristol. Graveney was prompted, having watched his guest hit a hundred against Gloucestershire, to offer the courtesy of congratulations. 'David' was duly complimented. The offence was brought to the notice of the Gloucestershire captain, B.O. Allen, who delivered another stinging rebuke.

Brian Close was blameless at Lord's but deference was not his strong suit. With others, his opponents on the cricket field, he was in control and able to admonish them with bat and ball. At Bradford, in the August of an auspicious summer, Close blazed a furious trail against Derbyshire. Yorkshire, wrote one correspondent, seized victory in the style of a schoolboy thriller, scoring at the rate of two runs a minute and winning by six wickets, with five minutes to spare.

Derbyshire had totalled 491 in their second innings and Yorkshire required 185 to win in 95 minutes. It was a formidable task against the redoubtable bowling trio of Gladwin, Jackson and Copson, all of them England players. Norman Yardley reshuffled his batting order to put the hitters in first, starting with himself and Lester. Yardley soon fell to a brilliant diving catch by the opposing captain, John Eggar. Lester was then run out and Lowson's dismissal, caught by Dawkes off Gladwin, left Yorkshire uneasily placed at 68 for 3. Even more important was the fact that the clock was ticking steadily on. The target was now 117 in 55 minutes.

Raymond Illingworth recalls the entry of Close and the subsequent barrage of strokes, which produced near-delirium in the watching spectators. It was a vital interlude and Bill Copson was one bowler whose reputation was severely bruised. Copson, a former miner, was renowned for the deceptive pace which he engendered at the end of a brief run-up to the crease. He was a late starter in first-class cricket; at 17, during the General Strike in 1926, he had been persuaded to join impromptu games on the local recreation ground. He then, almost without breaking stride, stepped up into the Derbyshire League where he took all 10 wickets for five runs in one match. Copson made rapid progress into the county ranks, reserving one special feat – 160 wickets at 13.34 runs apiece – for Derbyshire's championship triumph in 1936.

Copson conceded 45 runs in five overs in his bowling spell against Yorkshire at Bradford in 1949. As Illingworth recalls, one of Close's two sixes rose mightily to land on the roof of the stand. The *Yorkshire Post* correspondent enthused: 'Close gave the Derbyshire attack a Jessop-like hammering, using his long arms to hit out with terrific swings. He scored 34 in 20 minutes, and his innings also included four 4's before he was stumped off Gladwin.'

Coxon and, notably, Watson maintained the momentum. The fair-haired left-hander, normally a sedate batsman, now took up the cudgels, piercing the field with a flurry of shots. The fifth-wicket pair took Yorkshire to victory in such a manner that the last 35 runs came in 10 minutes against a side still bewildered by Close's onslaught.

Close and Lowson, together with three other Yorkshiremen, Ron Aspinall, Don Brennan and Dennis Brookes, were selected for the

North, captained by Freddie Brown, against the South in a Test trial at Edgbaston at the end of May. 'They must feel themselves to be living in a world of complete fantasy,' commented Jim Kilburn. 'A few weeks ago they were on trial for Yorkshire, not even the possessors of a second XI cap. Now they are near to international level.'

Kilburn issued a note of warning: 'Neither is quite ready. Lowson cannot field well enough as yet and Close does not know what to do when things are going wrong. But nothing is more certain in this uncertain game of cricket that in due course Lowson and Close will be international figures.'

Brian Close was the first to emerge as a Test player when he was selected in July to play in the third of the three-day Tests against New Zealand at Old Trafford. Only J.E.D. Sealey, who was 17 when picked for the West Indies against England at Bridgetown in 1930, had then taken part in a Test at a younger age.

Norman Preston, writing in *The Cricketer,* was generous in his praise after watching Close at Manchester. 'Whatever future honours are awaiting in cricket, there is no question that D.B. Close is the biggest discovery in post-war cricket, blessed with the ideal big match temperament. He was first change as a bowler at Old Trafford and struck a length immediately. The next time he was called upon for a turn with off-breaks round the wicket, and Close was just as accurate as with his faster style of bowling.'

Close was to gain a reputation as a lucky bowler and his first wicket in Test cricket did owe much to good fortune. All wickets are acceptable and not to be begrudged whatever the circumstances. It was obtained off a full toss, which Mervyn Wallace obligingly swung into the safe hands of Cyril Washbrook at deep mid-wicket.

Close, like his Yorkshire senior, Len Hutton in 1937, started his Test career with a duck against the same opposition. 'Runs were more important than wickets on the third morning, when England's last six wickets added 77 in an hour,' reported Reg Hayter. 'Close failed to score in his maiden Test but he deserved praise for his effort to follow the correct policy of big hitting.' Close himself recalls, 'I was under instructions from Freddie Brown to go for the runs. The

Old Trafford ground was then used to its maximum limits. Tom Burtt, the New Zealand slow left-armer, was bowling. I hit it like a dream but Rabone, a tall lad, fielding out at long-on, reached back to take the catch one-handed.'

The pride of a young cricketer in his first season was also measured in the company of a batting master. Close, the apprentice, looked on as Len Hutton displayed his inimitable artistry in a summer that was memorable even judged by his high standards. Of his own achievements, Close said it was like a 'very beautiful dream, and never did I want it to end. But what was real was the batting of Len. Not the least part of my education was being at the other end while he scored gorgeous runs. His timing, his balance, the elegance and grace of his cover-driving, the way he instinctively picked the right ball to hit made me glad I wasn't bowling, but even more delighted that I was just there to see it. And I was in the same team as that great man.'

This was statistically the Yorkshire maestro's finest season. Hutton completed 1000 runs on 8 June. His 1293 runs were accumulated despite the irritations of three consecutive ducks. He exceeded the total by any batsman for a single month, beating the 1281 by Wally Hammond in August 1936, and also scored 1050 runs in August. He joined Ranjitsinhji, C.B. Fry and Herbert Sutcliffe in recording 1000 runs in each of two months in the same season. His 3429 runs included 12 centuries – and a highest score of 269 not out against Northamptonshire at Wellingborough. Only Denis Compton and Bill Edrich (in 1947) and Tom Hayward (in 1906) have surpassed this aggregate.

Norman Yardley at Scarborough presented Close and Lowson with their coveted Yorkshire caps on August 17. Twelve days later their jubilation was increased when Yorkshire became a joint championship holder with Middlesex. They had won their previous five matches and the honour was sealed in an exciting transformation in the fixture against Glamorgan at Newport.

Yorkshire had established a commanding position on the Saturday evening but few observers were prepared for the ensuing dramatic turn of events. On the Monday morning Glamorgan lost their remaining six wickets. Yorkshire then raced to 239 for 8 before declaring at the tea interval. It was a combination of spin and pace that settled the match, which was extended by an extra half-hour. Wardle and Coxon each took five wickets as Glamorgan subsided to 69 all out.

Optimism brought a spring to the heart as stumps were drawn on Yorkshire's championship season. The adventurous spirit of Brian Close had earned him many friends in Yorkshire and elsewhere throughout the country. Everyone wished him well. 'Nobody would wish to withhold congratulations and hopes for a famous future, and there is no doubt whatever that Close has uncommon natural talents as a cricketer,' commented Jim Kilburn.

His next words might have been a premonition; they certainly reflected the anxiety felt by other admiring bystanders. 'Hero-worship and success make for a very heavy wine and it would be a cricketing tragedy if unbalanced enthusiasm were to lead a young player into a mood of complacency.'

Neville Cardus was later to refer to the 'ironic imps' which bedevilled Brian Close and, in the beginning, lavished rare gifts upon him. There were no second thoughts about these riches in the corridors of influence at Lord's. It was a post-war time of famine and Close appeared heaven-sent in an hour of need.

At a selection meeting at Lord's in 1950 the decision was taken, against Yorkshire advice, to thrust Close into the touring side. Ted Lester remembers receiving the news from Norman Yardley. 'They've picked Closey to go to Australia,' confided Yardley. 'Brian [Sellers] and I told them not to because he's too young.'

The die was cast for the raw and inexperienced Yorkshire boy. 'That was the worst thing that could have happened to Brian,' says Lester. 'The promotion was too sudden; he would, otherwise, have been in the England team for the next twenty years.'

2

Born into Cricket

'In school cricket Brian was absolutely brilliant. I opened with him and he got all the runs.'

BRYAN STOTT

Each day, as he hurried into class, an evocative photograph produced a twinge of envy. It was mounted on the wall of the school corridor and depicted a prematurely grey-haired man, Hedley Verity, resplendent in his England blazer. The picture stirred the ambitions of Brian Close, who was following in the footsteps of a great Yorkshireman as a pupil at Aireborough Grammar School. Also tugging at his thoughts was the knowledge that Verity, like him, had begun his own march to fame in the rural township of Rawdon on the road to the moors.

'Tha'll never be as good as thi' dad,' was the challenging message issued to the young Close by local cricket veterans. In time, the opinion would be reversed; when Brian made his county debut, one Yorkshire player said: 'His father and grandfather were good 'uns but Brian will be t' best of 'em all.'

Brian Close was born in Town Street, Rawdon, in one of a pair of stone-built cottages on 24 February 1931. He was the second eldest of a family of five boys and a girl. His father, Harry, who worked as a weaver at a mill in nearby Guiseley, was an accomplished wicket-keeper and hard-hitting batsman. He would have been good enough, says Brian, to have represented Yorkshire but for the plentiful talents available to the county in the years before the Second World War.

Harry Close played for Undercliffe in the Bradford League before moving into the ranks of the East Leeds club. At Rawdon, Brian, as a schoolboy, played with his father, as had Close senior with his own father at Undercliffe. 'I was very fortunate to inherit Dad's ability at ball games,' recalls Brian.

The elder Close is remembered as a man of dry humour, rather grumpy, and with very little small talk. His taciturn nature was probably forged by his harrowing experiences as an infantry soldier in the trenches of France in the First World War. He was undoubtedly a forceful character whose recourse to gamesmanship could place him at odds with opponents. As a wicket-keeper, he wore pads as large as those used by batsmen today. The top part of each pad was allowed to hang loose, and as he stood up he would give them a barely perceptible nudge to dislodge the bails.

From one piece of cricket folklore passed down to Brian it could be conjectured that a similar artifice was practised by his grandfather, Bill, also a wicket-keeper, at Undercliffe. The incident occurred in a Cup Final against Saltaire. Harry Close also played in the match. One of their opponents was the legendary Sydney Barnes, as cunning as either of the Closes. The umpires were in a quandary when Barnes indignantly rejected a stumping appeal against him and at first refused to leave the wicket. Tempers flared and the row reached such proportions that Harry had to come to the defence of his father. Whether Barnes was justified in his complaint in that it was a case of malpractice is not known. The outcome of the quarrel was that grandfather retired from the game and his son moved to East Leeds.

Esther Close, Brian's mother, had also been reared in a cricket family. Two of her brothers, Dennis Barratt, a leading light at the club in the 1920s, and Claude, both played for Rawdon. Bryan Stott, a village neighbour and future Yorkshire opening batsman, retains a picture of unfailing welcome on his visits to the Close home. 'Brian comes from a lovely family. His mother was beautiful, so generous and loving. His brothers and sister have all been smashing and turned out super.'

Peter, the eldest of the Close family, first worked for General Film Distributors and then, after army service in Palestine, joined the Metropolitan Police. Tony was a joiner; Kenneth, like his father, a weaver; and Alan was employed as a trades instructor in the prison service.

Mrs Close, cheerful and buxom, displayed a zealous devotion to her family. The management of six children in a small council house coupled with the attendant household chores meant that she herself had little time for cricket. She encouraged her husband to take the boys with him on practice nights and to Saturday matches at Rawdon. Brian says, 'We played much more serious cricket with other boys behind the pavilion and if we were beaten at cricket, we challenged our pals to a game of football.'

Brian's childhood was spent in council houses, first at Rawdon and later at nearby Guiseley and Yeadon. The modest dwellings had backyards within which his father provided early cricket lessons. He was a good learner and rattled the dustbins with shots to disturb their terrace neighbours. Home comforts were sparse but there were the more important blessings of warmth and affection to count in his upbringing. 'There were no luxuries but we didn't miss out on essentials.' There was only one family holiday to Bridlington before the Second World War to interrupt the year-long rounds of cricket and football in their seasons.

Brian's primary education took place at Littlemoor School, Rawdon, where he was taught by Grace Verity, sister of Hedley. Miss Verity, in her later years, would often remark on the impish nature of her pupil. The father of one of his friends was the village bobby, which ensured that he got a 'clout around his ears' if his mischief exceeded the proper bounds.

Two other friends were Hedley Verity's children, Wilfred and Douglas. The latter remembers one hair-raising sledge ride down a steep slope in the village. Shrieks of laughter were stilled in the rapidly accelerating descent. The sledge, with Brian on it, ran full tilt into an air-raid shelter at the bottom of the street. He was not quite out for the count but he was left only half-conscious. Douglas, almost as shaken as his friend, managed to drag him back home on the sledge to receive the ministrations of his anxious parents.

The perilous escapade was just one of many madcap frolics, but none was as potentially disastrous as an outing on a winter's day to

Larkfield Dam where nine-year-old Brian was again the daredevil. The dam was coated in a layer of ice sufficiently thick, as he thought, to bear his weight. There was a sickening crumble and he plunged through the gaping crevice in the ice. The frightened boy somehow managed, with flailing fists, to dislodge other fragments of ice to scramble to the side and safety.

Between times Brian was a diligent scholar to mollify his parents. He remembers their encouragement in the transition to higher education. 'They sacrificed a lot to see us through.' Brian was an outstanding student and soon after his seventeenth birthday he had passed his Higher School Certificate and seemed all set for university. Unfortunately, however, this would not have been possible until after he had completed his National Service, which was due to start when he was 18. The subsequent delayed entry would have important implications for him as well as Yorkshire and England cricket.

Brian's choice of a career as a professional sportsman might then have taken an entirely different turn. His headmaster at Aireborough Grammar School, John MacDonald, said that his student had a 'first-class brain' as well as being a good all-round sportsman. He had wanted Brian to study mathematics at Cambridge, but his pupil would have preferred medicine as a vocation. After Brian had made his first-class cricket debut against the Universities, MacDonald observed, 'He could have gone to Oxford or Cambridge, not with the Yorkshire team, but as an undergraduate.'

Sporting prowess was, it seems, always destined to hold sway in Close's life. The fitness of a boy growing in assurance and strength was reflected in the flying feet which took him to and from his studies at grammar school. From the age of 11 Brian used to run around eight miles a day. His daily pursuit appears similar to the challenge of a long-distance runner. He would arrive at school before classes in order to play football or cricket. This involved a race down to Rawdon Co-op by the traffic lights on the Leeds–Harrogate road to catch his bus. The school morning finished at 12.10, and then followed another dash to cling on to a Sammy Ledgard bus to return to Rawdon.

There was still another mile and a half to complete before he reached home. 'I used to kick the table leg for lunch and play hell if it wasn't ready,' says Brian. Within a few minutes he would be out of the house and on the bus back to school for more games with the other boys. It was a hectic timetable. The bell had scarcely rung to signal the end of lessons for the day before he began another return journey. 'I would belt home after school for tea before spending summer evenings at Rawdon cricket field.'

Peter Ellis, who lived next door to the Verity family at Rawdon, furnishes another tale of the zestful boy. Practice, with others mainly employed as bowlers and fieldsmen, was rigorously conducted in impromptu games on Micklefield Park. 'When Brian was batting,' recalls Ellis, 'all the other boys would wait in vain for their turn.'

Errant behaviour might have been construed as mere youthful extravagance except that Close belied his high intelligence in other cavalier adventures in adulthood. The contradictions in his personality have baffled even his closest friends. Bill Bowes once said that if a student of human nature had taken Close as a subject, he would have found the study rewarding but at times extremely confusing. The analyst would, on the one hand, applaud him as a 'grand chap', and then exclaim, 'but he is a funny mixture'.

Bowes considered that in any frank and brief summary of his Yorkshire junior it was unlikely any two opinions would coincide. His own neat assessment was that Close combined the character of a wise old owl with moments of childlike simplicity. Bryan Stott endorses these comments: 'Brian was a very bright lad but at school and later on he has done some of the most incredibly stupid things.'

Stott's friendship with Close did not begin until they came together as cricketing juniors at Rawdon. It has blossomed in abundance since their adolescent days. 'I have a great affection for Closey,' says Stott. 'He has always been brilliant at nearly everything I've seen him do. He could play football, golf, table tennis, tennis and swim.' In later life Close followed his father as an expert snooker player, once beating the world professional champion, Joe Davis, in an invitation event.

An impulsive nature, which is both endearing and irritating, has governed Close's life. Stott, three years his junior, recalls one instance of Brian's incorrigible playfulness during their days together at Aireborough Grammar School. At the school there was a swimming bath which had a rough bottom and there was the hazard of scratches if you dived in too deeply. The boys would shower after playing football or cricket and then have a swim. Brian also enjoyed the routine but in his case it had inevitably to be laced with daring. Surrounding the baths was a walking area behind which were curtained changing cubicles, six feet six inches in height. He could not resist the temptation. Watched by his friends, their faces glowing with expectation, he would clamber on to the top of a cubicle and dive into the deep end.

He was rebuked for this foolhardy act but the audacious pattern had been formed by the time John MacDonald, as the new head-master, arrived at the school. MacDonald was a strict disciplinarian and, as Bryan Stott says, 'he tried to curb Brian but didn't really succeed.'

On another occasion, Brian asked to be excused playing football for the school in the morning because he was due to turn out for Leeds United Reserves in the professional Central League in the afternoon. 'If you are selected to play for the school, you will play for the school,' was the head's instruction. Stott recalls that Brian did play for the school – in his 'civvies' and pumps – and that even in this attire he was far too good for the opposition. Brian wore his proper football kit, the blue and old gold colours of Leeds, in the afternoon match at Elland Road.

Another Rawdon stalwart, Jack Lees, who served the club as player and administrator for over 50 years, remembers that Close was always the 'boss' as a young boy. 'He was straightforward and spoke his mind and was frightened of nothing then or later.' Brian was a jack of all sporting trades at school. He was a fast bowler, opening bat and occasional wicket-keeper and captained his house elevens as well as the school's football and cricket teams.

Aireborough Grammar School was unbeaten in six cricketing summers during Close's time there. He remembers the encourage-ment of the teaching staff and the 'cracking lads' under his command. Most of them were also league players during this thriving period. 'All our matches were played over three hours on Saturday mornings. You had to bowl the other side out in time-governed matches. So we would rattle up a hundred or so and then bowl the other side out.'

The briefest of lunch intervals followed the school matches before the Aireborough contingent went their various league ways in the afternoon. All the clubs, compressed into a small catchment area, were cricket nurseries of distinction. Each of them could be reached in a short drive. 'Two or three of our seniors had cars,' recalls Brian. 'We would either cadge lifts or travel by bus on to the next cricket venue.'

Bryan Stott, an attacking batsman in his own right, has vivid memories of Close's leadership qualities. 'In school cricket he was absolutely brilliant. I used to open with him and he got all the runs. I perhaps scored 20 while he raced to a hundred.'

One of the most eagerly awaited fixtures on the school calendar was the match against Harrogate Grammar School. This was a big school with one wall directly facing the sports fields. Stott says, 'Brian used to take great delight in hitting the ball over the school or at the windows.' In one match at Harrogate, Close was at his exuberant best, flaying the home attack to score yet another century. Stott, his patient partner, was lost in admiration, once again marvelling at the effortless batting parade. 'All the time he was peppering those walls with his shots.'

Harry Close always sought to ensure that his son was given priority, wherever possible, in his cricket apprenticeship. In one match at Rawdon, he incurred the anger of the club captain. Close senior's instruction to his son to pad up ahead of him was of little consequence in the context of the game, but the Rawdon captain, rightly aggrieved that his authority had been overruled, strongly objected to the change in the batting order. Harry was, as ever, seeking to advance the claims of his boy. He thought that the minor infringement was justified in the circumstances.

At the age of 11, in 1942, Brian made his first appearance for Rawdon against Guiseley in an evening match in the Airedale and

Wharfedale Junior Under-18 League. It was a modest beginning, 11 not out as a tail-ender; but in the following match against Horsforth he shone as a bowler. 'Ken Worthy, our captain, called me up out of the wilderness in the deep and I took five wickets for 19 runs.'

As a result of his performances in the Junior Under-18 XI, Brian was promoted to play for the Rawdon second team that year but at the end of the season, when there was a late withdrawal, he was called up for first team duties against Menston in the Airedale and Wharfedale Senior League. He scored 11 and took two wickets, including that of Stanley Raper, the former Yorkshire Colts' captain.

Four years later Brian left Rawdon for Guiseley and the attentive county scouts acknowledged his progress by selecting him for the Yorkshire Federation Boys' team against Sussex at Harrogate. One of his mentors was George Hirst, the revered Yorkshire veteran. Brian was immensely favoured by the visit of the county coach to Rawdon to inspect him as a schoolboy. It was tantamount to the arrival of royalty in the Yorkshire village. 'He was like a god to all us youngsters,' he recalls.

Norman Threapleton, the current Guiseley president, remembers Close's time at the Netherfield Park ground. 'Brian just dominated junior cricket in the area,' he says. One instance of the authority displayed by Close occurred in a first eleven match against North Leeds. Guiseley were proceeding smoothly towards their victory target, then about 30 runs away. Threapleton, who had opened the batting, needed only a dozen runs for his fifty. 'I looked up at the scoreboard and thought, there are just enough runs left to enable me to reach this score.' He had not anticipated that another batsman would intervene to prevent this achievement. 'In marched Brian Close at number seven and I never got another ball. He knocked the lot off, all good cricket shots and no slogging, and I was standing at the other end just watching him.'

Threapleton also recalls the contributions of Close's brothers, Ken and Alan, at Guiseley. 'Ken was a very good second eleven player and got runs with them.' Alan, who also played rugby, he describes as 'quite a card . . . He used to wear a Yorkshire sweater passed down to him by his brother.' The younger Close wore glasses and was then working as a paint sprayer. 'Alan would come along to matches bespattered with paint. He did like to hit the ball but was not serious enough about cricket.'

Guiseley were founder members of the Airedale and Wharfedale Senior League in the 1930s. Among their outstanding products was the locally renowned Claughton family, including Hugh Marsden, who played for Yorkshire before the First World War. Another was Jackie Van Geloven, latterly Master in Charge of Sport at Fettes School in Edinburgh. He had one season with Yorkshire in 1955 before moving on to Leicestershire prior to his appointment as a first-class umpire. Guiseley can claim, however peripherally, that two of their bowlers – Van Geloven and Brian Close – shared the new ball for Yorkshire.

Close never forgot that it was in the Airedale Junior League that he first gained a foothold in cricket. He and Bryan Stott returned to play and help celebrate the Golden Jubilee of the league in a match at Guiseley in July 1989.

Jim Parks, a future England and Somerset colleague, was one of the Yorkshire Federation Boys' rivals on their southern tour in 1948. Parks was an emerging prospect with Sussex at Hove but his experience was restricted to schools and club cricket. Close scored a century against Sussex but, as Parks explains, 'It was no contest. They were such a good side and all had played league cricket in Yorkshire. Compared with us, they were hardened pros.'

Sharing the plaudits with Close in the visitors' ranks were Fred Trueman, Raymond Illingworth and Gerry Tordoff, who later played for the Royal Navy and Somerset. Parks remembers Close as a 'big lad', who ran in and bowled 'daggers'. Illingworth provides another telling perspective. 'Brian was as quick as Fred then – he had a lovely bowling action.'

The precocious talents that astonished Close's peers were always accompanied by an innate modesty. 'It wasn't in his nature to be big-headed and strut around as a boy champion,' asserts Bryan Stott. But Close was indisputably in charge during his one season at Yeadon, his final league staging post.

Yeadon, whose origins go back to the middle of the nineteenth century, were wreathed in garlands during the years following the Second World War. They were Bradford League champions four times and between 1944 and 1949 they appeared in four Priestley Cup finals and won the trophy three times. The club celebrities of this period included Charlie Harris, the puckish entertainer from Nottinghamshire; Les Berry, the resolute opening batsman from Leicestershire; Horace Fisher, the irascible but gifted Yorkshire slow left-arm bowler; and Jim Smith, the Middlesex and England fast bowler. Smith was also a ferocious striker as a batsman and once scored 50, genuinely obtained against front-line Gloucestershire bowlers, in 11 minutes at Bristol. Yeadon's professionals in 1947 included Ron Aspinall, the Yorkshire fast bowler, and the popular Australian Arthur Clues, the Leeds Rugby League forward who had played First Grade cricket in Sydney. Bert Cook, the New Zealand full-back and Clues's rugby team-mate at Headingley, also played for Yeadon as an amateur.

This was also the year when Bryan Stott departed from Rawdon to join the club where his father had given long and valued service. Harry Stott was a former Yeadon captain and represented the club for 25 years. As a 15-year-old, in 1949, the younger Stott played for Yeadon in the Priestley Cup final at Park Avenue, Bradford. Yeadon, after a lean league summer, were the victors against a Farsley team that included a future Yorkshire colleague, Raymond Illingworth.

In 1948 Close, under the leadership of Stanley Raper, won his own spurs with Yeadon in the testing arena of the Bradford League. After only two games in the second eleven he gained a regular place in the first team. He finished top of the batting averages, hit a century against Keighley, and was fourth in the bowling lists for the club. There was also one appearance in the Yorkshire second eleven against Nottinghamshire at Worksop. The match was rained off and he did not bat or bowl.

Close, aged 17, was old enough to captain the Airedale and Wharfedale Junior League eleven on midweek evenings as well as playing in the Bradford League. 'As a big lad, he kept us in order,' is the memory of Harry Dean, a former junior colleague who still lives within the vicinity of the White Swan ground. 'Brian was down-to-earth and blunt with it. He towered above everyone else and was the king of his castle. He was exceptionally gifted and it all seemed so effortless.'

Dean remembers one conversation in 1948 when Close was selected for the Yorkshire Federation tour of Sussex. Yeadon were heading for the title and Dean deputised for Close as the juniors' captain. 'Brian pulled me to one side, wagged a warning finger, and said: "Don't forget, you'd better win these bloody matches while I'm away."' After such a warning, the outcome could not really be in doubt. Brian returned from his exploits by the sea to find that his instructions had been obeyed.

Versatility as a sportsman was also evident in Close's fledgling years. Success as a footballer matched his cricket achievements. In his youth, Close believes, he was better known as a promising soccer talent than as a cricketer with a future. It was a time when it was possible to juggle the two sports, and many cricketers did so up and down the country. At the age of 14, Brian was on Leeds United's books as an amateur. Twelve months later he toured Holland with the West Riding F.A. Youth XI and subsequently became the first Leeds product to play for an England Youth team. In October 1948 he represented England against Scotland at Pittodrie Park in Aberdeen. Scotland won 3–1 but Close considers that they were indebted to the heroics of Ronnie Simpson, a future full international and Glasgow Celtic and Newcastle goalkeeper, in achieving a flattering scoreline. 'He produced so many brilliant saves.'

At Leeds, under the managership of Billy Hampson, Close played for the Central League side soon after his sixteenth birthday. His colleagues included the captain, Tom Holley, a centre-half in the stopper mould whose long legs would smother opponents in sweeping last-ditch tackles. There was the right-wing combination of David Cochrane and Aubrey Powell. Cochrane from Portadown in Northern Ireland, was a wizard to rank, in Yorkshire eyes at least, with Finney or Matthews when he was on song. His Welsh partner, Powell, with grooming to match his deft footwork, was the forager who clove the gaps for Cochrane's tricks.

The arrival of Major Frank Buckley as manager brought about a change in the regime at Elland Road. Buckley will always be known for his discovery of the great Welshman John Charles and his signing by Leeds from the Swansea area. Charles was a truly gifted player, remembered for his lithe power and grace. It was not just his tremendous physique which made such a deep impression on British – and later Italian – football and his followers. There were all his other virtues and, remarkably his fairness in the use of them.

In eight seasons at Leeds, Charles was idolised for his chivalry and artistry. In one season in 1955–56, in his striker role, he scored 42 goals to pilot Leeds to promotion to the First Division. In 2001, aged 69, Charles was belatedly honoured with the CBE for his services to the game. Close remembers his association with Charles at Elland Road. 'John is a wonderful chap – the greatest centre-half of all time – and not far from being the best centre-forward.'

The thrills of this and other alliances at Leeds could not overcome Close's disquiet at Buckley's methods. A natural inside-forward, he was played out of position on the left wing. Ken Willingham, the former England wing-half then playing in Leeds' reserves side, told Close: 'You want to get away from here. Look, you've been on the books since you were fourteen. You're not a "Buckley Boy" and the Major is only interested in his own products.'

In the meantime Close was posted to Catterick. A football injury caused the postponement of his call-up into National Service and led to him being able to play for Yorkshire at the start of the season in 1949. Later Maurice Webb, the Bradford MP and cricket enthusiast, acting on behalf of Yorkshire, was able to use his influence to obtain deferment until the end of the season and thus ensure Close's memorable entry into first-class cricket.

The glow of his achievements lingered but Brian was now a serving soldier. He was assigned as 22185787 Signalman Close as one of the intake of Army recruits at the North Yorkshire depot. What followed was a dire episode, which threatened to put an end to his sporting ambitions. In a Central League football game for Leeds at St James' Park, Newcastle, he collided heavily with Ted Robledo, one of the Chilean brothers, and smashed his thigh.

Substitutes were not allowed in those days and Brian, in an early illustration of his courage, actually played on for the last 30 minutes of the game. Hobbling on one leg, he was switched by Tom Holley from the wing into a central position. He volleyed twice against the posts and Jack Fairbrother, the Newcastle 'keeper, saved another shot from the crippled marksman as Leeds very nearly won the match.

The sequel to Close's bravery was a rapidly deteriorating injury problem exacerbated by the lack of urgent and expert attention. He reported sick to the authorities at Catterick after the match at Newcastle. It later transpired that the surface of the bone was broken, leading to ossification of the thigh: calcium was seeping out of the bone and into the muscles of his leg. Daily heat treatment was given by Bob Roxburgh, the Leeds trainer, but two weeks after the accident Close's leg was swollen right down to the ankle.

Close's career was now in the utmost jeopardy. He returned to Catterick to spend two months in the military hospital to receive specialist treatment which also involved enforced rest, a necessary but frustrating experience for someone of his temperament. The healing process was completed by a month's convalescence at Hereford. 'If I hadn't gone into hospital,' says Close, 'the injury would have finished me. I would never have bent my leg again.'

He returned to Catterick in the spring of 1950, happily restored in health and able to consolidate his cricket progress in services games during the following summer. He wryly notes: 'They never gave me a job while I was in the Army. Their reasoning was that I would be away more times than I would be there.' Certainly he was fully engaged in his sporting activities. His colleagues and opponents in midweek services cricket included many who would later move on into the first-class ranks. They included Jim Parks (Sussex) and Alan Moss and Fred Titmus (Middlesex), all future England players.

Close's feats in 1950 demonstrate why he was permitted to suspend his National Service in order to tour Australia in the following winter. It did place him unwittingly at the centre of a controversy. Why, it was asked, should he be released to play professional cricket for his country when many parents had asked for deferment to allow their sons to study in the professions and been refused? The dissension was not lessened when it was pointed out that professional sportsmen abroad are considered as ambassadors for their countries.

Close, for his part, could do no more than emphasise his credentials in this role. For the Army against the Royal Navy at Lord's he took six wickets for 38 runs with his off-breaks and finished with a match tally of nine wickets. At Chelmsford, playing for the Combined Services against Essex, he had match figures of 10 for 94, including 6 for 61 in the first innings. In another Combined Services fixture against Worcestershire he scored 92 not out and 60 and took three wickets.

There were also weekend leaves, extending over 48 hours, filled to the brim with more cricket. Close played for Leeds in the Yorkshire Council on Saturdays, and on Sundays he joined the throng of celebrity cricketers who took part in Jack Appleyard's charity games at Roundhay Park, Leeds. These included Eddie Paynter, the former Lancashire and England batsman, who enthralled the vast crowds with his big hitting, Horace Fisher, Bill Alley and the Australian bowler George Tribe, who later played for Northamptonshire and baffled many post-war opponents with his slow left-arm chinamen and googlies. Close fielded at first slip to Tribe in these games. 'It helped me later when we were opposed to him in the championship,' he says. 'I was one of the few Yorkshire batsmen who could play him.'

Jack Appleyard, a Leeds businessman, was a dedicated cricket enthusiast and organiser. He recruited as many big-name men as possible from the Bradford League, mixed them with local talent, and contrived to play an attractive cricket fixture every Sunday. These were staged in the Roundhay Park bowl – a huge natural arena near Leeds, which regularly catered for as many as 50,000 people on sunny afternoons.

One writer remembered the refreshing informality of the cricket, common to both players and spectators at Roundhay. 'The batsmen, without averages to think about, can shed decorum completely and hit sixes in rapid succession. The small boys of Leeds can clamber about sightscreens with impunity and even set up competitions on the boundary edge – things which could never happen at Headingley. And what county ground could contemplate the idea of entertaining spectators by relaying Strauss waltzes over the loud-speakers during the tea interval?'

Just as appealing was the diversity of the crowds drawn to the programme of matches, which had started as a Holidays-at-Home attraction in the dark days of the war in 1940. The assembly included busy housewives, relaxing on a Sunday on a spree in the park. 'They come with bulging picnic baskets, balls of wool and quite often babies,' related another observer of the scene. The cricket, he said, also had a strong appeal to the younger generation contemplating matrimony. 'They congregate high up on the hillside at the Mansion end, too far away to be victims of big hits should their attention wander from the game.'

Appleyard could not charge admission for the games at Roundhay. He had to rely on collections, rarely more than a penny a head, to meet expenses. These consisted in the main of a guarantee that he would cover the cost of getting every player to and from the ground. In addition, there was a maximum fee of £2. Many charities benefited from Appleyard's industry during those years. One important legacy was the endowment of a bed at Leeds Infirmary, for which Appleyard handed over a cheque for £4000 in 1943.

When he finally disbanded his organisation in 1963, Appleyard had raised over £20,000 for charities and, in particular during the war years, had provided enjoyment and relaxation for hundreds of thousands of sport-starved spectators. On one memorable occasion, when he organised a match in aid of the Hedley Verity Memorial Fund, the Leeds City Transport Department estimated that they had moved 70,000 people to and from Roundhay Park.

Brian Close was honoured and reprimanded at the same time after one weekend outing to Roundhay in early August 1950. The bizarre episode coincided with his selection to tour Australia. He had been instructed to play in a trial match at Catterick, but thought this was a little pointless when he could be helping to raise funds for charity in Leeds. Accordingly he explained his predicament to Captain

Duncan Pocock, who skippered the Royal Signals team. 'Yes, we can let you off; go home and play there,' was the response.

Rain washed out the cricket at Leeds but it was fine at Catterick. At the time Brian opened the batting, and in his absence the Signal Training Corps major, normally number three in the order, opened the innings. Brian's fortunes would have been better had his senior officer scored runs. Unfortunately, he was dismissed for a duck, whereupon he demanded to know what had happened to his subordinate. 'He's gone home,' he was told. The major spluttered with anger: 'Then he's absent without leave.'

Brian arrived back at Catterick on the Sunday night to learn about his misfortune. 'On the Monday morning I found myself on a charge. I was admonished for missing the match and given seven days CB [confined to barracks].' He confesses that he was not particularly aware of the more esoteric aspects of Army life. 'Someone explained to me that "confined to barracks" did not relate to being kept in after school. It involved parading daily in something called Field Service Marching Order and that meant having the FSMO equipment to parade in.' At the outset of his service this had been deposited, along with his cricket gear, with a trusted friend at the unit's Camp Centre. It was a precautionary measure because, as Brian says, he was frequently away and there was always the danger of the equipment being stolen if left unattended.

Brian travelled down to Camp Centre to reclaim his equipment, unaware that he was guilty of another offence in leaving the barracks. His departure, as if on cue, was combined with the news of his selection to tour Australia. He returned to discover a state of turmoil. Everyone was beaming with pleasure but hordes of newspapermen had by now converged on Catterick. The Army Press Officer was appraised that Close, the newly sung hero, was, in fact, in disgrace. He sought to ensure that the misdemeanour went unrevealed.

Arrangements were made that night for a press conference in the NAAFI club. All but one of the Fleet Street contingent were there to file their stories. Unbeknown to the press corps, a reporter from the *News Chronicle*, who did not know about the conference, had turned up late. He had visited the guardroom while Brian was down at the press conference. The *Chronicle* man introduced himself and asked if he could speak to Signalman Close. 'Well, he should be here because he has been confined to barracks this morning,' he was told.

The reporter was then directed to the NAAFI club and arrived just as the conference ended. But he already had his story, and pleas not to divulge it fell on deaf ears. 'He waited until the conference was over,' recalls Brian. 'Then he went up to the press officer and said: "Well, what about this then? Signalman Close is on CB, isn't he?"' It was too good a yarn to keep to himself. The back-page headlines on the following day revealed all. They told, in gloating details, the tale of a cricketer for once caught off guard.

All was forgiven in the euphoria of Close's cricket honour. But despite the surge of acclaim for him, the situation did demand a suitably measured Army response. Close's commanding officer issued a statement which emphasised that the privileges of a cricketer did not give him immunity from Army discipline. 'We treat him as we treat any National Serviceman. If he contravenes military regulations he must be treated in the same manner as any other signalman.'

So it was that Brian Close was uniquely summoned as a cricket tourist while under detention for misconduct in the Army. The soldier in dudgeon was released from his shackles to journey on to an even sterner parade ground as a cricketer in Australia.

3

Toppled from his Pedestal

'In a world of men the boy had to assume a cloak of confidence that was bound to prove threadbare in the cold winds of criticism.'

JIM KILBURN

A bright star was dimmed in the demanding fields of Australia in 1950–51. The sorrowful Yorkshire elders had counselled against the too-sudden selection of one of their own apprentices. The rejection of their advice was to cast a long shadow over the career of Brian Close. As Neville Cardus would later relate, the tour presaged a story of bitter-sweet years, the fates of which might have been devised by a Thomas Hardy of cricket fiction.

Close had set out on a coveted mission rich in expectations. At the start of a great adventure there was no inkling of the perils ahead. The change from austerity rations in England to a glut of unimagined food was pronounced. 'We went out by ship, first-class passage on a big boat, the 29,000-ton *Stratheden*. I had never seen food like it,' he recalls. It was reported that, in his delight at embarking on the voyage, he explored the ship from top to bottom within 24 hours of departure. 'I was young and fit and by eight o'clock each morning I was running round the decks.'

Here was a boy with boundless energy and self-assurance. His buoyancy would all too soon be quenched and his confidence undermined by crass management. Close's experiences in Australia as a friendless youngster changed his character; some people believe that he never fully erased the mental scars inflicted on the tour.

Close today exonerates those seniors who withheld their support. The forgiving attitude exemplifies his lack of vengeance and his status as the gentlest of men. 'It was an unfortunate scene; the elders in the MCC party did not want to be saddled with an inexperienced and immature youngster. I was a scruffy young Yorkshire kid mixing with my idols. They had lost six years to the war and were perhaps making their last trip to Australia. There were no youngsters of my own age with whom you could mix easily.'

Alec Bedser, who would take 30 wickets in the series – the first of three such aggregates or over in the 1950s – nobly held sway as England's bowling hero in an ill-starred series. Bedser has lamented the emphasis on untried youth on the Australian tour and the decision to leave more experienced campaigners kicking their heels at home. Among those left out were the ill-rewarded Jack Robertson, two seasoned and combative men in Bill Edrich and Joe Hardstaff, and George Emmett, Tom Dollery and Dennis Brookes, all with credentials beyond those selected.

Only seven of the MCC party had previously toured Australia and the judgement on the others (Parkhouse, Dewes, Sheppard, Warr and Close, the youngest at 19) was that they had been thrown into the sternest of contests too quickly. Trevor Bailey, also making his first tour but with six home Tests behind him, believes that Close was at a disadvantage because of the 'unfortunate mixture of a side out there with him'.

Doug Insole, touted as captain in Australia at one stage, expresses the view that Close would have benefited from rooming with a sympathetic 'older hand'. Going out on a tour as a newcomer knowing very few players, as was the case with the Yorkshire boy, was bound to be a trial. 'Unless those people make a specific effort to bring you into things, it can be very lonely,' says Insole.

Events would demonstrate the significance of this statement. Bryan Stott, a future Yorkshire colleague and close friend, was told after the tour about the nightmare experience. 'Brian was totally raw and inexperienced. There was not one person, Leonard [Hutton] included, prepared to take him under his wing. Brian has needed this aid all his life but it was especially important then.' Ted Lester, another county team-mate, concurs: 'The senior players in Australia treated him very badly. Nobody wanted to know him, so he spent his time playing golf. He cried himself to sleep many times out there.' Stott also remembers that Close, at this time, did not smoke or drink. He was ill at ease in the traditional Saturday night club on board ship. This often entailed heavy drinking sessions and the MCC seniors ragged him because he only drank orange juice.

Frank Tyson, the former England fast bowler now resident in Australia, also regrets the lamentable management. 'Freddie Brown and the senior professionals on that tour had a lot to answer for in their handling of Closey. They would have made rotten teachers. They were completely unable to understand the lad's immaturity and certainly did not make allowances for it.'

Another aspect of the estrangement was the atmosphere of snobbery prevailing over 50 years ago. John Dewes, the Middlesex amateur and a fellow tourist, recalls: 'As amateurs, we were not allowed, or encouraged to mix too freely with the professionals. And, therefore, as a person, I did not get to know Brian too well. Because of my Christian background, I did try to be approachable. Brian did then have a very broad accent and this did not help him.'

The key factor was the stewardship of Freddie Brown, who, having urged Close's selection, was virtually to disown the recruit as the tour progressed. Brown was in fact the third-choice captain in Australia, after George Mann and Norman Yardley had made it known they were unable to tour because of business commitments. It is interesting to reflect on whether more lenient measures would have prevailed had either been available.

Mann was disappointed at the omission of Bill Edrich, his Middlesex colleague. He offered a general statement on misguided tour management, in which he suggested that it was a reflection of confidence, or lack of it, in dealing with problems. 'If a player is picked for England, it does not mean that he is naturally an easy, or even a nice person. What it does mean is that he is a bloody good cricketer. As a manager, or captain, you have to cope with misdemeanours and try to help players to avoid them . . . As a touring captain, you take out a team of cricketers, who are a cross-section of the community. You cannot expect them all to come out of the same mould.'

The leadership style of Freddie Brown did not permit compromise. He could be bossy and brusque – then as captain and later as an MCC manager. The iron fist was rarely concealed, especially where professionals were concerned, and prejudices often distorted his judgement. Trevor Bailey presents a wry appraisal: 'Freddie was a brave player in some respects. But he was the sort of person who would lead an attack from the trenches but then forget to deploy covering fire as a smokescreen. Everyone would have been killed and he would have gone down first.'

Brown's adventurous approach as a player was not dissimilar to the qualities which had at first attracted him to Close. The appreciation was stifled in his subsequent disregard for the Yorkshireman. The posture of a 'poor character and not a likeable man', in the words of Bryan Stott, is indirectly confirmed by another amateur more generous in spirit.

Raman Subba Row, the former Surrey, Northamptonshire and England batsman, refers to the bullying environment which existed then and lingered on after the abolition of the Gentlemen and Players in 1963. 'The influence of former amateur captains continued after they had moved into cricket administration. They had grown up as autocrats and persisted with the same attitudes.'

Tom Cartwright is the epitome of a social democrat in his outlook on life. He was to share a rare cricketing bond with Close during his swan-song in Somerset. He talks earnestly about the unfairness of expecting a cricket novice to go on the field and do a man-sized job in Australia. Off the field, the rationale changed; the deficient mentors reverted to treating him like a child.

Cartwright also had his tussles with authority. He comes from similar humble stock to that of Close, discovering his socialist doctrine as a boy amid the deprivations of miner neighbours in the East Midlands. He is understanding in his reflections. 'It's not just about cricket,' he maintains. 'Suddenly, for boys like Brian, they are confronted with general table etiquette and meeting people from all walks of life. It's a complete social upheaval, producing bewilderment as to what it is all about. What is definitely not required is someone squashing people at that age.' He refers to the pecking order in cricket and a social climate which permits Australians to fulfil their promise as compared with the restrictive influences obtaining in England. 'The legacy of elitism still exists and every day it makes you want to scream.'

Alan Davidson, the former Australian all-rounder, examines the differences in grooming young players in both countries. 'In England the professionals would be seeking to protect themselves unlike in Australia where our seniors sought to encourage those trying to get a foot on the ladder.' He cites his own example as a rookie in his first game in England against Leicestershire in 1953. Neil Harvey had already scored a hundred when Davidson went in to bat. Harvey went on to a second hundred but he was outpaced, whether by design or accident, by his new partner.

Their seventh-wicket stand produced a yield of 117 runs in 65 minutes; more pertinently, it was Davidson who dominated the proceedings with 63 before Harvey resumed his assault. Afterwards, Lindsay Hassett, the Australian captain, took Davidson to one side and said, 'I didn't know you could bat like that. I'm going to promote you in the order but don't let me down.' Davidson says of this incident and other encouraging signals that it was all 'part and parcel of our cricket education'.

Trevor Bailey still maintains that it was a viable decision to select Close for the Australian tour in 1950–51. The terse manner of the isolated newcomer did deter a meaningful dialogue in the shape of advice. It was clearly a handicap then and later and the result was that he was regarded as a bumptious and irresponsible young man in Australia. Bailey says, 'Unfortunately, Brian was under the impression that he knew everything. He was quite convinced that he was always right. If he made a mistake it took him longer to realise his error. It did become very difficult for him.'

Close does not disagree with the tenor of this assessment. 'I made some mistakes,' he concedes, 'and kept getting out in the twenties and thirties. Put it down to exuberance. I was still playing cricket for fun and could have done with a few bollockings.'

John Dewes observes that Close's big strength at the time was his physical ability. 'Brian didn't then have the temperament to wait for things to happen. He always wanted, not often wisely, to dominate affairs.'

Alan Fairfax, the former Australian Test player, sounded a warning note for the MCC travellers in a pre-tour commentary. 'There is 11,000 miles of difference between playing cricket at Lord's and at Melbourne. Too few English players realise this when they set out on their first Test tour down under. Australia can make or break an English tourist. Some come over with big reputations, only to fail when they try their skills in the new conditions.'

Brian Close at first seemed likely to live up to his billing as a gifted young talent. Amid the piercing winds of the 'Fremantle Doctor', reminiscent of an April day at home, he hit an unbeaten century against Western Australia at Perth. 'Close's century was the thing of the day,' commented Raymond Robertson-Glasgow. 'It might be compared to a school exercise written by a very promising pupil.'

David Sheppard, who opened the MCC innings at Perth, reveals the differing reactions of Len Hutton to his own and Close's performances. 'I was dismissed for five after struggling for fifty minutes against two good fast bowlers on a lively pitch.' After much badgering he was given an audience by Hutton. The Yorkshire master was complimentary in their post-match talk. 'Well played,' he said. Sheppard thought this was a sample of Hutton's droll humour; it seemed a flattering verdict on a minor effort. He asked for an explanation. Hutton told him, 'You made it easy for the rest of them. You battled it out.'

Close's extravagant display was less to the taste of Hutton. The latter recalls, 'Brian had a lot of luck, got away with it, and went on sweeping and pulling.' The outcome was that Hutton, feeling responsible for his fellow Yorkshireman, sternly reprimanded Close for not learning from his escapes. Sheppard concludes, 'I think this story tells as much about Len as Brian and me. I was trying to play his way. He could not approve the dashing and risky strokeplay that was Brian at his best.'

Close, the adventurer at Perth, was raw in cricket experience. Raymond Robertson-Glasgow reported that Herbert, the West

Australian leg-spinner, twice persuaded him into 'how-not-to-do-it' positions. 'Each time Close answered with sizzling drives and lived in happy alternation between the misprint and purple passage.' So happy was Close in his assault that he did not refrain from stealing the bowling on the eighth ball. 'They're good at arithmetic in Yorkshire,' declared Robertson-Glasgow.

Jack Fingleton also cast a watchful eye on a spectacular innings. 'Close is the man of the moment; he is obviously going to be either a terrific success or a hopeless failure on this tour.' The fluctuations of the innings, veering from vulnerability to steadfast defence, did not dissuade Fingleton from expressing cautious optimism. 'Close was so full of aggression and, in a manner so typical of him, he tried to hit a six on the verge of his century.' The ball soared towards the waiting guard on the long-on boundary. Close, believing he was out, slapped his pads with his bat in annoyance. The steepling catch, in fact, had eluded the grasp of the fieldsman. The reprieve was just and Close went on to mount his first hurdle in Australia with a fine hundred. He had batted for three hours and 20 minutes and his innings included 12 fours.

Jim Swanton also applauded an innings of great significance, if of mixed merit. 'There were blemishes, certainly, but between times, Close's batting burgeoned with promise and possibilities. His best hits were sweeps and off-drives and his power was unmistakable.' Swanton added: 'He is indeed a precocious 19-year-old, chock full of cricket. His only serious enemy seems to be an overflowing confidence that accompanies great natural gifts.' The licence exercised by Close caused Swanton to ponder on the fashion of the cricket of Denis Compton in his early days. 'It does not do to be censorious. When the selectors surprised the majority by choosing Close they were no doubt alive to the prospect of his playing as an all-rounder in the Tests.'

Compton, with a century, was allied with Close in a stand of 54 runs against Victoria at Melbourne in November. It provided the tourists with their first glimpse of Jack Iverson, who was to confound them in the forthcoming Tests. Robertson-Glasgow, in typically humorous vein, offered a verdict on an extraordinary bowler. 'His bowling method has been described in nearly every Australian newspaper and will soon surely reach the columns of the more advanced engineering journals in England.'

Iverson, then aged 35, was regarded as the rawest of Test debutants. Yet he enjoyed remarkable success. Sid Barnes, excluded from the Australian ranks in the series, related the opinion of one Englishman that Iverson's deliveries had more curves than a six-day bike race. This was the Victorian's finest hour. He headed the Australian bowling averages against England: his 21 wickets cost him only 15.23 runs each. But he would all too soon be stunned into submission by more daring batsmanship and depart abruptly from first-class cricket.

Iverson's puzzles were not yet fully unveiled against the MCC at Melbourne. The focus for English observers, such as Swanton, beamed happily on Brian Close. 'There was not only nerve and spirit in his batting, but a number of beautifully timed leg hits that were authentic and admirable,' reported Swanton. Discretion, he thought, would emerge in due course. 'The question is whether it will be soon enough. Our hearts were in our mouths once or twice when Close attempted liberties.'

A string of low scores for Close preceded another century, against the New South Wales Southern Districts at Canberra in December. Sheppard also hit a hundred and the pair shared an unbeaten fourth-wicket stand of 179 in 90 minutes. As one writer put it, 'they made their runs in a hot, fly-infested sunshine with a kind of careless rapture.' Close's 105 included 64 in boundaries. 'The young Yorkshire all-rounder showed that he was not daunted by his recent failures,' commented Reg Hayter.

The exhilarating overture proved to be a false dawn. Bill Bowes knew that Close's quick and unfettered rise to stardom had antagonised many cricketers who had struggled for years on the verge of honours. The day of reckoning was not far distant. Sheppard, as another beginner called to the England colours before his time, believes that the 'enormously talented' Close had achieved his distinctions in England in 1949 without having to work really hard for them.

Neville Cardus observed that it was best to pick your date in history carefully to do justice to your talents, especially if you happened to be merely a boy. Waiting for Close was as superbly contrasted a company of Australian bowlers as ever honoured the field. They included the massively formidable pace trio of Lindwall, Miller and Johnston that had exploited batting frailties in England in 1948. Their threatening presence did not escape the notice of Bill Bowes. It did not take them long to find a weakness in Close's armour. 'They found they could hurry Brian into error with a short-pitched ball on the leg stump,' he said.

Bowes recalled that Close's dilemma was rendered less easy by a badly pulled groin muscle. 'Some of his colleagues thought he was malingering. One can only guess at the feelings of a young man, hitherto superbly fit and successful in everything he did, relegated to passenger status.' As a member of the press corps in Australia, Bowes was limited in his access to Close. At opportune moments he tried to reassure his fellow Yorkshireman. He did speak with the voice of experience, but, as he confessed, the exhortations to 'keep on trying and everything will come right sooner or later' sounded hollow and abysmal in a difficult time.

The injury which was to curtail Close's cricket and finally lead to his demotion was sustained in the match at Canberra. During the course of his century innings he tore the roots of a tendon in the groin. Close was then selected for the second Test at Melbourne. It was undeniably a feather in his cap and a thrilling promotion, but he now admits that he shouldn't have played in the match. 'It jiggered me up for the rest of the trip.'

Freddie Brown had told him, 'We want you in the side to give it the right balance.' With hindsight, Close's decision to accept the invitation can be seen as the moment when his tour of Australia fell into disarray. 'Well, I can still feel the strain,' he advised Brown. 'But if I have my leg strapped up I'll be all right.'

England, beaten by only 28 runs, held the advantage on the first day at Melbourne. Alec Bedser and Trevor Bailey, with sustained hostility in the heavy atmosphere, each took four wickets. Australia was dismissed for 194. A trailing leg did not deter Close in his supporting role. In his spelling duties, at medium pace, he bowled six economical overs and broke a menacing fifth-wicket stand when he dismissed Loxton, whose partnership of 84 runs with Hassett was the highest of the innings. Close was a fraction away from what would have been a prized scalp. Hassett was so nearly his next victim. 'I bowled him an absolute jaffa on leg and middle. It pitched and swung late and went over the top of his off stump.'

The critical tirade which greeted Close's debut innings against Australia disregarded other elements of weakness in England's reply. As on other occasions, he was blamed although others had equally failed. The skies had cleared and conditions were more propitious for batting on the second day. Yet England surrendered the initiative and had lost five wickets for 54 runs when the sanctuary of lunch beckoned.

'Gilbert Parkhouse [lbw to Johnston] had got out just before the interval,' recalls Close. 'I had to go in and face Jack Iverson for the last over.' Iverson, according to Close, had not posed a special threat in the earlier match against Victoria. 'When I played against him I'd spotted him, worked him out. He slightly dropped his arm to bowl the leg-spinner; his orthodox ball was the wrong 'un.' Close did not give himself time to substantiate this claim in the Test. His confidence betrayed him in a fatal over. 'I played a couple of balls and then he bowled one nine or ten inches outside my leg stump. I tried to sweep it, got a top edge, and Sam Loxton caught me behind square.' He had not calculated for the harder wickets in Australia and the extra bounce, which contributed to his downfall.

He was an abject figure as he returned to the England dressing room. The silence there was heart-stopping and fraught with scarcely concealed anger. 'I remained there through lunch, almost in tears and sick with misery,' he recalls. The unspoken words told him plainly that he was a 'silly young bugger'. Many years later one of his Australian opponents, Ian Johnson, told Close that he had observed his distress at Melbourne. He had asked Brown to speak to the distraught boy: 'Young Close is a bit down. Go and have a word with him.' Brown allegedly replied, 'Let the blighter stew. He deserves it.'

Worse was to follow this day of disgrace when Close travelled to Tasmania in January as a member of the MCC party captained by Compton. Why he was included on the trip when he was plagued by a persistent injury is a puzzle. There were to be accusations from other players that he was 'swinging the lead'. 'I was only a kid,' says Close. 'All I wanted to do was hit the ball and take wickets. I hadn't got the sense to think about swinging the lead.'

Playing cricket seemed an unlikely prospect for Close in Tasmania. He was advised that on the team's arrival in Hobart he would be sent to a specialist for an examination of his injury. A lunchtime appointment was arranged, probably at short notice, on the first day of the opening match. Compton had presumably not been alerted to the visit to the clinic, and he instructed Close to change and act as twelfth man. It seems fair to judge that the appointment with the specialist had to take priority over cricket. Accordingly, Close sought the aid of Parkhouse, his roommate on the tour, who agreed to deputise as twelfth man while Close was away.

The verdict of the specialist, expressed on the medical note, was that Close was not fit for cricket and furthermore that he should not be expected to play for at least a month. On his return to the ground in the afternoon, Close handed the note to Brigadier Michael Green, one of the two MCC managers. Green read it and then, with a hint of apology, remarked, 'You'd better show this to Denis when he comes off the field because he's going to play you in the next match.'

The next development seems out of character for a usually fair-minded man. It was perhaps yet another instance of the yawning gulf between Close and his seniors. The severity of Compton's response could be attributable to various factors. As acting captain in Tasmania, he was operating with limited playing resources. He had been allotted only 13 players, effectively only 12 with Close handicapped by injury. Eric Bedser, who had accompanied his brother Alec to Australia, was recruited to supplement the meagre ranks, and played in the match at Hobart. It was also a stressful time personally for Compton. He was deeply upset by his form in Australia, where his batting in the Tests yielded only 53 runs at an average of 7.57. It must be regarded as the worst-ever series for a player of his calibre.

The sympathy of the captain was notably absent after a hard afternoon in the field at Hobart. Close chose the wrong moment in which to add to the pressures afflicting Compton. He recalls, 'I should have waited until after tea because Denis was in an angry mood.' In his version of the incident, Close says that Compton gave the medical note a cursory glance and then proceeded to rip the paper into pieces and throw them on the floor. He then abruptly dismissed his junior with the words, 'I don't care what the doctor said. You will play in the next game.'

The situation deteriorated at Launceston, Close's first appearance since the Test at Melbourne. Close fielded at first slip and batted at number three in the order. Parkhouse was drawn into another row. 'You'd better get your pads on. I've had no practice,' Close told Parkhouse. The remark was overheard by one of the amateurs and reported back to Freddie Brown. The request was of minor importance and probably was given other overtones in the telling, but it could not help but increase the fury of the England captain.

Back on the mainland, Close took part in a two-day fixture against a South Australian Country XI at Renmark in the heart of the wine-growing area. Before the match he was detailed to report to Brown, who was roused from his rest in his shuttered hotel room to admit him. The conversation was brief and to the point, with Close not allowed any rejoinder. Brown raided his store of invective in upbraiding Close for his misconduct in Tasmania. 'I was given a right dressing-down and told that it was my duty as a professional, irrespective of injury, to obey the orders of my captain.'

The censure, so roundly administered, told Close that he was considered unreliable. Before long he would be regarded as an outcast. He now knew that his tour of Australia was moving towards a sad finale. His last game, under the captaincy of Cyril Washbrook, was against a Victorian Country XI at Geelong in February. His leg was once more strapped up and he opened the bowling with John Warr on a swelteringly hot day. Close actually took the first wicket and then, as he relates, 'I felt my leg go, really properly.' He tumbled to the ground and was half-carried off the field. His leg was packed with ice and he remained prone in the dressing room for the rest of the day.

Cricket can be cruel and this was never more apparent when Close was ostracised by his team-mates. 'They all bloody crucified me because, as the opening bowler, I'd cracked up after bowling only four overs.' His reputation was now in tatters; he was, as Jim Kilburn said, in the touring party but not of it. 'There was no lonelier young man in the Commonwealth,' declared Kilburn.

Close, as if to emphasise this disclosure, shied away from further contact with the team. In happier times he would have shared the jubilation of his colleagues when England achieved their first victory over Australia for 13 years in the final Test at Melbourne. He was an absentee, preferring to play golf away from the celebrations. It was a heavily criticised act and perhaps justifiably so on a proud day. 'I was no longer on speaking terms with the team and so my presence would have been fairly pointless,' is his wan explanation.

In a post-tour report, *Wisden* adopted a measured and sympathetic tone. 'As a natural all-rounder, who may become a top grade left-handed batsman, Close might have been a vital link in the Test team chain but his bowling suffered from a lack of accuracy and his batting from want of discretion. In view of his extreme youth,' continued the summary, 'Close should escape harsh criticism. Rather the hope should be expressed that if he ultimately learned the lessons that were available, his tour would have been worthwhile.' Close today agrees with this assessment. 'I did grow up very rapidly in Australia. It wasn't like the Yorkshire scene. You literally had to make your own way because no one was going to help you.'

John Dewes also comments on an arduous assignment in which he, along with Close and other newcomers, was ill-equipped to prosper. He refutes allegations that Close was a serious misfit in Australia. 'Sometimes his tongue ran away from him and he said things that he shouldn't have done. But he was growing into a team member. He very much had his L plates up.' Close's taxing groin injury, aggravated because of the insistence on match play, is also remembered by Dewes. 'I was disappointed that this very promising all-rounder was below his best because he was physically below his best.'

Two warring adversaries in Yorkshire were for once in accord on the consequences of the misadventure in Australia. Ironically one of them, Johnny Wardle, paid a severe penalty for a breach of discipline when his county sacked him in 1958. Wardle, in a telling appraisal, said, 'Had Brian been given greater protection on his first tour by senior members of the team he would have been England's answer to Keith Miller.'

Ronnie Burnet, who, as Yorkshire captain, had been the instigator of Wardle's dismissal, was the other Yorkshire witness. He adamantly declared that Close should never have been out of the England side. He told a revealing story of the impact of the demoralising experience in Australia which had, he recalled, almost resulted in Close giving up the game. In one long conversation at the Station Hotel, Crewe, Burnet had tried to dispel the clouds of depression. 'You're wasting your breath, Ronnie,' said Brian, 'I'm finished.'

4

Seasons of Frustration

'He was acknowledged to be one of the best all-rounders in the country but never had the luck or opportunity to prove it internationally.'

BILL BOWES

Brian Close had to live with his tarnished image for many years after the Australian misadventure. He returned home from the tour as a disillusioned young man. The resilient and unshakeable warrior of later times was totally at variance with the downcast cricketer of the mid-1950s. Raymond Illingworth, who grew up in thrall to the imperious giant by his side, reflects on an uneasy second phase in Close's career. 'He was a completely different person; it was quite unbelievable.'

Jim Kilburn said that Close drifted near to the resignation of fatalism. 'However skilfully and convincingly he climbed, the rope always seemed ready to break when he was nearing the top. Nobody could doubt his batting ability – which steadily took precedence over his bowling – but many could and did doubt his powers of application.'

Illingworth says that those younger Yorkshire recruits who played under Close's mature leadership in the 1960s were astonished and disbelieving that their captain could at any time have been labelled as fainthearted. Close did linger on the brink of despair; and, as he admits: 'The criticism in Australia did strike me hard. For the first time I got over the hot flush of youth and realised that people can be cruel. I had been hit for six by the critics and yet I wasn't guilty of anything.'

His unpredictability brought expressions of regret. One great friend in Yorkshire, not identified by Bill Bowes in his recollection, watched Close at the wicket. He would shake his head in dismay at the needless risks taken and the impulsive big hitting. As he witnessed yet another spectacular downfall, he remarked, 'A pity Brian doesn't get married and settle down.'

Doug Insole, as a southern observer, expands on the cavalier theme, saying Close's cricketing map should have excluded having a 'whoosh' and heedlessly squandering his wicket. It was exasperating to watch a player of his ability go down this route. His command was such that, while others faltered, he could have played with the proverbial stick of rhubarb.

Ronnie Burnet, a future Yorkshire captain, also favoured a less wayward approach. 'Brian possesses, without doubt, more natural talent than most players in the game today,' he observed. 'It is for that reason that we are disappointed when he fails, and we are inclined to criticise him.'

The general consensus focused on a betrayal of uncommon gifts. Illingworth firmly believes that his friend should never have been out of the England team. 'Brian had the ability to force recognition through the 1950s. His opportunities at Test level were restricted because he failed to produce consistent performances with Yorkshire.'

The cricketing balance sheet, at least in the short term, reveals a discrepancy in Illingworth's account. Close accomplished the double in only his second full season with Yorkshire in 1952 and was only three wickets short of a third double three years later. There was, in addition, a fruitful spinning partnership with Johnny Wardle. This was curtailed by a knee injury, which thereafter caused much discomfort and had to be carefully nursed.

The dramatic emergence of Bob Appleyard coincided with Close's absence on National Service. Appleyard took 200 wickets in his first season with Yorkshire in 1951. The achievement was regarded, in Yorkshire circles at least, as the most sensational performance by a debutant since the days of Wilfred Rhodes. Appleyard finished top of the England averages and bowled Yorkshire to second position in the county championship. Jim Swanton said that

Appleyard had a distinctly individual talent. 'I cannot think of a close parallel to him as a bowler. He had a deadly accuracy and the ball was sharply spun and cut.'

Close, despite his displacement as Yorkshire's offspinner, expresses his own regard for a great bowler. 'Bob was favoured by wet wickets in 1951. But he was so accurate and able to disguise his changes in pace. Pitching on the leg and middle stumps, he could bowl at a right-hander with no more than a couple of fieldsmen on the off side.'

Illingworth was also a beneficiary as Close was relegated to the role of deputy spinner. His diligent application to his bowling meant that he became the first to be tried with off-spin. Illingworth, at 18, had been invited to special coaching classes with Yorkshire. One of his instructors was Bill Bowes. 'This was the most important incident of my career,' he says. 'Bill changed me from a medium-pace bowler to an off-spinner.'

A measure of renewed purpose was apparent when Close resumed his National Service in 1951. There was valour amongst the other aspiring young men of his generation on the cricket fields of England. Close represented the Combined Services and warmed to a near-hopeless task against the touring South Africans at Portsmouth. In two innings he scored 201 runs and almost single-handedly saved his team from defeat against a Springboks attack that included veteran pace bowler Geoff Chubb and spinners Hugh Tayfield and Norman Mann. Close's unbeaten 135 in the second innings, after the Combined Services had followed on 264 runs behind, was then the highest of his career and his first century in England.

Close also scored 66 in the first innings; his partner was a perky Aircraftsman, Jim Parks, who hit 51 in an hour. The bullish juniors contributed more than half the Combined Services' total and avoided a complete rout. In the second innings, after two wickets had fallen for 13, Close shared stands of 86 with Parks and 143 with John Manners. His century, occupying three and a half hours, included three sixes and 15 fours.

There were other noteworthy performances to demonstrate his

assurance on home pastures. Close hit another century for the Combined Services against Cambridge, 96 not out in the victory by six wickets over Oxford University at the Parks, and another hundred, an unbeaten 134, for the Army against the Royal Navy at Lord's. Between times he made one appearance for Yorkshire seconds against Lincolnshire at Grimsby. Yorkshire won by an innings and Close, in all-round good fettle, scored 108 and took 10 wickets for 62 runs in the match.

Neville Cardus was present on a whim, which often takes people to cricket, to see the burgeoning stroke play of Close in the Army ranks on a July day at Lord's. 'My first acquaintance with Brian was in this Services match. I had never seen him before; and, after he had thrilled me with two sparkling off-drives, I said to myself, "Top class!"'

Brian Close left the army in October 1951. At that time his sporting ambitions continued to favour football as well as cricket. Arsenal had first expressed an interest in him while he was still a schoolboy and on the books of Leeds United, and he was now invited to join the august company at Highbury. Alex James and George Male, two renowned internationals of yesteryear, were on the coaching staff. Among those wearing the famous red playing colours were Dave Bowen, Laurie Scott, Jimmy Logie, Jack Kelsey and Arthur Milton.

Milton was the last of the cricket and soccer internationals, and had joined Arsenal straight from school in 1946. He represented England, deputising for the injured Tom Finney, on the right wing against Austria at Wembley in November 1951. Milton, as a callow West Country boy, remembers his daunting first visit to the luxurious stadium at Highbury. 'It was a fantastic place, just like a first-class hotel and had been built on the successes of the legendary manager, Herbert Chapman.'

A lifelong friendship between Milton and Close was first established at Highbury. They played together in Arsenal's second team in the London Combination League. Milton recalls, 'Brian wasn't a bad centre-forward but not that good in the air.' Tom Whittaker, the Arsenal manager, was concerned about Close's heading abilities. In one match Brian had missed chances through heading fractionally upwards and over the bar. 'So it was decided that we must have some practice,' continues Milton. 'I spent a couple of mornings crossing the ball for him to head it down. Brian seemed to be getting the hang of it.'

There was an immediate opportunity to put the practice to the test in the next match at Lowestoft. After ten minutes, Milton accelerated down the wing past his floundering opponent. He darted towards the by-line and centred with mathematical precision. Close, as instructed, was beautifully positioned at the correct height to meet the pass. There was power, perhaps too much, and conviction in his header as it struck the firm ground. 'Up he went, headed the ball down, and it bounced over the bar,' says Milton. 'We all fell apart laughing.'

So was Close an indifferent header of the ball? One former captain of Leeds United said: 'I don't reckon Brian was a great footballer – but he could head the bloody ball harder than most of us could kick it.' The jurors on other players such as Bobby Charlton and Stanley Matthews would claim that their fame in soccer was achieved by the skill of their footwork. Like them, perhaps, Close was happier with the ball at his feet and his goal scoring earned him rapid promotion to Arsenal's London Combination reserves team.

The advance in form brought him into contention for a first-team place. Alex James recommended Close for promotion when his fellow Scotsman Jimmy Logie had to stand down with an injury. As luck would have it, Close was also unfit and he missed the opportunity to justify James's confidence in him.

It was quite maddening how the imps of fortune tripped him up at sporting hurdles. Close was restored to fitness and selected to play for Arsenal in a London Combination Cup Final at Highbury on a Wednesday evening in April 1952. Unfortunately, this coincided with Yorkshire's opening match of the cricket season against the MCC at Lord's, to which Close was also committed. All seemed well when he received permission to fulfil his soccer date from Norman

Yardley, the Yorkshire captain. 'Don't worry, Brian,' said Yardley. 'We'll let you go at tea-time.'

Yardley's assurance proved unavailing when he was detained in Yorkshire on more pressing business. At home in Sheffield his wife, Toni, would soon give birth to twins. Don Brennan was Yardley's deputy as captain at Lord's. He deferred the matter of Close's withdrawal from the game to John Nash, the Yorkshire secretary, who was managing the team. Nash was informed about the sporting clash and instantly dismissed the request. 'Your job is cricket,' he told Close. 'You will be here until the end of play at 6.30.' Despite the rebuff, Brian rather optimistically thought there might just be time to cross London for the soccer match. It was a bad calculation. He did not arrive until half-time and, to make the situation worse, Arsenal had been forced to field the skip boy, an 'A' team player, in his absence.

Arsenal, in the event, were beaten 3–1 and this result in an important match had special significance for George Male. He was one of two candidates on the Highbury staff – his rival was another former England international, Jack Crayston – seeking preferment in succession to the ailing and esteemed Tom Whittaker as manager. On his return to the Yorkshire team's hotel in London, Close was told to ring Arsenal the following morning. George Male, understandably angry about the lax behaviour, made clear his displeasure in a brief conversation. 'We have decided to release you on a free transfer.' The dismissal completed a depressing interlude in London. Yorkshire were beaten by an innings at Lord's, though Close did have the consolation of taking five wickets in the match. They included three internationals, Jack Robertson, Bill Edrich and Freddie Brown.

In 1952, Surrey began their impressive reign as county champions, a position they did not relinquish for seven years. Yorkshire were close on their heels but the loss of Appleyard, through illness, and Trueman, carrying out his National Service, were key factors as they slipped into the second-place berth. Surrey won the title with 256 points, the highest total since the resumption of first-class cricket in 1946. Yorkshire were strong in batting, with six players scoring more than 1000 runs, but this could not compensate for their depleted bowling resources. The constraints did not prevent Yorkshire from reaching an aggregate of 224 points. We may be sure that the irony of scoring eight more points than Warwickshire had achieved as champions in the previous season was not lost upon them.

Close and Johnny Wardle were the pivotal figures in the absence of Appleyard and Trueman in an ill-fated summer. Between them they bowled nearly 2500 overs in the championship and took 256 wickets. They were the spinning masters in the innings victory over Leicestershire. The home side was routed for 88 in their second innings and the Yorkshire pair shared nine wickets. Then at Bradford, Warwickshire, seemingly safe from defeat, lost their last seven wickets for 37 runs and Close and Wardle were again the seducers with nine wickets in the innings.

Close demonstrated his all-round skills in completing his double in the victory by 17 runs over Hampshire at Scarborough. He first rescued Yorkshire with a fiercely struck 55 and then turned the scales in a tight struggle by taking six wickets. He aroused memories of his debut season in 1949 with spectacular hitting against Middlesex at Sheffield. His 87 included three sixes, two of which clattered alarmingly on to the pavilion balcony. At Worcester, Close was again in punishing mood. In a major partnership with Bill Sutcliffe he hit 78, including 50 in half an hour.

It is a matter for conjecture whether Close would have maintained this rich vein of form had he not elected to pursue his soccer career with Bradford City. Certainly the repercussions of an injury while in City's colours were immense and culminated in a lost season of cricket when his renaissance could well have been confirmed. His absence in 1953 following his decision to continue in what was perceived as a secondary talent met with much disapproval in Yorkshire cricket quarters.

Close's return to football in Yorkshire, at the instigation of the Bradford player-manager Ivor Powell, the Welsh international, came three years after his last appearance for Leeds United. He was given a month's trial at Valley Parade before scoring seven goals in nine games for Bradford's Third Division team. The accident, which enforced his retirement from the game, occurred in a match at Port Vale in December 1952. It was a typical episode of sporting fervour. The 'smash-up' came in one City attack. As the ball came over from the right wing Close chested it down and moved in on goal. 'The centre-half tore in and wrapped his legs around mine,' he recalls. He tried to elude the challenge by veering to his right but could not correct his stride and went straight on into a sickening collision.

The outcome was torn cartilages, one of which had to be removed, and his knee was still heavily swollen by the start of the cricket season. 'I was lucky to get myself right for 1954,' says Close. 'It was touch and go whether I would be fit. I played for two-thirds of that season with Yorkshire with a pressure bandage on my knee.' Bill Bowes, writing in 1960, revealed the extent of the handicap over several seasons. 'Only now is Brian able to bat or bowl with confidence. A twist while fielding, a long bowling spell, or a partner sending him back after he had got started on a run, many times caused swelling and acute pain.'

It was becoming a grievous journey with blows to diminish his confidence. It may have been during his season of idleness in 1953 that Close was moved to express his dissatisfaction with the game in the conversation with Ronnie Burnet. These stresses in a seesaw time were doubtless contributory causes of his puzzling bouts of depression and indecisiveness.

Jim Kilburn remembered the disturbing years before Close regained his assurance and peace of mind as Yorkshire captain. 'He had begun to doubt his commitment to the game and to feel the world was against him.' Raymond Illingworth, as a friend since boyhood, was also anxious and baffled by the switches in mood. 'Brian did keep breaking down and he was warned that he would be out of the team if he didn't pull himself together.'

In one match against Kent at Headingley, so Illingworth relates, Close was unable to bowl because of a bruised heel. Illingworth bowled more than 40 overs on the opening day. 'We were getting far more work than we should have had to do.' Bob Platt, another Yorkshire bowler, remembers that Kent batted all day on the

Saturday and Colin Cowdrey did not force a closure until one o'clock on Monday afternoon. Close was sufficiently recovered after treatment to play two rounds of golf on the rest day on the Sunday, after which, Platt says, he was urged into cricket action on the Monday. 'Ronnie [Burnet] threw him the ball, and after Brian Sellers, the Yorkshire chairman had given him a rollicking, Closey took eight for 41 with his seamers, a career best performance.'

Platt, the current Yorkshire cricket chairman, witnessed other curious lapses into erratic conduct. Another Yorkshireman, Charlie Lee, described Close as a 'Rolls-Royce with a cylinder missing'. Platt gives his own currency to the view that genius is not always accompanied by a stable mind, but, he stoutly maintains, 'Brian never harmed anyone but himself.'

He remembers another instance when Close veered wildly from indisposition to recovery and a match-winning performance. 'Middlesex had given us a pasting in one match at Headingley in 1960. Brian only bowled twelve overs in the match and watched them pan us all round the field.'

Vic Wilson, the Yorkshire captain, was incapacitated by illness in the next match against Derbyshire at Chesterfield. Close took over as his deputy. 'I was running down the hill to bowl for the first time at Queen's Park,' says Platt. After five overs he was called over by Close. 'All right, Bob,' he said, as a preliminary to a bowling change. Platt vigorously protested: 'But you're not fit to bowl, Closey!' It elicited the confidential reply: 'Well, have you noticed where they played yesterday?' He pointed to the footmarks in the bowlers' follow-throughs. 'I think I can drop my off-spinners in those marks,' he said. The invalid of the previous day thereupon took six wickets and Yorkshire won by 58 runs.

Close was vindicated in his decision at Chesterfield but there were other more bizarre episodes, including one that severely taxed the nerves of Dickie Bird at Worcester. Dinner was over and Bob Platt was enjoying post-prandial drinks together with Ronnie Burnet, the Yorkshire captain, at the hotel bar. 'Suddenly, Dickie steamed in, completely out of control,' recalls Platt. ' "Skipper," he cried, "I think Closey is trying to drown himself. All his clothes are on the river bank."' Soothing murmurs greeted his distraught announcement. It was not yet time to call for a rescue party.

The worries ceased when Close returned unharmed. It transpired that he had stripped down to his underpants to undertake another trial of strength by swimming across the dark waters of the Severn. The feat, accomplished after a full dinner, might well have been his response to the kind of dare that astonished others in his schooldays. Close could never resist a challenge.

If Close was taxing to others in these strained relationships, it may be assumed that he was fighting to overcome some demons within himself. There was, moreover, the heavy affliction of migraine which must have affected his nervous system. It first surfaced after his first century for Yorkshire against the Pakistanis at Bramall Lane, Sheffield, in 1954. 'I was sitting in the dressing-room when suddenly my eyes became blurred and I was as sick as a dog,' remembers Close.

It was a persistent and recurring ailment which led to bad lapses in form and his omission from the Yorkshire team. He was given twelfth-man duties in the match against Middlesex at Lord's in July 1955. 'I was dreading having to go out on to the field. It wasn't going right and I had no answer to the problem.' Medical advice was sought in London, after which Norman Yardley asked his team-mate if he would prefer to go home rather than travel on to the next match against Somerset at Taunton. Close hoped that his recuperative powers would prevail and said he would accompany the team. 'I was still not out of the doldrums when we arrived in Taunton.' He was selected to play in the match and in the first innings batted at five.

For the second innings, Yardley, with a perception to match his sympathetic management, produced the elixir of a challenge to rouse the despondent Close. 'Pad up, Brian,' came his urgent exhortation. 'You're going in first with me.' Yorkshire had been set a target of 285 runs in three and a half hours. Close, in company with fellow left-hander Vic Wilson, was a man transformed. The salve of aggression raised his spirits. The intoxication of chasing runs against the clock could not have been bettered as a tonic.

His application to the task produced 143 runs out of 212 in less than three hours. The second-wicket partnership with Wilson garnered 191 and Yorkshire galloped to victory by eight wickets. There were quiet smiles to greet the rejuvenated Close. 'It literally changed everything,' he recalls.

Refreshing overtures of this order only intermittently commended Close to the attention of the England selectors. He played in only four Tests in five years: one against South Africa at The Oval in 1955, two consecutively against the West Indies at Edgbaston and Lord's in 1957 and one against India at Leeds in 1959. There was one other Test, against Australia at Old Trafford in 1961. Astonishingly, 14 years would elapse after his first appearance against New Zealand in 1949 before he played in a full series for England.

While it is true that there were ample resources available to England in the 1950s, Close's performances in the matches allotted to him were by no means negligible. He deserved but did not get prolonged scrutiny. The gremlins still dogged his footsteps; he was, it seems, not forgiven for blotting his copybook in Australia as a boy. Neville Cardus, one of his admirers, thought the exclusion unfair. 'We should assess a cricketer by his best form,' wrote Cardus. 'I am convinced that he should have been persevered with by England's selectors.'

In any definition of Brian Close as a cricketer, what is beyond doubt and uppermost among his virtues is that he wanted to win at all times. He was the worst of losers. This abhorrence of defeat must have added to the pains of failure as a boy in Australia and the travail of lapses of form in the Yorkshire camp in an exacting decade. 'The only reason I went on to a sports field was to win,' he says.

Geoffrey Howard, his manager on the MCC 'A' tour of Pakistan in 1955–56, remembers one instance of Brian's zeal in a game of tennis on the sub-continent. Howard was then in his forty-fifth year and Close, 20 years his junior, was not disposed to make any concessions or surrender graciously to his senior. 'I won one set but that was all. I didn't win another point against Brian in that contest.' He also recalls the impromptu games of soccer in the gardens of their hotels. 'Brian did not hold back even then; he treated each one as if it was a Cup tie.'

Close's selection for the tour of Pakistan, under the captaincy of Donald Carr, placed him among a group of aspiring young men, all either internationals or on the verge of recognition by England. The party included Allan Watkins, Ken Barrington, Fred Titmus, Tony Lock, Alan Moss and Jim Parks. Bill Sutcliffe, as vice-captain, Peter Richardson, Roy Swetman, Peter Sainsbury and Mike Cowan were others looking to advance their claims on this tour. Howard is complimentary about his charges. 'It was a well-selected team. They were all young men and we had a lot of fun, mostly of our own making. I must have appeared to them almost like their grandfather.'

Pakistan did, though, present formidable opposition. In their ranks were Fazal Mahmood, the brothers Hanif and Wazir Mohammad and Imtiaz Ahmed, a fine wicket-keeper/batsman. The captain, Abdul Hafeez Kardar, was rich in cricket experience. He was a contemporary of Donald Carr at Oxford and led his country in their first 23 Tests. 'Pakistan had beaten England at The Oval in 1954,' recalls Howard. 'It was very quickly apparent to us that they were not going to lose to an "A" team.'

Pakistan were conclusive victors in the first two of the unofficial Tests, at Dacca and Peshawar, winning by an innings and seven wickets respectively. Tony Lock, with tour figures of 81 wickets at an average of 10.72 runs each, was a major bowling force in Pakistan. In the final match in the series, at Karachi, he took five wickets for 49 runs in a marathon spell of 40 overs. This first-innings analysis and the dismissal of Pakistan for 178 gave the MCC the ascendancy. Close, who finished third in the batting averages, hit 71 (out of 184) and 30 as the MCC won by two wickets.

'Certainly not, Alex, these are good chaps,' was the response of the Pakistan Board of Control to the offer to call off the tour by the MCC President, Lord Alexander of Tunis. The hue and cry and the flurry of cables between England and Pakistan followed an innocent jape which ruffled the dignity of the umpire Idris Begh. One of the standing jokes on the tour between the MCC players themselves had involved the use of cold water in the manner of ragging by students. The high spirits got alarmingly out of hand in an incident involving

Begh on a February evening in Peshawar. *Wisden* reported: 'More important was the unhappy timing of the affair during the course of a match in which umpiring decisions had been criticised.'

Donald Carr admits his complicity in the teasing interlude. 'It was a prank which ultimately got out of hand.' Carr remembers that he was in overall command and that he and Close and Roy Swetman took leading roles in the pre-arranged escapade. 'The party as a whole were in agreement. Closey was such a strong fellow and he took it upon himself to transport Mr Begh by a tonga to our hotel.'

Begh was known for his unfailingly immaculate appearance. It was rudely disturbed at the hotel when a huge cauldron of water emptied its contents on him. All the MCC players, themselves drenched, thought he was a willing victim. It had been gently explained to the umpire that this was an application reserved for special friends. 'Begh was a little shaken up,' says Carr, 'but he was treated reasonably and was really quite enjoying what was only fun in our company.'

Unfortunately, for the delighted parties, the news of the 'kidnapping' of Begh had come to the attention of two other Pakistanis. One of them, says Carr, was 'my friend, Hafeez Kardar'. They arrived at the tail-end of the deluge to see Begh in unusual disorder. Their laughter at the wet and bedraggled umpire changed the situation. Begh, hitherto disarmed by the mischief, now took offence and disappeared from the room.

In retrospect, the boisterous parade at Peshawar deserved little more than mild wigging for the guilty youngsters. It was, though, rapidly magnified in proportion and urgent diplomacy was required to defuse the row. Geoffrey Howard, on his return to England, issued a public statement. He said the folly was now fully understood. 'I can assure you that our young team are bitterly sorry about it and have suffered a good deal as a result.'

There was another sequel, a gesture of goodwill by the MCC tourists, in the arrangement of a soccer game following the incident at Peshawar. Their opponents were the reigning Pakistani Cup finalists. It was played at Multan, after the completion of a cricket match at lunch on the third day. The tourists had a number of footballers, some of professional status, in their ranks. They felt they would not be outclassed, even against a team crowned with pride in Pakistan.

Willing helpers were set to work in marking new lines for the match played on the cricket field. 'We had a good crowd for the cricket and even better one for the football,' remembers Howard. At half-time, Bill Sutcliffe and Alan Moss emerged, like mischievous waiters, carrying buckets of water, and proceeded to show the cheering spectators that the MCC footballers were just as subject to a dousing as their umpire. Less to their satisfaction was the result of the match – a 2–0 defeat. Close, at centre-half, was hugely formidable against the dethroned champions. 'Closey was largely responsible for our victory,' says Donald Carr.

The daring at Peshawar was misguided but would doubtless have appealed to the impulses of Brian Close. He drove his cars with a similar madcap air and scant regard for his own safety and that of others. One near-disastrous accident occurred soon after his return home in 1956, when heavy rain caused the abandonment of Yorkshire's match against the visiting Australians at Bradford.

Arrangements had been made for a round at a Halifax golf course with Bob Appleyard and two Australians, Ray Lindwall and Keith Miller. Close usually carried his golf clubs in his car for just such an occasion, but this day had left them at home because the car was undergoing repairs. He returned home to collect his clubs and then, in a hired vehicle, set off for Halifax. 'I decided to take a short cut over Thornton Moors. I was driving down a road unknown to me, and went over a hump-backed bridge leading to a T junction.'

Approaching in the opposite direction was a monster obstacle – a three-ton lorry. He slammed on his brakes but there was no avoiding the collision. It threw him forward under the dashboard and his knee was ripped open. He was lucky to escape with nothing worse in the headlong clash. Raymond Illingworth, when advised of the accident, exclaimed: 'Has he killed himself this time?'

Good fortune was to aid Brian in other motoring adventures, but there was conflict of another kind in the highly combative Yorkshire dressing room in the 1950s. A picture of a battle as savage as a Scarfe cartoon was presented by observers both inside and outside the county. Leadership that was complacent and frail in discipline was cited as the main cause of the disaffection. Norman Yardley, as Yorkshire's captain, was criticised for failing to exert his authority in a more vigorous manner. Ted Lester remembers, 'Norman was such a nice bloke but he couldn't control people and there were some who took advantage of him.'

Yorkshire are sometimes charged with taking their cricket pleasures too seriously, and in the 1950s the belief still persisted that the county had an inalienable right to the championship pennant. The triumphant march of Surrey only served to heighten criticism of the team. Close maintains that the antagonism was exaggerated by observers. 'When you've got strong characters, all very competitive, as Surrey also had, you do need strong leadership. Don't forget that from the end of April to the beginning of September, players are virtually living in each other's laps. It is only human nature that you will not always see eye to eye with your team-mates. Envy is the inevitable consequence if the form of one player differs from another.'

Close, like other Yorkshiremen, strongly believes that it was the captaincy of Stuart Surridge at The Oval that swung the scales in Surrey's favour. 'Norman Yardley was a good captain, technically, a naturally gifted batsman and useful change bowler. But he wasn't a disciplinarian; if anything he was too mild in dealing with the senior players with whom he had grown up.' By contrast, Surrey had a leader who, while in every degree Yardley's inferior as a cricketer, was indisputably the boss. Surridge was immensely skilful in welding the mix of disparate personalities within his team. His discipline was often harsh and he did not mince words with amateurs or professionals. 'No one was under any illusion as to what the score was when Stuart was in charge,' recalls one admiring colleague, Raman Subba Row.

There was, however, the narrowest of divides between two great teams. It can best be judged by the fact that in one season Yorkshire and Surrey, between them, supplied 13 players to England. Yorkshire were four times runners-up in the championship and third on two occasions in the 1950s. Appleyard's absence for two seasons and injuries to other key bowlers diminished the challenge. Other contributory factors were inconsistent batting and an inability to find another bowler to aid Trueman in his opening thrusts. Yorkshire could no longer call on Close, whose knee problems sidelined him as a quick bowler.

The boundless energy of Fred Trueman salvaged pride on so many occasions. Ken Taylor, one of the emerging young players in this period, remembers Trueman in action at Park Avenue, Bradford. The hilltop ground had the atmosphere of a bullring. It was so called, said another Yorkshireman, Jim Laker, 'because once you had descended the three steps and gone on to the field, you saw brick walls around and a circle of intent Yorkshire folk watching you'.

Trueman, his dark hair tumbling, bristled with menace in his accelerating approach down from the whitewashed walls at the pavilion end. He was the exultant matador who pierced the defences of all but the most resolute opponents. A cordon of slips encircled the batsmen in his opening spells. Ken Taylor, patrolling the covers, and Don Wilson, on guard at mid-wicket, were the only men in front of the wicket.

'Fred had a magnificent action. He never broke down and he would bowl all day given the chance,' recalls Taylor. Ted Lester remembers his own qualms even though he was not on the receiving end. 'You felt frightened for the batsmen.'

Trueman was superbly equipped to be Yorkshire's spearhead. He measured up to one description of the ideal fast bowler as having 'shoulders that could brush each side of a barn door, a backside like a Belfast drum and the heart of a lion'. His stamina, though, was severely taxed as he persevered with a multitude of bowling partners. Many were tried and found wanting. The list included Eric Burgin from Sheffield, Brian James, a Barnsley recruit, and Philip Hodgson and Bill Holdsworth, candidates from Todmorden and Leeds. The best among the long stayers were Mike Cowan, another Leeds man whose career was disrupted by injury and illness, and Mel Ryan and Bob Platt, who had business commitments to subvert their claims.

One other bowler, the Halifax-born David Pickles, gave evidence for a brief time that he possessed the required credentials. Ted Lester recalls the comradely banter with Trueman on the introduction of Pickles. He suggested, with a twinkle in his eye, 'David is as quick as you.' The implication did, of course, have the desired effect of making Fred bowl even faster.

Pickles took 31 wickets in 12 matches for Yorkshire in 1957. His tally included three wickets in six balls, with Insole and Dexter among his victims, against the MCC at Scarborough. There were match figures of 12 wickets against Somerset at Taunton. In the first innings, armed with the new ball, Pickles took five wickets for six runs in 29 deliveries.

Lester, his captain in the Yorkshire seconds, remembers that Pickles had an unorthodox bowling action. On one occasion, during a Scarborough Festival, he tried to persuade Pickles to resist attempts by the county coaches to change the action. Unfortunately, this did not happen and the muddled young bowler completely lost control. A distraught Pickles told Lester, 'I used to love to bowl and aim at those three stumps. Sometimes the ball went one way and sometimes the other and I never knew where it was going.' Coaching can be a bugbear in arresting natural gifts. Lester adds sadly, 'David never got it back again.'

Brian Close, surveying a challenging decade, acknowledges that Surrey with their winning hand of four Test bowlers – Alec Bedser, Peter Loader, Tony Lock and Jim Laker – were better than Yorkshire in dismissing opponents. Bill Bowes also believed that Yorkshire lacked the bowling strengths to match Surrey, who had bowlers for all conditions, both at The Oval and on other grounds.

There were exaggerated claims that The Oval wicket was expressly tailored for the spin of Laker and Lock. Winning games in responsive conditions at home does, though, breed confidence, a fact that served to increase the displeasure of the Yorkshire partisans. Close and Bob Appleyard, as purveyors of off-spin, enjoyed their tussles at Kennington. There was an extra swagger in Appleyard's stride when he bowled on wickets supposedly prepared for Surrey's spin twins. If it helped them, he thought, there would be spoils for him, too.

Close, however, also maintains that a provoking ruling put Yorkshire at a disadvantage on their own grounds in the 1950s. The groundsmen held sway in producing the best possible wickets. Before one important match at Harrogate the players sought to obtain a more sporting wicket. 'We didn't mind an increased challenge. All the Yorkshire lads could play on turners,' says Close. The response of Brian Sellers, the Yorkshire chairman, when he heard about the request, was brusque and dismissive. It told the team that the preparation of wickets was none of their business.

The furious departure of Johnny Wardle, a bowler of genius, in 1958 polarised opinion in Yorkshire circles. On the one hand it was deemed necessary to restore discipline, and on the other it robbed Yorkshire of the most experienced player in the team. 'He was a man who knew more about bowling than any of us,' says Appleyard, his former partner.

Close was another of Wardle's allies in a regrettable situation. He believes that Wardle's expertise should have ensured that he followed Bill Sutcliffe as Yorkshire captain. Even those players who incurred his displeasure acknowledged Wardle's rating as a model professional. 'From all the people I came across I learned more from Johnny on how to play cricket. He was as cute as a box of monkeys, with all the tricks up his sleeve, and all perfectly honourable.'

The dismissal of Wardle, then a premier bowler at the height of his powers, was the inevitable consequence of his feud with Ronnie Burnet, the newly appointed Yorkshire captain. It was a fall from grace conducted in the glare of national publicity. A controversial series of articles in the *Daily Mail*, which Wardle regretted almost as soon as they were printed, dwelt upon what he considered a lamentable decision to install Burnet as captain. The core of his complaint was that Burnet, then aged 40 and without any previous first-class experience, was ill fitted to command seasoned professionals. Burnet was not without his devotees, though, especially among those he had captained to win the Minor Counties championship in 1957. They would form the nucleus of the team that ended Surrey's championship reign two years later.

Geoff Cope was one of the later school of Yorkshire cricketers who benefited from Wardle's wisdom. When Cope, as an off-spinner, was banned for 'throwing' in the 1970s, Wardle was deputed to act as his bowling tutor. Their friendship during this time blossomed into a father-and-son relationship. Cope began to appreciate the frustrations of Wardle in previous years. 'I know the kids thought the world of Ronnie Burnet. He had done a super job with the second eleven. But he could not adopt the same measures in the first team,' said Cope.

Stories of dissension did, however, filter through to the younger brigade. There were charges of a chaotic dressing room in which arguments raged and, said one observer, the wrangling did not always stop when the team went out on to the field. The position changed when Burnet assumed command. The disputes ended and a new belief took hold: the importance of fostering the merits of a team game as opposed to individual interests. It was, as events were to prove, the difference between winning the championship and languishing in second or third place. Burnet, whatever his deficiencies as a player, was able to marshal the resources of the boys who had won their spurs under his leadership as Minor Counties champions. He always insisted that his mandate as first eleven captain was to get the team playing together again and not to pursue any vendetta against Johnny Wardle.

Brian Close accumulated his store of knowledge as a cricketer during this troubled time. Provisions for success were stored to stimulate his appetite in other happier times. Captaincy, he was later to state, was a labour of love; he would also find it thrilling to be allowed to dictate matters. More immediately he was conscious of the plight of the besieged Wardle. 'Ronnie Burnet was a good leader but his awareness of the ins and outs of cricket was limited,' he maintains. Cricket, Close says, is a thinking game and the hardest job for any captain is in the field.

In his view, Wardle's quarrel with Burnet stemmed from lack of consultation at key moments. 'We were all complaining in our different ways but Johnny was the senior player and the most voluble.' One outburst summed up the general disaffection. 'We came off the field in one game and told Ronnie: "We are trying our damnedest and you will not do the things we suggest. As a result, you are making us look like fools out there." '

Watching the profitless campaigns preceded a renewed surge of interest in the game. Close knew then that he was about to enter into his true calling. Captaincy was not yet within his grasp but he sensed the time was drawing near. 'Brian began to take a deeper interest in the Yorkshire cricket scene once the reorganisation under the captaincy of Ronnie Burnet had taken place,' recalls Bryan Stott. Close was now beginning to steer the fortunes of the team. 'As time went on, you watched Brian as well as the skipper,' continues Stott. 'It did not require a second glance when he moved you in the field. Quietly he would indicate that this was the better place for you to be.'

The captain-in-waiting was polishing his skills for the future, though he was not yet an infallible guide. Burnet's circle of advisers also included two others astute in the ways of cricket, Raymond Illingworth and Jimmy Binks. They would make sure that an inspirational leader did not stray too far in his direction in a magnificent era.

5

A Championship Cruise at Hove

'The championship pennant has been taken away from Surrey with the sheer will to win. Yorkshire have gone for the runs when they seemed impossible.'

YORKSHIRE POST

'Oh, what a beautiful day,' enthused the leader writer, as if larkishly regaling his audience with a chorus from a Rodgers and Hammerstein musical. The flurry of runs on an August afternoon at Hove in 1959 had a comparable jollity. It was a gallop that defied the odds against them; the victory over Sussex carried Yorkshire to their first championship for 13 years.

The congratulations reflected the distinction achieved by the youngest team, with an average age of 22, to claim the title. Yorkshire had begun the season with only eight capped players, four of whom had only been capped in the previous two years. The match-winning total, scored at the rate of 127 runs per 100 balls, was then the third fastest recorded in first-class cricket.

There was, amid the delight, a typically downbeat footnote to halt undue euphoria. Rashness in compliments is never permitted in Yorkshire. The Richardson cartoon in the *Yorkshire Evening News* carried the caption: 'Don't let Yorkshire winnin' the championship go to your head an' start backing Leeds United to win the Cup.' It was a reference to the sporting status of the soccer club, then the poor relation of rugby and cricket in Leeds.

'If there is any moral to this proud cricketing feat, surely it must be that no star is indispensable,' was the verdict of another captivated commentator. 'At a time when three players of Test experience – Wardle, Appleyard and Lowson – dropped out of the side last year the wailers could see no future for Yorkshire. To axe from the attack one of the greatest exponents [Wardle] of left-arm spin bowling in the world and stride on to honours is just as surely an indication that the team is always greater than the individual.' It was, as Yorkshire's caretaker captain Ronnie Burnet concluded, a complete vindication of the disciplinary measures he had been forced to put in place.

Burnet remembered the pre-season lunch in 1959 at which Brian Sellers, the newly appointed chairman, had expressed the opinion that it would take at least three years for Yorkshire to emerge as a championship side. Sellers had been the captain when Yorkshire last won the title outright in 1946. His cautionary overture was under-standable, but it also constituted a challenge to a new generation to prove him wrong.

Yorkshire were set a target of 215 runs in 105 minutes at Hove. The pugnacity of their response had all the fury of a Sunday League knockabout. The strokeplay, with Bryan Stott and Doug Padgett in the vanguard, was violent and breathtaking. Stott remembers that the Sussex captain, Robin Marlar, had resisted the pleas of his team-mates to declare at lunchtime. 'He'd nothing to gain, we didn't expect him to declare.'

Marlar contributed to a thrilling finale by his conduct of the game. 'Sussex weren't proppin' and coppin',' says Stott. 'They were giving us a chance, however slim, and Jackie Birkenshaw took two superb catches on the boundary to dismiss Dexter and Parks off the bowling of Don Wilson.' The winning quest was aided, as on other occasions during the season, by the total involvement of Yorkshire's senior professionals. 'They were absolutely on full power in their contributions,' adds Stott. For the first time in many years there was ample evidence of a commitment to the team's cause.

Brian Close recalls that victory for Yorkshire had seemed an unlikely outcome. 'At lunch I thought we'd blown it. Sussex, with seven wickets down, were around two hundred in front, and time was running out for us.' A measure of concerted action was needed and this was agreed in a discussion between Burnet and Close on the resumption. The Yorkshire captain considered that the introduction of Fred Trueman was the best means of making a breakthrough.

Close, however, had noted the strong wind blowing from the Cromwell Road end down towards the sea. 'Forget Freddie,' urged Close. 'Let Raymond have that end. He likes to bowl with the wind at his shoulders.' Close prevailed in the talk; it was a timely intervention, and Illingworth took the last three wickets, including that of Pataudi, who had been missed off a skier before lunch.

The omens in 1959 at first seemed to support the circumspection of Brian Sellers in his luncheon address. Bryan Stott believes that Yorkshire rode their luck. By mid-June, their progress had been undermined by lost tosses. They were then positioned only halfway up the table. Three victories towards the end of that month carried them into first place. Yorkshire were never subsequently out of the top three in the order for the rest of the season. But they had to withstand a discomfiting tour of the West Country during which Somerset and Gloucestershire beat them in consecutive matches.

At Bristol they suffered a stunning reverse. They were beaten by an innings and bowled out for 35 in the first innings in 75 minutes. Bolus, unbeaten, was top scorer with 12 and the last six Yorkshire batsmen all registered ducks. Tony Brown, making the ball swing in the air and move alarmingly off the pitch, took seven wickets for 11 runs in a spell of 11 overs. It was Yorkshire's lowest score since 1935, when Essex dismissed them for 31. If this could happen to seasoned campaigners, it seemed preposterous to imagine that an immature team could recover and place their names on the championship roll call.

Yet they did find the resolve to disregard the dip in form. In the crucial final phase Yorkshire's young men gambled on taking risks to ascend in triumph. 'We started to achieve winning targets and our confidence rose sky high,' remembers Stott, reflecting on the extent of a revival when the most imposing tasks began to be accomplished with astonishing ease. The disappointments of the earlier struggles gave way, in the space of a handful of games, to the fervour of an unbeatable combination.

Stott concedes that Yorkshire were fortunate to carry the day against Sussex at Hove. It was a match they had to win to ensure the championship. Surrey were edging towards an eighth title, but they would have had to beat Middlesex and Northamptonshire at The Oval, and failed in both matches. Yorkshire, on the other hand, took full advantage of the indecision of Robin Marlar. 'He didn't quite grasp the situation,' says Stott. 'He was too late in trying to shut up shop, so we had to go for the runs.'

Close remembers the spurt for runs. 'Ronnie's boys were all fired up. They all got stuck in and it was a marvellous feeling to bring Surrey's reign to an end.' It was, though, an episode of calculated bravado, almost absurd in its outcome. An outrageous romp began with 15 runs in the first over. Within half an hour the score had advanced to 77. The hundred was hoisted in 43 minutes and the total had doubled before the clock ticked on another 45 minutes. Yorkshire, in fact, had seven minutes to spare in winning by five wickets.

'Robin Marlar had set off with a normal field,' recalls Stott. 'We were so far in front after two overs that he just couldn't pull us back. We had beaten them. Their bowlers didn't know what to do.'

Jim Swanton, writing in the *Daily Telegraph,* reported whimsically: 'There was a strange notion during the interval between the innings that Yorkshire had only the slimmest chance. They had to try, of course, because they had nothing to lose.' Swanton enthused about the daring onslaught. 'Yorkshire won the championship,' he said, 'thanks to two innings of exemplary hitting by Stott and Padgett. In 61 minutes they scored 141 together, starting at 40 for 2, and took their side to the brink of victory.'

Swanton also commended the sporting tactics of Sussex. 'They contributed generously to the occasion by refusing to "play safe" and bowling at the stumps. The strokeplay of Stott and Padgett was unforgettable. It was not in any sense blind hitting. They made ground to everything, so dictating the length, and in turn they showed every stroke. By the time Padgett was caught at deep mid-wicket by Dexter off Thomson, Yorkshire had only to coast comfortably and keep their heads.'

In the small hours of the following morning a convoy of cars carrying the jubilant Yorkshire cricketers arrived in Scarborough.

The time was a little after four o'clock and silhouetted in the distance was a great mass of welcoming followers. The beckoning applause soared into a full-throated greeting as the happy party turned down the main street to find the pavements packed with excited townspeople.

The glamour of the splendid terraced ground in North Marine Road was a magnet for players and supporters alike. It has, at the curtain fall of each season, been the venue for special events. Huge crowds watched over the years the traditional fixtures – Yorkshire v MCC, Gentlemen and Players, and H.D.G. Leveson-Gower's XI against the touring team.

Jim Kilburn remembered the unchanging routine at Scarborough. Train seats were as scarce from King's Cross as from West Riding towns before the opening of the festival. The luncheon gongs in the boarding houses in adjacent Trafalgar Square clanged hundreds away at one o'clock. Other spectators did not stray from their favourite benches. They opened their packets of sandwiches and listened to the cries of the vendors – 'ripe William pears' and 'chocolates, clear-gums and pastilles'. On the field there was the ritual of refreshments carried out by a uniformed butler and a retinue of waitresses. Through the intervals and during play the town brass band was another entertainer, striking vigorous notes in musical medleys. Johnny Wardle, never one to resist a jest, caught the mood of the festival. The band played a Johann Strauss polka and he would move in jauntily to bowl – one, two, three, hop – to the rhythms like a dancing master.

It is debatable whether all, including tourists faced with the equivalent of another Test, would agree with Kilburn that festival cricket at Scarborough was first-class cricket on holiday. But it was an immovable family date in September. 'Mother and daughter would perhaps count nine days on a cricket field as an inadequate holiday,' reflected Kilburn. 'Scarborough offers them other attractions, still permitting father and son to indulge their particular delight with a peaceful conscience.'

The rejoicing at another Yorkshire championship in 1959 brought other fathers and sons to witness more exhilarating exploits.

Doug Insole, a stern competitor, captained the MCC against the newly crowned champions. 'Yorkshire kept up their season's custom and lost the toss,' reported Bill Bowes in the *Yorkshire Evening News*. Ronnie Burnet was due to play for the MCC, but at the request of the Festival chairman, Tom Pearce, he retained the Yorkshire captaincy. 'I think you should have the great honour of leading your champions on to the field,' said Pearce.

A tight duel for first-innings honours, with Illingworth on the brink of a double as a century maker, was followed by a tardy declaration by the MCC. Brian Close recalls: 'Doug set us about a hundred and twelve an hour and said: "There you are, have a go at that!"' The actual target was 260 in two and a half hours. Yorkshire, high on adrenalin, won by seven wickets with 25 minutes to spare. Close led the way in another victory against the clock. His unbeaten 88 included 50 in 35 minutes.

Yorkshire sealed a hat-trick of spectacular triumphs in the traditional fixture between the Champion County and the Rest at The Oval. 'We had had a fair celebration time at Scarborough,' remembers Close. 'And we were now faced by an England side in all but name.' The festival revelries might just have caused them to blink wearily at the names of the impressive opponents, 10 of them internationals, intent on stopping them in their tracks. Three of the Rest team – Geoff Pullar, Ken Barrington and Trevor Bailey – had season aggregates of over 2000 runs and another, M.J.K. Smith, had topped the averages with 3245 runs. Bailey had also achieved a notable double as the first player to score 2000 runs and take 100 wickets since 1937.

Yorkshire seemed destined to lose this particular battle as they followed on 224 runs behind the Rest. Pride was salvaged by Close and Vic Wilson, the latter making a century, and Yorkshire hit back to total 425, their highest score of the season. Accounts vary of the selection of the 38-year-old Wilson, who had suffered lapses in form and, at his own request, was relegated to the second team.

According to Close, it was at his instigation that Wilson played at The Oval. Jackie Birkenshaw would have been the choice of Ronnie Burnet. Close pointed out that Yorkshire already had two off-spinners in the party – Illingworth and himself – and that to include Birkenshaw, another offspinner and a modest batsman, would create a lack of balance in the team.

Stott presents a different version of Wilson's selection, portraying it as a request from Burnet. He remembers that at team discussion before their departure for London the Yorkshire captain had advanced the claims of the veteran. 'Ronnie said: "This is Vic's last season. He has played so long without being a member of a championship team. I would like him to play at The Oval."' It was considered a fair proposal, as was the consensus that Dickie Bird should also be included in the party. It was thought unlikely that financial aid would be forthcoming from the Yorkshire committee and the team decided to pool funds themselves to meet the expenses of Bird's journey.

Wilson's readmission to the Yorkshire team was then seen merely as a courtesy to a man at the end of a worthy career. His century, a good one, at The Oval, not only delayed his retirement but produced, as it turned out, an extension of three years.

Close was also determined that Illingworth should not be displaced by injury. 'Illy's spinning finger was a little worn after a hard season, but I told him to assure Ronnie that he was fit to play.' The troublesome finger was nursed sufficiently to enable Illingworth to flourish against the Rest. The off-spinning duo of Close and Illingworth snared nine wickets to bring about another remarkable somersault. The Rest were routed for 135 and Yorkshire, once more against the odds, won by 66 runs.

There was an intriguing sequel to a season of high accomplishment. In October 1959, Ronnie Burnet and Johnny Wardle met for the first time since their dispute, at a dinner in Doncaster. 'Johnny walked across the floor to greet me and said: "Congratulations, skipper. Well done."' Burnet replied: 'You should have been with us when we won the championship.' Wardle's response was a mixture of self-rebuke and amazement. 'I know I should. I'm sorry. I didn't think you could do it.'

Vic Wilson, the brawny and handsome farmer from Malton, was, in the words of Close, 'a sound, solid citizen in cricketing terms'. In

17 seasons with Yorkshire, his powerful forearms wielded a bat whose breadth recalled the fields he farmed, and he accumulated 21,650 runs, including two double centuries. His sure hands, mostly employed in the leg trap, also grasped 548 catches. This ability as a fieldsman was a key factor in his surprise selection for the tour of Australia under the captaincy of Len Hutton in 1954–55. Hutton, as a fellow Yorkshireman, knew from experience that he could rely on Wilson's merits as a catcher in any emergency.

Burnet related to me the sequence of events that led in 1960 to Wilson's elevation as Yorkshire's first professional captain in modern times. In the previous winter Brian Sellers, the Yorkshire chairman, had invited him to lunch. The substance of the meeting at the Raggalds Inn, near Bradford, was that Burnet was asked to stand down as Yorkshire captain. With some justification, Burnet believed that his successful leadership entitled him to continue in the post for at least another season. He had learned enough from the lessons of the tragic affray in 1958 to restore the reputation and esteem of the county. Sellers, never a man to be dissuaded, strongly argued that it was in the team's interests that Burnet should make way for Wilson. Burnet thought long and hard about the proposal before giving his consent.

It was a strange cricketing coronation for Wilson, a near discard at the end of Yorkshire's championship season and seemingly just waiting for the handshakes at the end of a long and honourable career. The 'interests' referred to by Sellers implied that Yorkshire needed a safe pair of hands at the helm and Wilson was judged the man for the job. It was also a snub for Close, who might have expected preference as captain ahead of the veteran.

Bryan Stott believes that Wilson's appointment was misguided. 'Vic should never have followed Ronnie. He was an absolute disaster as captain because he had had no reason to think as a captain for the whole of his career.'

Wilson, despite the reservations about his captaincy, did have an excellent record in an unexpected finale to his career, though his two championship successes owed much to the team under his command. They were able to overcome the tactical errors of a quiet, private man. Close speaks of a 'hell of a nice chap', wryly adding that Wilson was not one of cricket's philosophers.

Stott also makes the point that Close, a fretful guide, would in this period have been trying to make up for the deficiencies of his captain. There had been a similar imperative during the reign of Burnet. According to Close, Burnet had initially welcomed the advice of his senior professional and then become a little blasé and stopped listening.

There seems little doubt that Close also attempted to engage in a supportive dialogue with Wilson. This liaison probably foundered when Close started to move players around in the field. Bad feelings came to a boiling point in what appeared to be a struggle for authority. There was a major row between the two players in a match at Hull. 'You're a professional and I'm a professional,' raged Wilson. 'And as long as I'm captain I'm also senior professional and I don't need your advice.'

The refusal to accept assistance is at variance with the view of Raymond Illingworth, perhaps a more discreet helper. 'Vic was a good honest bloke,' he says. 'He would listen to what you suggested. Brian gave him some hard times.' However, others buffeted Vic Wilson in the Yorkshire team, all vainly urging Close to use his powers of persuasion to exert tactical changes. 'So I did keep on asking and Vic kept refusing until he finally told me: "If you open your mouth once more I'll send you home on the train."'

These were irksome times for the magnificent team under Wilson's command. But Yorkshire were now an experienced unit, able to pull together and override all hazards. They achieved their second successive championship in 1960 despite two wounding defeats by Lancashire. Geoff Pullar scored a century at Headingley – his third in successive Roses matches. Yorkshire, overwhelmed by the leg-spin of Greenhough and Barber, lost by 10 wickets in two days. The other reverse, in a dramatic conclusion at Old Trafford, was by two wickets off the last ball of the match.

The Whitsuntide defeat at Leeds came as a severe shock after three weeks of convincing victories. Yorkshire returned to the winning path in June, but, as Jim Kilburn reported, 'The crack in the plaster of self-esteem was never again entirely renovated.' Wilson's captaincy brought praise from the *Yorkshire Post* cricket correspondent, who was clearly one of his admirers. 'His overall strategy never wavered in its devotion to enterprise . . . in the bright and dark hours he was always obviously the leader.'

Certainly Wilson displayed a startling disregard for personalities in his jousts with his fellow professionals. It took a brave man to discipline Fred Trueman, then at the height of his fame. When Trueman arrived late for a match against Somerset at Taunton, the Yorkshire captain dropped him from the team. He fuelled the fury of his fast bowler by telling him to return home and report to the Yorkshire committee.

Yorkshire slipped to second place in the championship behind Hampshire, who won their first title in 1961. It was, observes Close, little short of a disaster for a team once again the undisputed challengers. 'If we didn't now win championships there were inquests at all levels, from the county committee to the smallest cricket society.'

Yorkshire had looked certain to win their third consecutive championship in 1961. They claimed seven victories in their first eight games, but a slump followed as Hampshire leapfrogged above them – and the other contender, Middlesex – in a rousing finish to the season. Close, while conceding first place to Hampshire and their buoyant captain, Colin Ingleby-Mackenzie, does identify declarations by opponents as one reason why Yorkshire were deposed as champions. 'They declared in eleven matches won by Hampshire, while that happened only two or three times to us.'

There was a return to winning ways and another championship to send Vic Wilson off into cheerful retirement in 1962. Yorkshire bowled out Glamorgan for 65 at Harrogate in a match they had to win to regain their status as champions. Twenty wickets fell for 166 runs on the first day and Glamorgan were 23 runs behind with all their wickets intact at the close of play.

'Glamorgan's first innings was Yorkshire's justification and joy,' wrote Jim Kilburn. 'It never approached prosperity on such a pitch as spin bowlers sometimes find in their dreams but rarely discover in their waking and working hours. The ball turned readily, but, more significantly, it turned beyond prediction.'

Yorkshire gained a lead of 36 on the first innings, thanks mainly to Ken Taylor, whose batting at Harrogate was invested with a steel that should have brought him more than three England caps. He surged to a polished 67 and batted for all but 10 minutes of the innings. Only Phil Sharpe among the other batsmen reached double figures.

Torrential rain descended on the Harrogate ground on the last day. The resumption of play was in the nature of a miracle. It was made possible only by the remarkable drainage of the field and the diligent labours of the groundsmen from before dawn. By lunchtime seven wickets were down and Glamorgan held the narrow advantage of 39 runs.

Yorkshire were held at bay for 40 minutes in the afternoon. Don Wilson and Illingworth spun in vain on a rapidly easing wicket. Evans and Ward were the dogged batsmen. They only scored 29, but it was the biggest and longest stand of the innings. Yorkshire turned to Close, who not only broke the stand but also finished the innings. Close ended his championship bowling for the year with three wickets for four runs in nine balls. Sharpe took his seventy-first catch of the season when he caught Evans off Close to beat a Yorkshire record held since 1901 by John Tunnicliffe.

Yorkshire were left a modest target of 66 in three hours, but they had to weather the shock of the dismissal of their first-innings saviour, Ken Taylor. He was yorked first ball by Jones, who thus was credited with an unusual hat-trick after having taken the last two wickets of Yorkshire's first innings. Sharpe and Close also fell to handsome catches, but Jackie Hampshire forced confident boundaries, Stott's first scoring stroke was a six and in less than an hour the game was won.

The happy tidings of another championship were exceeded for Close with his belated appointment as Yorkshire captain in 1963. 'Captaincy came to me as a joyous relief rather than strain,' he says. 'I could follow my own instincts, put my own ideas into operation. To back me up I had a team of superb professionals who were not only great, or very good, players but who all thought about their cricket day and night.'

The mental confusions which, said Kilburn, had driven Brian Close to the verge of instability were now cast aside as he embarked on an illustrious decade. He braced his shoulders for captaincy and the new responsibility concentrated his cricketing mind. It was always his true calling and, as he says, there were many thrills to be had as the director of Yorkshire's fortunes.

6

'They Didn't Know How to Lose'

'His side of the Sixties, though occasionally exasperated when he went on one of his mental walkabouts, nevertheless regarded him in affectionate wonderment and professional respect.'

DON MOSEY

The curtains parted to usher the word-perfect understudy into the captaincy spotlight in Yorkshire's centenary year in 1963. Brian Close, aged 32, and after waiting so long in the wings, knew his lines backwards. He was immediately dominant in a coveted leading role.

Close's appointment in succession to Vic Wilson was the turning point in his career. Bill Bowes, one of Yorkshire's champions of the past, expressed his astonishment at the impact of a man whose promotion was tinged with circumspection. He was pointedly on trial. 'Almost overnight it seemed that Brian Close matured,' wrote Bowes. 'Close's field placings were as intelligent and antagonistic as any seen in the county for 25 years.'

Jim Kilburn was equally admiring as another witness of a transformed cricketer. 'In his first season of the Yorkshire captaincy Close not only played decisive innings but adopted fielding attitudes, philosophical and physical, that were an inspiration. Yorkshire won their twenty-eighth championship. Close won respect.' A lonely cricket adolescence, said Kilburn, came to an end with the responsibilities of captaincy. 'The office was not given without misgiving and Close was aware of the misgiving. He knew that because he was senior he must act like a senior.' Raymond Illingworth, Close's canny brother in arms, declares that this was the moment when Brian became the hard man. 'No one could destroy him.'

Close's leadership qualities had been honed and polished during a gruelling apprenticeship. He had learned much from success and failure. His powers of communication had been forged during the years of turmoil in the 1950s. 'I'd had a lot of experience playing under various captains, good and bad,' says Close. 'I knew how people's minds worked and developed an understanding as to how to bring the best out of my team.' Just as important was the need to engender a good spirit in the dressing room, especially on days of ill fortune. 'We always had a laugh about things which went wrong.'

He would later stress the keynote of captaincy, which was in line with his own unselfish approach to the game: 'I've always believed that the team is more important than the individual.' At the outset of a distinguished reign he restated his credo as a cricketer. 'I've always been a winner – and this is how I wanted things to be for Yorkshire.' Pride and satisfaction were the driving forces. 'Whatever the match, I wanted to win. I wanted to compete and put my skills to the test against others. That, for me, is what sporting life is all about.'

The awesome rule of a great soccer motivator, Bill Shankly, would find its parallel in the cricketing mind games of another master psychologist. 'We used to go out on to the field with Brian fully expecting to win,' recalls one colleague, Bryan Stott. 'We couldn't see any reason why we should lose a game.' Don Wilson, a happy entertainer in his own right, adds: 'He made us feel like we were the greatest bowlers in the world.'

Brian Close at Yorkshire replicated the unassailable authority exerted by Bill Shankly at Huddersfield and Liverpool. Ken Taylor, a sturdy centre-half under Shankly's management at Leeds Road, discovered a comparable strategist in Close. 'Shanks used to tell us that we were the best eleven players on the park. The others didn't deserve to be playing against us.' The pattern of command continued in Taylor's cricket seasons with Yorkshire. 'Shanks made you want to play for him. Closey was the same.'

Mike Brearley, with similar qualifications as a captain, referred to Close as a physically hard and shrewd competitor with whom it was wise not to risk provocation. As a fine attacking captain, said Brearley, Close was much happier when his team was 'on the go' in the field, trying anything to get a wicket. 'He would caper about at the batsman's feet as happy as a hippo in wet mud.'

Stott presents a picture of the sometimes outrageous passages of play and the excitement that Close brought to Yorkshire's adventures in the 1960s. 'When you played for Yorkshire you always knew something was going to happen. You didn't necessarily rely on Brian. But in the big games he was rock solid. The harder, stronger and more competent the opposition – this was when he came into his own. You knew then that he would take some getting out. Nothing would move him on those occasions.'

Yorkshire's duels with Surrey carried a weight and a challenge that summoned the audacious response of a great player. As Close invariably attributed his dismissals not to his own indiscretions but to some alien source, he was pardonably aggrieved at The Oval in June 1960. He chose Tony Lock's benefit match to play an innings that had veteran onlookers entranced by strokeplay reminiscent of Frank Woolley.

Yet his anger was unconfined as he left the field, having been caught by Tindall off Loader, just two runs short of a glorious double century. Gordon Ross, the Surrey historian, recalled, 'Close departed with an expression of disdain and anguish never leaving his face on the long trek to the pavilion. Anyone just arriving might have thought that Close had been put out first ball. He had hit 22 fours and four sixes. Here was an innings to keep the saloon bars around Kennington well stocked with conversation for months.'

Tony Lock, the hapless beneficiary, returned figures of 0 for 127. Prodigious hitting sent the fieldsmen scurrying in fruitless pursuit. Close thrice struck Lock for sixes into the spectators' laps in the pavilion seats – once sending the ball clean through the open windows to clatter on to a table in the committee room. Amid the riot of sixes, a major disappointment was that he failed in his aim to hit Lock over the pavilion.

Bob Platt remembers 'an incredible innings' at The Oval. Even more vivid in his memory is Close's furious reaction to his dismissal.

The roars of acclamation were ringing in his ears as he disappeared from view. His footsteps pounded on the stairs leading to the Yorkshire dressing room. 'The bat came in first before Closey,' says Platt. 'It bounced on the table and nearly shot through on to the members' balcony outside.'

Close's third-wicket partnership of 226 with Doug Padgett was the rousing prelude to Yorkshire's victory by nine wickets. Fred Trueman took 14 wickets in the match, including three wickets in five balls in each of the Surrey innings. The thrilling exploit by Close at The Oval was succeeded in the same season by another onslaught against Nottinghamshire before his own supporters at Scarborough. Once again the double century narrowly eluded him but his 184 was a pulsating example of his inspirational batting.

Peter Roebuck, one of Close's pupils during his later term with Somerset, was among those enthused by an incorrigible cricketer. 'Sometimes his inspirations triumphantly succeeded; at other times they fell into ruins. Brian was an extraordinary man, a mix of King Lear storming in the wilderness and Churchill defying 'em on the beaches.'

Apocryphal stories pursue larger-than-life characters and Close was no exception. Bryan Stott gives substance to one anecdote involving Close in a match against Derbyshire at Queen's Park, Chesterfield. Les Jackson, always a mesmeric force on the Peak county's green wickets, came under Close's scrutiny.

Close, sitting with his pads on, spent the first hour of the morning on the pavilion balcony, watching Jackson. At last he told his team-mates, 'I've got it.' He flourished an imaginary ball to explain when and where Jackson bowled his leg-cutter. Shortly afterwards he went in to bat, shouldered arms and was bowled by what was an off-cutter to him as a left-hander. Close returned to the dressing room and, after the customary pause for reflection, there was a considerable explosion of mirth. 'We all collapsed with laughter,' says Stott. 'It was an hilarious experience.'

Brian Close, with his exceptional fervour, was an irresistible gladiator. A host of acclamations ensued as Yorkshire swaggered to four championships and two Gillette Cup triumphs in an invincible decade. 'The 1960s side was the greatest sporting and entertaining team in the world – on and off the field,' he says. 'You should have seen our version of the Black and White Minstrels Show.'

The ardour of the Yorkshire captain also prevailed in another even more important conquest. His marriage to Vivien would bolster him in the perils ahead and would become a unity of devoted partners. Vivien, extrovert and engaging, is a Devonian and a former BOAC flight attendant. She is a rewarding discovery, as Brian decided within a few minutes of meeting her at the Breakers Beach Club, Bermuda in 1964. Brian was a persistent suitor. Obstacles, such as the fact she was already engaged to an airline pilot, also called Brian, were brushed aside as irrelevant. He embarked on a romantic siege. The stubborn Yorkshire admirer became an earnest student of airline timetables. Whenever Vivien landed in Britain, Brian was there waiting to meet her.

Brian had asked Vivien to marry him at their first meeting and his courtship never wavered. Vivien was equally determined as she refused the overtures. 'I didn't think he was my type, and anyway I didn't particularly want to get married so soon. I was having a lot of fun as a single girl.'

Vivien, who now shares her husband's obsession with golf, was also an all-round sportswoman. She threw javelin and played netball in school events, and she was also a keen tennis player and swimmer in her native Devon. At 19, after a year in France, she joined the International Telephone Exchange as a linguist. Appointments followed with BEA and later BOAC and she graduated to regular three-week journeys on routes embracing New York and San Francisco, Honolulu, Tokyo and Hong Kong.

Exchanging these exotic odysseys for unpredictable domesticity must have been a difficult decision. She did not then know about Brian's resolute character as a cricketer, but she assuredly knew of his tenacity as a courtier. She received an ultimatum on New Year's Eve 1965. 'If you don't agree to marry me,' announced Brian, 'I'll never see you again.'

In the following March they were married at Vivien's home at Ottery St Mary. The nuptials were cunningly timed so as not to coincide with the cricket season. 'Brian still maintains that I would probably never have married him if I had known what a cricketer's life entailed.'

Merging with the happiness of the newlywed pair was the satisfaction of rousing cricket campaigns. Close dwells on the versatile talents that lay at the heart of Yorkshire's successes. 'Illy and I both bowled off-spinners as well as seamers apart from our batting. At a pinch we could call on as many as nine bowlers. Don Wilson had established himself in the team in succession to Johnny Wardle. He was an exceptional fielder at mid-wicket or wide mid-on – both key positions – and a good hitter as a tail-ender. We all pulled together and fought like hell for Yorkshire. And we had the know-how to outwit other counties.'

Don Wilson refers to his former captain as a man who showed no fear or panic in seemingly impossible match situations. There was an ever-present tactical awareness and willingness to offer the bait of runs to lure Yorkshire's opponents to their doom. 'Closey would often instruct me to give away as many as five runs an over, and the wickets would fall as the batsmen fell for the trick. We would whittle them down to nine, ten, jack, and Brian would then call upon Fred to clean up.'

The riches of Fred Trueman were an inheritance bequeathed to Close. Their relationship was sometimes stormy but governed at all times by a sure and mutual respect. Jim Kilburn, in his post-season summary in the *Yorkshire Post* in 1963, remembered Close's magnanimity in his first season as captain, when he ignored his own credentials as the most significant force in the team. 'He publicly conferred that distinction on Trueman, who was, of course, the one bowler of unquestionable quality with a match-winning capacity made manifest again and again.'

Close himself places strong emphasis on having a great bowler at centre stage in his operations. 'You can get all the other bowlers to play supporting roles and improve them by allotting them short spells.' He defines powers of concentration as the difference between

'Belligerence at the batting crease, always rock solid on the big occasion.'
(Somerset Cricket Museum Limited).

From school to county: Top: Aireborough Grammar School 1st XI, 1945 (Close is pictured on front row, second from the right). Dominant in league cricket: His first captaincy role with Yeadon, the Airedale Junior League champions in 1948; the Yorkshire team which played the Army at Hull in 1949. Back row (left to right): Fred Trueman, Vic Wilson, Frank Lowson, Gerry Smithson, Close, Jack Firth, Herbert Walker (scorer). Front row: Bright Heyhirst (masseur), Willie Watson, Johnny Wardle, Ellis Robinson, Geoffrey Keighley (captain), Alec Coxon, Ted Lester.

Celebrating a glorious summer: Left and right: Characteristic aggression as top scorer for the Players against the Gentlemen at Lord's in July 1949. Fast and true in his bowling style in the Test Trial at Edgbaston.
Bottom (left): Test debutant with New Zealander John Reid, who also represented his country for the first time at Old Trafford.

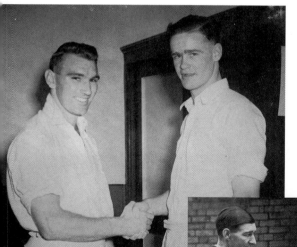

Norman Yardley, the Yorkshire captain, presents Close and Frank Lowson with their county caps

Next test—a trade test Brian Close, 18-year-old Yorkshire and England discovery of last cricket season, became 22188787 Signalman Close, B., yesterday. He was one of an intake of National Service recruits kitted out at Catterick, Yorks. Close is the youngest cricketer ever to play for England in a Test match, youngest to gain a Yorkshire cap and youngest to achieve the cricketer's double of 1,000 runs and 100 wickets.

Top left: A proud mother shares the joy of his selection for the tour of Australia in 1950–51. Right: Signalman Close begins his National Service at Catterick. He was released to travel to Australia. Bottom (left and right): A farewell kiss from sister Mary before his departure. Quoits on the deck of the *Stratheden*. Trevor Bailey waits for his turn.

The MCC party:
Back row (left to right): Arthur McIntyre, Bob Berry, Trevor Bailey, Close, J.J. Warr, David Sheppard, John Dewes, Gilbert Parkhouse, Eric Hollies.
Front row: Brigadier M.A. Green (joint manager), Alec Bedser, Godfrey Evans, Denis Compton, Freddie Brown (captain), Len Hutton, Reg Simpson, Doug Wright, J.H. Nash (joint manager). (Sussex CCC).

Scorecard recording Close's first 1st-class century in England for the Combined Services against the touring South Africans at Portsmouth in June 1951.

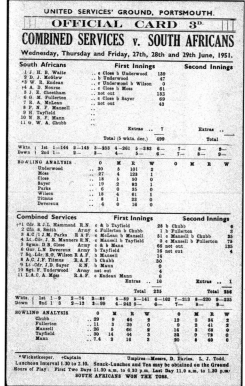

UNITED SERVICES' GROUND, PORTSMOUTH.

OFFICIAL CARD 3D.

COMBINED SERVICES v. SOUTH AFRICANS

Wednesday, Thursday and Friday, 27th, 28th and 29th June, 1951.

South Africans	First Innings		Second Innings
1 J. H. B. Waite	c Close b Underwood	139	
2 D. J. McGlew	b Underwood	47	
*3 W. R. Endean	c Underwood b Wilson	0	
†4 A. D. Nourse	c Close b Moss	61	
5 J. E. Cheetham	not out	133	
6 G. M. Fullerton	c Close b Sayer	69	
7 R. A. McLean	not out	43	
8 P. N. F. Mansell	..		
9 H. J. Tayfield	..		
10 N. B. F. Mann	..		
11 G. W. A. Chubb	..		
	Extras ..	7	Extras ..
	Total (5 wkts. dec.)	499	Total

| Wkts. | 1st 1—144 | 2—145 | 3—253 | 4—261 | 5—383 | 6— | 7— | 8— | 9— |
| Down | 2nd 1— | 2— | 3— | 4— | 5— | 6— | 7— | 8— | 9— |

BOWLING ANALYSIS	O	M	R	W	O	M	R	W
Underwood	30	5	101	2				
Moss	27	4	123	1				
Close	18	5	50	0				
Sayer	19	2	83	1				
Parks	6	0	35	0				
Wilson	18	4	61	1				
Titmus	8	1	23	0				
Devereux	4	0	16	0				

Combined Services	First Innings		Second Innings	
†*1 Cdr. R.J.L. Hammond R.N.	c & b Tayfield	28	b Chubb	6
2 Cfn. S. Smith Army	c Fullerton b Chubb	1	b Fullerton	3
3 A.C./1 J.M. Parks R.A.F.	c McLean b Mansell	51	c Mansell b Chubb	35
4 Lt.-Cdr. J. K. Manners R.N.	c Mansell b Tayfield	3	c Mansell b Fullerton	75
5 Sgmn. D.B. Close Army	c & b Mann	66	not out	135
6 Gnr. L.N Devereux Army	b Tayfield	16	not out	4
7 Sq.-Ldr. R.G. Wilson R.A.F.	b Mansell	14		
8 A.C./F. Titmus R.A.F.	b Chubb	30		
9 Lt.-Cdr. J.D. Sayer R.N.	b Mann	0		
10 Sgt. F. Underwood Army	not out	4		
11 L.A.C. A. Moss R.A.F.	c Endean b Mann	6		
	Extras ..	16	Extras ..	1
	Total	235	Total	256

| Wkts. | 1st 1—9 | 2—74 | 3—88 | 4—89 | 5—141 | 6—162 | 7—213 | 8—220 | 9—225 |
| Down | 2nd 1—3 | 2—13 | 3—99 | 4—242 | 5— | 6— | 7— | 8— | 9— |

BOWLING ANALYSIS	O	M	R	W	O	M	R	W
Chubb	29	9	64	2	12	3	34	2
Fullerton	11	3	29	0	9	2	41	2
Mansell	26	5	66	2	14	3	68	0
Tayfield	30	14	44	3	32	9	72	0
Mann	7.4	2	16	3	20	8	40	0

*Wicketkeeper. †Captain.   Umpires—Messrs. D. Davies, L. J. Todd.
Luncheon Interval 1.30 to 2.10. Snack-Lunches and Tea may be obtained on the Ground
Hours of Play: First Two Days 11.30 a.m. to 6.30 p.m. Last Day 11.0 a.m. to 1.30 p.m.
SOUTH AFRICANS WON THE TOSS.

Starring first at soccer, but cricket priorities held sway to check his progress in the sport. Top: Wearing the blue and old gold colours of Leeds United in the club's Stormcocks nursery side; and below (pictured back row, fourth from the right) as a member of the England Youth FA XI against Scotland at Aberdeen in 1947. Bottom (left and right): Building up fitness with the medicine ball. A Yorkshire 'gunner' on parade with Arsenal after his transfer from Leeds.

Yorkshire captaincy years: Left: Close and Fred Trueman, his bowling ace, raise their glasses to toast another championship in 1967.

Below: cartoonist Roy Ullyett's reflections on the allegations of 'time wasting' in Yorkshire's championship match against Warwickshire, 1967.

Below: A winning combination (back row, left to right): Doug Padgett, John Hampshire, Don Wilson, Mel Ryan, Tony Nicholson, Brian Stott, Philip Sharpe, Ted Lester (scorer). Front row: Jimmy Binks, Fred Trueman, Close (captain), Raymond Illingworth, Ken Taylor.

Top: A match on their hands. The
Yorkshire bridge school (left to right):
Ted Lester, Raymond Illingworth, Don
Wilson (standing as an observer),
Tony Nicholson and Close. Right: An
England trio, Illingworth, Trueman
and Close, meet the Yorkshire
patroness, the Duchess of Kent.
Below: Gillette Cup triumph, 1965. A
victory speech at Lord's. Doug Insole,
the match adjudicator (half hidden,
far left), Billy Griffith, MCC Secretary,
and Gubby Allen listen on the
rostrum.

a major bowler and an ordinary one.

As a prime asset, Trueman was given special attention under Close's captaincy. One of Close's key principles was never to exhaust his main bowlers. He instinctively knew when to slip the leash or conserve their strengths. 'Freddie was a brilliant bowler but his previous captains had overbowled him,' he says. 'And, as was natural in such circumstances, he would bowl within himself. We had been pals since we were sixteen and I knew him pretty well. In my first two seasons as captain I cut his bowling down so that he would not tire himself out.'

Close was instantly alert to any slackening of effort. 'I'd get the feeling that it was time for a rest and ask him to take his sweater.' A splutter of surprise was Trueman's first reaction to the unaccustomed withdrawal, but it did have the positive effect of reinforcing his menace when he returned, refreshed in fitness and outlook, to spread-eagle the wickets. Bill Bowes remembered this adroit instance of man-management. 'Close kept the fiery and volatile Trueman happy, used him in short bursts, and balanced those occasions when he asked for long and sustained spells with opportunities to bowl at tail-enders.'

The prowess of a superb fielding side was shaped in the mould of Yorkshire's other great championship teams. Close reflects on the demands of outcricket. 'The hardest job is in the field. It is up to the fielding side to attack and pose questions with constant variety, bowling paces and field sets.'

All the Yorkshire bowlers profited from the vigilance of their wicket-keeper, Jimmy Binks. 'Jimmy did his job so well that you never noticed him,' says Don Wilson. 'He used to take marvellous blind catches off me – the little leg-side tickles when the batsman's pads and everything was in front of him. He stood up to Tony Nicholson and his leg-side stumpings were wonderful to see. He had such superb anticipation but he didn't say a lot and he was never flashy.'

John Arlott said of Binks: 'He has a lively boyish manner, moves with an air of eagerness, retains his sense of humour – often valuably when nerves are on edge in a taut game – and never loses his zest for cricket.' Binks's fellow craftsmen in other counties were unanimous in their praise of the Yorkshireman. 'Up or back, Jimmy is the most consistent wicket-keeper in the country.'

Binks was called upon to take the lightning pace of Trueman and the contrasting spins of Wardle, Wilson and Illingworth. All was done with a quiet, unfussy efficiency, except his appeal, which, as one writer said, was more a triumphant statement than a question.

Binks made his debut for Yorkshire in June 1955 as a replacement for the injured Roy Booth, who later moved to Worcestershire. He was to establish a county record of 412 consecutive appearances up to his retirement in 1969. In 1960, Binks dismissed 107 batsmen (96 caught and 11 stumped) and his total of catches set a new record for a season.

Only seven wicket-keepers have dismissed 100 batsmen in a season. Les Ames achieved the feat three times – in 1928, 1929 and 1932 – and his Kent predecessor Fred Huish reached the milestone in 1913. Each was helped by major spinning partners, Tich Freeman and Colin Blythe respectively. Jimmy Binks is ranked fourth, jointly with Duckworth and behind Ames and Hugo Yarnold of Worcestershire, in the list of wicket-keeping centurions.

Philip Sharpe's standards of excellence as a slip fieldsman also played a vital part in Yorkshire's successes. Sharpe's 71 catches in 1962 gave him a county record and only Hammond, Micky Stewart and Peter Walker have taken more catches in a season. His status as a fieldsman was so high that he was selected for England against the West Indies at Edgbaston in 1963 when his batting form did not justify the honour.

Don Wilson remembers how Sharpe used to take the ball with his 'small, very small hands' a long way behind his body, which argues superb anticipation and reactions in delaying the catch until it was a certainty. 'He instinctively knew which way the ball would go as it left the bat. He stood a little wider to me, covering first and second slip, and his agility gave us a spare man in the field.'

Bill Bowes said that Sharpe, at five foot seven, gave the impression of being dumpy although he was in fact stocky and compact in physique. The misleading appearance was the result of his preference for baggy and capacious flannels, with plenty of room in the beam. Sharpe explained: 'I like to move and bend in comfort.'

At Leeds University a series of trials was arranged to assess human reaction times. Three Yorkshire players, David Bairstow, Geoff Cope and Sharpe, were invited to catch tennis balls thrown in a darkened room with controlled intermittent flashes of light providing glimpses of the ball in flight. Bairstow was exceptional in the test and the bespectacled Cope emerged with credit. The fact that Sharpe saw the ball much later in the light of actual match play was shown by his inability to line up the ball in a dark period of flight. Although he was acknowledged as one of the finest of close catchers, his record in the university test was by far the worst of the three county men.

In six years at Worksop College Sharpe was an all-round sportsman, playing hockey, squash, tennis and rugby, as a scrum half. At 18, as captain of cricket in his last year, he scored 1251 runs, including five centuries and two double centuries, at an average of 113. It was only 26 runs short of the schools' record set by Ian Campbell at Canford School.

Sharpe was capped by Yorkshire in 1960 but his form underwent such a decline that it seemed he was played primarily for his slip fielding. Twelfth-man duties were often allotted to him and he even spent some time deputising for the sick incumbent as the county scorer. Close remembers that Sharpe was basically a back-foot player. One tactic that helped to restore his confidence occurred when Close deliberately elected to play off his front foot to assist his partner. 'Sharpie benefited because they had to change their length to him,' adds Close.

In 1962 Sharpe began to apply the concentration previously lacking in his batting. The change in attitude reaped immediate benefits; he scored 2352 runs at an average of 40.94 and finished top of the Yorkshire averages. The Cricket Writers' Club named him as the Best Young Cricketer of the Year. He plunged from these imposing batting heights in the following season, but the England selectors took the view that his fielding in the key position at slip merited his inclusion. In the event, he prospered in both departments. In his three Tests against the West Indies he topped the averages with 267 runs at an average of 53.40.

Sharpe played in 12 Tests, scoring nearly 800 runs and holding 17 catches. He compiled a score of 111 against New Zealand and three in the mid-eighties against the West Indies. The prevailing view was that if he had had greater consistency in county cricket he would have played longer for England.

A memorable day 'oop for the Cup' at Lord's in 1965 was by way of a pleasing diversion for Yorkshire. Worcestershire, county champions in two consecutive seasons, had usurped their rivals on the title path. It gave Yorkshire the opportunity to inspect another field of conquest. Close, forced to re-examine his cricket priorities, announced himself ready to address a new challenge.

He was, and remains, a stern critic of the follies of limited-overs cricket. It was, as Tom Cartwright, a future colleague in Somerset, said, anathema to the Yorkshire captain. The negative form of the game was a betrayal of his attacking instincts. Close confirms his disapproval: 'It is stereotyped, literally putting your fielders in the right place to stop runs and not getting people out.'

Close could, though, play Scrooge as well as anybody. Moreover, in his term as Yorkshire captain he had the bowling resources to exert a stranglehold, so that 'batsmen fell over themselves to get out and played silly shots'. The means to success was unwelcome but it did not deter him from following the formula to put the chains on Lancashire in one game. 'We kept one slowcoach in and by the time Clive Lloyd and the other strokemakers emerged it was too late for Lancashire.'

The way to Lord's and the Gillette Cup final in 1965, and Geoffrey Boycott's sparkling match-winning century against Surrey, was opened up by the taut control of Don Wilson. It was his miserly bowling that overcame Warwickshire in the semi-final. Warwickshire needed only 178 to win but were driven to the suicide of five run-outs. Wilson conceded only 15 runs in taking two wickets in his 13 overs. At one stage he bowled four overs without a run being taken off him. What should have been a cosy saunter for

Warwickshire became a frantic race. It vied with the Keystone Kops for lunacy.

Surrey were out-generalled and outclassed at Lord's. The weather had threatened to wreck the proceedings. Incessant and driving rain had not relented for 24 hours before the final. 'What the ground staff accomplished from dawn until noon was little short of a miracle,' reported Gordon Ross. 'They were reinforced by men and equipment from The Oval, and under the direction of the Lord's groundsman, Ted Swannell, with enough sawdust to have supplied every butcher's shop in the country, they had the arena ready for play to start at a quarter past twelve.' Ian Peebles, writing in the *Sunday Times*, thought Lord's looked more suitable for receiving Bertram Mills' circus than two teams of cricketers.

Close says that Surrey transferred the initiative to Yorkshire by putting his team in to bat, which was not then, as today, a common practice for sides winning the toss. It was a damp wicket and he believes that Surrey were loth to bat first for fear of not setting Yorkshire a suitable target. For his part, he was aware that the team in the field fell between two stools – whether to bowl out their opponents or save runs.

Geoffrey Boycott – the bore who became the whizz-kid, as Terry Brindle neatly put it – was to dominate the day. It does need reiteration that it was Close who championed him amid dissenting voices when he was a young cricketer. Vic Wilson, Close's predecessor, was one who would have dispensed with his services. Boycott's elevation to opening batsman after a chance vacancy was also at Close's instigation. As an industrious apprentice, his consistent scoring had kept him in the team in this summer, and his prospects were so enhanced as to encourage his decision to adopt cricket as a career. 'Competence in his new calling is already evident,' commented Jim Kilburn. 'Distinction is clearly within reach.'

The opening passage of play at Lord's appeared to ratify Surrey's chosen course. Yorkshire, after 10 overs from Geoff Arnold and Dave Sydenham, had scored only 20 runs. Boycott, the severely practical technician, was tight in defence against both bowlers. Close recalls: 'We had to quicken up the run-rate. I was down to bat at four or five. Dougie [Padgett] was padded up and due to go in at number three. He was always a little frightened of having to run with Boycs. Dougie said: "Look, skipper, I think you ought to go in before me."'

The outcome, after Taylor's dismissal – caught by Barrington off Sydenham – was an extraordinary display by Boycott. Jim Kilburn reported: 'If Close's presence dictated the mood, Boycott's emergence from the chrysalis of defence changed the scoring rate. In the thirteenth over he drove Arnold for two fours and hooked him for three runs. Thereafter, to the end of the innings, a maiden over was a matter for remark and congratulation. Surrey's bowling was firmly and systematically destroyed.'

Close remembers the serene composure of Surrey when he came in to bat. 'They were pleased and easy with a normal field.' A brisk exchange of words with Boycott preceded a furious change in tempo. There was an urgent command from Close to his junior partner. Arnold was about to begin an over at the pavilion end. 'If he pitches it up, go for it,' said Close. He recalls that the first ball was a succulent half-volley. 'Boycs laid into it and cracked it through extra cover for four runs.'

In the ensuing bombardment Micky Stewart, the Surrey captain, was left to rue his decision not to include any recognised spinner, especially Pocock, a lauded off-spinner, in the side. Whether they would have subdued Boycott in his mood at Lord's must be a matter of doubt. Close was, though, aware that Boycott might decide to temper his approach in order to save his wicket. It was not a time to slumber or deal in courtesies. Close was not a man to trifle with when roused to action. Boycott was promised a violent chastisement if he disobeyed his captain.

Surrey shuffled their bowling pack and Gibson and Storey entered the fray. 'If they pitch it up, hit it anywhere – from long on to square leg,' was Close's next instruction. Boycott was thrust, however unwillingly, into an orgy of savage shots. Close looked on with pleasure as Boycott pounced on another half-volley. 'Where do you think it went?' he enquires rhetorically. 'Over long on for four. The next ball was a little shorter and Boycs whipped it to mid-wicket for another four. We thrashed Surrey and Boycs played the innings of his life.'

Boycott, in his autobiography published in 1987, was at pains to deny that his innings was in any way the result of Close's rugged intervention. 'It was obvious that we had to pick up the pace of the innings. As far as I am concerned, at no time did Close tell me to get on with it. The myth about my attitude and motivation that day supports the image of a bold, decisive captain dominating a reluctant subordinate by the force of his personality. But not once did he threaten or cajole me into playing the strokes I played.'

Despite these protestations, the pattern of Boycott's innings was then in stark contrast to his normal sedate progress. It went against the norm, as Gordon Ross recorded in an article in *Playfair Cricket Monthly*. 'Boycott reacted to his captain's presence in an amazing fashion; it was a Boycott many of us had never seen. He just hit Surrey out of sight.' The dedicated, thoughtful young cricketer had slipped his technical chains. His 146 included three sixes and 15 fours. It is still the highest score in the history of the competition.

Jim Kilburn charted the exhilarating progress of the partnership between Close and Boycott. 'They drove, cut and hooked boundaries and scampered short singles. A century stand was created from 22 overs. Tindall and Barrington conceded 90 runs in eight overs.'

Close, with 79, and Boycott added 192 for the second wicket and Trueman and Hampshire gorged themselves freely in a riotous finale to the innings. Yorkshire's total of 317 was the highest in the competition before Sussex and Warwickshire overtook it in the renamed NatWest final in 1993. While Sussex faltered at their final hurdle, Yorkshire's attacking campaign did not permit a somersault of this order on their great day.

'Pride and the satisfactions of vicarious accomplishment swelled to a bursting point in the ninth over of the Surrey innings,' observed Jim Kilburn. 'Trueman took three wickets in four balls.' Tindall batted with courage and skill to complete a half-century but for the rest it was a sorry story. Five players made one run between them and Illingworth, with five wickets for 29 runs, was also able to savour the downfall of three batsmen in one over. 'As their last wicket offered token resistance,' wrote Kilburn, 'the shadows of the pavilion and the stands covered half the ground but the sun had long since set on Surrey's hopes and ambitions.'

Yorkshire resumed their championship quest in 1966. The margin of victory over Middlesex in an astonishing upheaval at Sheffield was 120 runs. This concealed an unexpected turn in the fortunes of the game. Middlesex were shuttered tight in defence and seemed assured of survival. They had lost only two wickets for 85 by mid-afternoon when, like floodwater bursting through a dam, Yorkshire surged on with an uncontrollable force and swept away the rest of the innings in 40 minutes. Middlesex lost eight wickets for 29 runs and Don Wilson finished with 6 for 22, including a final spell of 5 for 12 in eight overs.

Yorkshire's championship stride lengthened against Gloucestershire at Middlesbrough. Wilson and Illingworth shared 10 wickets and a hapless Gloucester struggled in their spinning trap. They collapsed to 69 all out and lost their last nine wickets for 33 runs. The tale of havoc continued at Worksop where Wilson recorded the second hat-trick of his career against Nottinghamshire. He had match figures of 9 for 112, including 5 for 46 in the second innings. Close struck a ferocious century as Yorkshire added 147 runs in a hectic morning session. On a turning pitch Nottinghamshire narrowly averted an innings defeat but Yorkshire needed only seven runs to win by 10 wickets.

The destiny of the championship depended on the last match, against Kent at Harrogate. Yorkshire a month before had left Old Trafford after the Roses match as heirs-apparent to the title. They were 40 points ahead of Kent and 42 in front of Worcestershire. August was a cruel month and they completed only one outright victory, against Glamorgan, in eight matches, leaving themselves vulnerable to the late rally by Worcestershire.

Rex Alston recalled that the weather did its worst to ruin the closest championship finish for many years. Yorkshire entered their final engagement knowing that outright victory would assure them of the title but that any other result might leave them in second place. The thrilling denouement was signified in the circumstances prevailing on the last day. Kent needed 163 with eight wickets standing and Worcestershire, at home to Sussex, required 133 with seven wickets intact.

Alston reported: 'The pros and cons were anxiously debated by Yorkshire's supporters at Harrogate, as they watched the ground staff feverishly mopping up after a night of rain.' At midday play looked a forlorn hope and the news was even bleaker from Worcester where the home side were nearing their target, with Tom Graveney apparently in command. 'Suddenly the tension eased,' continued Alston. 'Worcester were heard to be almost out – 122 for eight – with all their big guns gone and 60 more runs needed.'

Play was resumed at Harrogate at 2.15. Two and three-quarter hours remained and Kent now had to score at a run a minute. 'The faces of the Yorkshire team, seen through the binoculars, were a study,' observed Alston. The next message was broadcast at three o'clock. Worcestershire had advanced their score to 146 and Roy Booth, a Yorkshire exile, was leading the recovery.

Ten minutes later those Yorkshire faces were wreathed in smiles. A thunderous roar shattered the eardrums. Someone shouted to the fieldsmen: 'Tha's won it, lads.' Over the loudspeakers came the laconic confirmation. 'Worcestershire all out, Yorkshire are the champions.'

Sunshine and a drying wind shone and blew in unison as if in response to the glad tidings from Worcester. Illingworth and Wilson, who gained a hat-trick, found profitable purchase for their spin and Yorkshire were the victors by 24 runs. Six minutes from the end of extra time the Yorkshire players fought their way through the ranks of excited spectators as winners of a game which had seemed for so long certain to end in frustration.

This was a match that could easily have been abandoned by the umpires in the morning had the captains disagreed about the state of a sodden pitch, but Close had let it be known that he would play whatever the conditions. 'Under normal circumstances the pitch would not have been considered fit to play. But no Yorkshireman likes to sit on his backside and watch championship points taken away from him.'

Colin Cowdrey, the Kent captain, was equally anxious to continue because a victory would have given his team third place in the championship. His acquiescence was also rooted in fair play. There was the knowledge, too, that if they had refused to play and Worcestershire had won and retained the championship, Kent might have been accused of aiding the cause of the holders. Yorkshire's title bid had only flagged on the last lap of the season and so, in the end, justice was served in the eventful hours at Harrogate and Worcester.

Far-reaching developments were beginning to exercise cricket minds when Brian Close – and Yorkshire – completed a hat-trick of championships in 1968. It coincided with the introduction of overseas players and then, a year later, an extension of limited-overs cricket with the new Sunday League. Sounding the end of an era in Yorkshire were the retirement of Fred Trueman, then nearing his thirty-eighth birthday, and the departure 12 months later of Raymond Illingworth to other glories as Leicestershire and England captain. Between them Trueman and Illingworth had taken 3135 wickets for Yorkshire. The combination of explosive pace and intelligent spin was fit to rank with Bowes and Verity in their years of supremacy in the 1930s.

In the wider arena, the changes in the regime of cricket would have a major impact on the game in the ensuing years. The heirlooms of the county championship, for so long in safe keeping, would be tossed aside in the revolution. Brian Close prophetically foresaw the popularity of the one-day game as the destroyer of what had been, for him, the finest competition in the world.

While Close went on his barnstorming way – and he was to linger ferociously for some time yet – he remained as one contender able to radiate the old ardour and communicate the immutable standards of his cricketing birthright. His last winning championship campaign, in 1968, bestowed upon him the distinction of being the third most successful captain in Yorkshire's history. Only Lord Hawke, with eight titles in 28 seasons, and Brian Sellers, with six in nine seasons, surpassed Close's record of four in eight seasons at the county helm.

Bonus points designed to reward enterprising cricket hoisted

Yorkshire above Kent in the championship race in 1968. Kent were runners-up and won one more game but 14 fewer bonus points, the exact margin which gave Yorkshire the advantage. The bravery of Close was never more evident in the tussle that sealed the championship against Surrey under grey skies at Hull.

Yorkshire at one stage in their first innings tottered at 221 for eight. Close had hit 72 but the recovery was effected by a late stand between Illingworth and Don Wilson who added 85 runs in 70 minutes. Younis Ahmed, Surrey's top scorer with 75, and Arnold Long resisted the Yorkshire advance for an hour and a half in a palpitating finale. The partnership ended fortuitously when Younis essayed a fierce pull off Wilson; the ball struck the arm of Close, fielding at short square leg, to rebound into the hands of Binks behind the wicket. Two overs later the match was over. Surrey lost their last three wickets and Yorkshire had won by 60 runs.

Mike Selvey, in an article in the *Guardian*, recalled that as a Surrey player he had witnessed the summary end to the proceedings at Hull. 'Closey was fretting, fiddling around, trying everything to make a breakthrough.' Like Don Wilson's, Selvey's memory played tricks in the actual events leading to the conclusion of the game. 'My recollection, and the one I want to be true,' wrote Selvey, 'is that the ball struck Closey full on the dome. He reappeared after a visit to the hospital, with his gap-toothed grin, a fag cupped in his palm, and a cross of white sticking plaster on his head.'

Close's treatment in the local casualty ward was not a consequence of Younis's dismissal. It did, however, involve the Surrey left-hander and Don Wilson. Wilson recalls: 'Younis whacked this bloody ball from me and it hit Closey smack on the shin. We looked at Brian and there was blood pouring out of his boot.'

The captain's bravado usually provoked admiration but this went beyond the bounds of hardship. There was consternation among the Yorkshire players. 'Get off the field,' they all said. Wilson, the guilty party in the horrendous injury, was sternly told to get back to his bowling mark. Close did not flinch at the sight of the seeping wound. 'Get on with your bowling,' he told Wilson. 'I'm not leaving this field until we've won the match.'

Close, not to be intimidated, moved even nearer as Wilson bowled his next delivery. Younis went down on one knee to strike the ball again. It thudded into Close's body and thence into the hands of Binks. Afterwards the champagne corks popped merrily in the Yorkshire dressing room. Amid the euphoria, the absence of the captain, who had at last been persuaded to go to hospital, went unnoticed. 'Closey returned, all stitched up,' says Wilson, 'and there wasn't a drop of champagne left for him.'

If anyone deserved the brimming tonic as a salute, it was the undaunted leader, but his rueful smile belied his thirst. More important to him was the fact that he sported the ravages of his day's work with justifiable pride.

7

Close and Illingworth

'They worked beautifully together. Brian was the flair man
and Raymond, like a computer calculator, knew his statistics
backwards.'

KEN TAYLOR

Collectively they were a brilliant pairing, an amalgam of extravagant
audacity and penny-wise security. The two boyhood friends pooled
their resources to complement each other in one of the most
productive alliances in first-class cricket. 'Neither of us had jealousy
for each other,' asserts Raymond Illingworth. 'It did not worry me
that Brian was captain and he reciprocated by asking me for advice.
We knew each other inside out.'

The depth of their friendship was shown when Close was best
man at Illingworth's wedding. 'Brian has always been a kind bloke.
He never missed visiting us on Christmas Day and, as her godfather,
bringing a present for our eldest daughter each year up to her
twenty-first birthday.'

Togetherness can produce mixed blessings, even when the ties are
strong. As a bachelor, Brian could be unnerving as a regular guest.
'Before his marriage,' says Raymond, 'he used to spend a lot of time
at my house. He is distinctly accident-prone. On three consecutive
visits he cost me money. The first time he had his leg in plaster and,
as he pushed his chair back from the table, he fell back and broke the
chair leg.' Seating accommodation in the Illingworth household
became more depleted when Brian contrived to repeat his chair-
breaking in the following week. 'After that he gave our chairs a rest
– and as we were by that time down to two I felt quite relieved. But,
as he was yawning and stretching on another day, he pushed his fist

into a light fitting.' The Illingworths had some reason to be thankful when Brian married and the siege of their home was lifted. 'He was fast becoming a luxury we couldn't afford.'

Luxuries were too hard-earned to be surrendered heedlessly. The one exception to Illingworth's thrift was the 'one little fad in my life', a coveted Jaguar car. He had assessed the purchase as a good business proposition, in the knowledge that he could trade in the car and make a profit on his investment. Prudence in outlook and a good sense of how to live within his means was an abiding principle. As a canny Yorkshireman, his first objective was to win his county cap, gained at the age of 23 in 1955. Then, with money in the bank, he deemed the time was right to get married.

Illingworth's frugal nature was also strongly apparent in his cricket. While Close would prefer the adventurous route, he exuded caution as a bowler, begrudging every run. Trevor Bailey, similarly circumspect, was an appreciative observer. He applauded the pinpoint accuracy and rare deviations from line and length. 'This means,' said Bailey, 'that a batsman has to take positive action against him, if he wishes to score runs, because he will have to wait a long time for a loose delivery.'

Johnny Wardle was one of the respected Yorkshire elders who planted the seeds of Illingworth's patience and precision as a bowler. In one conversation he related his philosophy: 'There is a batter at one end who you would rather did not stay too long. You have got the ball and it is up to you to dictate how long he remains at the crease. You work and work away until the batter makes a mistake.' One vital lesson passed on by Wardle was the need to 'educate the rest of the lads in the dressing room as to the way you, as a bowler, are thinking'.

As one of the recipients of Wardle's guidance, and with the benefit of his own maturity, Illingworth was well versed in the Yorkshire way of playing cricket. He and Close shared an approach founded on the experience they had accrued as batsmen. 'We both knew how it felt to bat for half an hour and not score a run. The frustration meant that you were liable to do something silly. That's how batsmen think and it is the way you've got to think as a bowler.'

Don Wilson, the former Yorkshire slow left-arm bowler, remembers the immeasurable benefits of bowling in tandem with Illingworth. The association prospered because Close revelled in the art of spin and was able to assess how to use it in the right conditions. The plan of action would be drawn up in concert with Illingworth. Wilson was advised: 'If they haven't scored a run off us in the first ten overs, don't give them anything. They'll try to break out and if they don't we'll win the battle.'

Wilson says, 'Raymond was mean, really top-class. On a turning pitch he would bowl any side out. My job in those circumstances was to get as many wickets as I could. On bad pitches opposing batsmen often thought: "My goodness, I'm not going to get anything off Raymond. My best chance will be to get them off Wils." I often copped for wickets on those occasions.'

Close and Illingworth, with their mix of spin and seam, took over 3300 wickets between them in their seasons with Yorkshire, and then respectively with Somerset and Leicestershire. Close's career aggregate of nearly 1200 wickets belies the general judgement that he overrated his own bowling. He was said to be a lucky bowler, but the records reveal that he broke major stands at both Yorkshire and England levels. It is true, that like Ian Botham, one of his protégés in Somerset, he did have the inestimable knack of taking wickets with bad balls. Ted Lester remembers the deliveries that tempted batsmen into eager aggression. He and Willie Watson were the fielding sentinels who helped Close to achieve the double in his debut year in 1949. 'Willie and I took a lot of catches off Brian in the deep field.'

David Allen remembers one amusing example of Close's 'golden arm', a piece of unintended trickery in a match between Gloucestershire and Yorkshire at Sheffield. It was a modern version of Spedegue's dropper and Barrie Meyer was the embarrassed victim. 'Closey came in to bowl and the ball slipped. It was coming straight at Barrie's head. He ducked but it came through so slowly that he ducked again and finished up with his head almost on the ground.' The hilarity in the Gloucester dressing room was unrestrained as the looping ball rose above Meyer to dislodge the bails.

Illingworth recalls that Jackie Birkenshaw, another off-spinner with Yorkshire and Leicestershire, was similarly blessed with good fortune. 'How do you get wickets with that rubbish?' he once teasingly asked Birkenshaw. 'Well, why don't you try it?' was the droll rejoinder. Illingworth did try it but the batting counter was a warning not to indulge in generosity. 'I bowled a waist-high full toss and it went straight out of the ground for six.'

Tom Cartwright has paid tribute to Close as one of the great attacking captains. 'If he could have translated the messages of his vision into defence he would have been rated even higher.' There was, however, no gainsaying the threat he posed as a fieldsman. The intruding physical presence hung like a dark cloud over opponents.

His daring, as David Allen remembers, confounded even as astute a captain as Don Kenyon at Worcester. Kenyon took great pride in his batting ranks, and especially Tom Graveney and Basil D'Oliveira at the top of the order. 'Closey was up for the bat-pad catch on the off side. It was a decisive fielding position he had created for himself.' It was the height of temerity to offend and distract the two Worcester batsmen. 'They had never seen anyone field so close to them before. It upset both Tom and Basil and knocked them sideways for at least one innings.'

Close, as Allen also recalls, never wore a cap – or any other protection for that matter – on the hottest of days. Close once explained that he crouched as low as possible in order to provide the smallest target possible for opponents under his gaze. The peak of a cap would have forced him into a higher stance and unable to make adjustments when the ball was delivered.

He now makes his own observations on his awesome domination. 'You soon get to know the players who like a fight and those who don't, and you can make cricket a very difficult game for them. I only had to perch myself at short leg and just stare at some of 'em to get them out. They'd fiddle about and turn away and then look back to see if I was still staring at 'em. They didn't stay long.'

It was an antagonism that provoked opponents and dovetailed perfectly with Illingworth's unswerving accuracy as a bowler. 'Brian was brave and set a marvellous example to the team by fielding where he did. He had supreme confidence in me. I bowled such a good line that he never felt in danger.' Don Wilson also enthuses about an 'incredibly brave man' whose presence in the field gave him 30 wickets in a season.'

Illingworth remembers one occasion, in a Test match against Pakistan at Lord's, when they exchanged roles. 'Billy Ibadulla was batting and I was fielding at forward short leg for Closey. He bowled two full tosses and one whistled past one ear and the other past the other. Both went for four.' At the end of the over Illingworth could not hide his disgust. 'What the hell is going on?' he asked Close, who replied, 'I got a little bored.' It was hardly an explanation to defuse the situation. Illingworth exploded with anger. 'Well, don't get bloody bored with me standing there,' he said.

The Yorkshire combination was on a firmer and friendlier footing when Illingworth was the bowler. They were the first to devise the plan to discourage bat-pad play. Close was then stationed at silly mid-off. 'Brian was so near and straighter and the position meant that he was catching the ball directly from the bat,' recalls Illingworth. 'It was even more important then that I bowled a good line. Otherwise he would have got killed.'

Ted Lester believes that Close's daring as a fieldsman and his disregard for personal safety enhanced his status as a captain. 'It was frightening to watch him at times.' In one match against Kent Yorkshire were wheedling out the tail-enders. One of them was Alan Brown, a powerfully built man and a fierce and rather wild hitter with a preference for the long handle. He did not deal in the niceties of batsmanship. 'Brian was getting nearer and nearer,' says Lester. Suddenly Brown decided on furious action. 'The ball whistled over Brian's head and finished just short of extra cover. If it had hit him, he would have been seriously hurt.' Lester adds, 'It didn't deter Brian. He was still there for the next ball.'

Arthur Milton recalls another occasion at Bristol when Close narrowly survived a fierce blow from Martin Young. Illingworth was the bowler and Close was stationed at short square leg. 'Youngie lapped one and it hit Brian. The ball was deflected off his head to be caught by Sharpe at first slip.' Later in the day Milton was sharing a pot of tea with Close. 'Brian,' he said, 'if that ball had struck you full on the temple, it would have killed you.' Close nodded his bruised head and replied, 'Yes, that's true, but he would have been caught at cover.'

Illingworth remembers another occasion when Close did briefly falter, in a match against Hampshire at Portsmouth. The opponent was Richard Gilliat. Don Wilson, not always at his best against left-handers, strayed in direction, and Gilliat swung mightily in an attempted pull shot. Close could not take evasive action to escape yet another agonising blow on the forehead. The ball ricocheted past Ken Taylor, fielding at cover, and sped to the boundary. Close was at the time bowling in tandem with Wilson. The blow caused him to see 'stars with every step' when he began his next over. Illingworth had noted the grimace of pain accompanied by heavy breathing after the incident. After a while he suggested that Close take a respite away from the wicket. The response was an unusual concession: 'My nerve went for a couple of overs,' he admitted. Close was, though, a man with a high pain threshold. The fearful crack did cause a momentary qualm but he was not prepared to leave his post. 'I'm all right now,' he said, planting himself even more defiantly in front of the batsman.

There are expert voices in Yorkshire who insist that Close is the best left-handed batsman England has produced since the Second World War. The allegations that he under-achieved for a player of his gifts are refuted by others who say that he was sadly denied more opportunities to prove his worth at Test level. In the reckoning of many contemporaries, Close has never been fully credited for his abilities as a batsman. Had he played for any other county but Yorkshire, where he so often sacrificed his wicket, maintains Tom Cartwright, he would have substantially increased his aggregate – which even so was nearly 35,000 – of runs. 'He would have scored more *important* runs – centuries and double centuries – to increase his ranking alongside others of his time.'

Ted Lester talks about the batting swell who could 'hit the ball many a mile' but was equally resolute in defence. One telling example of Close's fortitude and unselfishness as a batsman occurred in a match against Derbyshire on a spiteful pitch at Headingley in August 1963. Rain and bad light severely curtailed play on the first day, but the match, which Yorkshire won by seven wickets, lasted only two days. Yorkshire led by 29 runs on the first innings and they were indebted to Close and Illingworth in achieving this narrow advantage.

Eric Todd, the *Guardian*'s northern cricket correspondent, remembered a display of self-discipline and devotion to duty seldom equalled in his experience in county cricket. Close demonstrated his obduracy in a crisis, holding the fort at the 'awkward end' for over two hours. The hostility of Harold Rhodes, the Derbyshire fast bowler, on a broken pitch was sustained and unrelenting. It was a vicious barrage, with the ball lifting head-high at times. Every run had to be eked out with the precision of a sculptor.

After Close's arrival at the crease, Rhodes delivered 88 balls. Brian took 81 of them, all the while instructing the other batsmen to try and get runs – twos or fours – at the other end. His strength of purpose is shown by the pace of his innings: he batted 50 minutes for one run and had scored only 12 after an hour. Defiantly he held sway and struck one boundary to increase his total to 20 five minutes before he was at last scuttled by Rhodes.

Illingworth remembers the pandemonium at Headingley. Angry voices roared in disapproval as Rhodes bombarded their champion; the Yorkshire partisans roundly booed the bowling aggressor. Amid the uproar the vigil of Close was a masterclass in concentration. 'I was in for a long time with Brian,' Illingworth recalls. During their partnership he offered reassuring words: 'You're doing a great job at that end, kid.' For his part, he undertook to tackle the off-spinner, Edwin Smith, at the other end. 'You can't hit him on this wicket,' he said.

Although this was true in the sense of the problems Smith would set a left-hander, it also expressed Illingworth's greater ease in the circumstances. 'Brian was hit on the head three times by Rhodes. The ball was quite literally taking off.' The Headingley exploit afforded ample evidence to support the tribute of Ted Lester. 'No one played the quicks better than Closey when the ball was whistling around his ears.'

Alan Gibson observed that Illingworth best demonstrated his worth for Yorkshire in 'pulling them over the hump' of the season, when the championship battles were at their toughest. He was also sage in counsel and colleagues stress the extent of his rapport with Close. All of them say that Illingworth would have been the first choice in any team selection determined by Close, for Yorkshire or England. More evidence was provided when Tony Greig took over as England captain. 'Where are the players who can stand up to these Aussies?' he inquired of Close. 'Well,' answered Brian, 'there's me and Illy.'

Illingworth believes that day by day he had greater concentration than Close. Boredom in a stalemate situation on a good wicket could cause the Yorkshire captain to disengage his attention. There were times when wicket-keeper Jimmy Binks, another shrewd adviser, would seek Illingworth's assistance. 'Have a word with Closey,' he would say. 'I think the rudder's gone.'

A direct approach from Binks, as occasionally happened, would fall on deaf ears and might risk an early bath for the player. 'Fortunately, knowing Brian so well, I could say what I wanted to him,' reveals Illingworth. 'The lads would come to me if there was a problem. He would accept suggestions from me, as his mate, but he was less receptive to Fred [Trueman] or others. I could give Brian a kick up the backside. He would then snap back into action.'

Yorkshire's winning strategies – and the degree of intensity with which they were endowed – had as a parallel the acuteness of the bridge school which operated on rain-affected days. The card-playing elite in the Yorkshire dressing room often included Close and Illingworth, either as partners or in company with Philip Sharpe and Tony Nicholson.

Don Wilson, not a member of the school, remembers that conversation abruptly ceased during the card sessions. 'We weren't allowed to talk. It was like a Test match in the way they used to go on at each other.' He believes that the spirit of these struggles overflowed on to the cricket field. 'Raymond would step in, as at cards, when Brian's interest was waning.'

Illingworth remembered one occasion when their joint endeavours at cards foundered because of Close's inattention. He was in charge of a straightforward hand – four spades – and took the chance to go to the toilet. He returned to discover that Close had finished up three short. Illingworth expressed his astonishment and demanded an explanation. Close ruefully said that his attention had drifted off the hand. He was sternly admonished: '*Don't* drift your attention off when you're playing with *my* money.' They were playing for a penny a hundred!

Golf was, and remains, a ruling passion for Close. He has been a member of the Bradford Golf Club for 50 years. The late Don Mosey wrote that Close was gifted enough to have won renown at the highest level had he had the time to concentrate on the game. He has still been good enough to earn distinction in celebrity pro-am tournaments over the years. Close today plays off a handicap of nine but in his younger days, as an ambidextrous golfer, it was as low as two right-handed and five when he changed to the left hand.

The switch to playing left-handed occurred in the late 1950s. The impetus for the change was a round with Johnny Wardle, another left-hander. Wardle was an outstanding golfer, consistently playing to a handicap of two. He was captain of the Wheatley Golf Club at Doncaster. In 1978, at the age of 55 and in his first year as a senior, Wardle won the Yorkshire County Seniors' Amateur Championship.

Close remembers borrowing a six iron from Wardle during their earlier partnership. 'The balls went away like bullets,' he said. He was an immediate convert to the new style. It transformed his game and he found that he could hit the ball further than with the right-handed approach. The method was given an extended trial at the nearby Ganton golf course following the Scarborough Festival that year. 'I played some of the best golf of my life at that time,' Close recalls.

Bob Appleyard, another Yorkshire colleague, has a theory about Close as a golfer. He remembers the time before Close turned to the option of playing left-handed. Appleyard – and Frank Lowson, another cricket and golf friend – would often strike a greater length down the fairway. 'We would hit the ball past Brian to get him going! I believe that he changed to the left hand so that he could gain an advantage over us.' Tom Graveney is another long-standing single handicap golfer who could have earned a living in the professional game. Of their jousts around the fairways, he says: 'Brian struggled if I hit it past him.'

Frank Twiselton, the former Gloucestershire cricket chairman, remembers that Close could be peevish when his performances on the golf course did not come up to his demanding standards. On one occasion in South Africa their playing partners were the Gloucestershire and Leicestershire cricketers Tony Brown and Roger Tolchard. 'For the first six holes Brian was not playing well, consistently hooking his tee shots, with his left hand, into the trees on the right of the fairways.'

Close appeared genuinely puzzled at his waywardness. 'When we reached the seventh tee,' continued Twiselton, 'he suddenly stood back and gazed down at the fairway.' Brian announced: 'I can see now what my trouble is, this is a bloody right-hander's course!' He then proceeded to explain in precise detail his theory. It did not convince his partners, but it was enough to satisfy himself that he had solved the problem. Thereafter he drove with assurance, straight and true, down the fairway. As in any game, he was the master of the unexpected, unfailingly confident in his ability to effect a cure and never at a loss for words when he failed.

Whenever a group of cricketers gather together, the talk is bound to turn, sooner or later, to Close's driving not of golf balls but of cars. He was, to be frank, a menace on the road and those who travelled with him as passengers quickly learned their folly. As Tom Cartwright says, Close displayed an entirely different side of his personality on the road. On the cricket field he was totally unselfish and would 'give you his life'. Off the field he could be labelled selfish, especially when he reduced unsuspecting car companions to a state of near-hysteria. Their lives were imperilled at such times.

Close was constantly seeking new recruits to join him on his harum-scarum journeys. His watchword was speed, looking to negotiate any distance in the shortest possible time. For all his passengers it was important to stay on the alert and keep awake.

Illingworth was one of the first people to accompany Close on these madcap travels. 'I had a few adventures with Brian. It was really frightening to be with him in a car.' Boredom afflicted Close and he lost concentration in much the same way as when cricket failed to stir him in dull passages of play. Illingworth would berate his friend for not taking avoiding action when collisions loomed but were miraculously averted.

'You would see this bloke turning right but Brian carried on and he was almost up his backside. Sometimes the motorist would actually apologise for being late in giving a signal.' Illingworth, having survived this latest episode of driving brinkmanship, would vigorously protest: 'Bloody hell, Closey, you could have stopped twenty yards short of him.'

But it was the marathon journeys before the arrival of motorways that really tested Close's passengers. The horrors of one outing, a trip of 300 miles from Scarborough to Torquay, are still a vivid memory for Illingworth. His nerves were shredded long before their arrival in Devon.

Their travels together ended, at the insistence of Illingworth's wife, Shirley, after a dinner at Ilkley. She accompanied the pair and was exceedingly frightened on the return journey. 'We came back over the moor,' recalls Illingworth. 'There was quite a steep drop on one side of the narrow road. Closey was driving with one hand and twiddling the knobs of the car radio with the other.' They were highly relieved to reach home safely. Shirley was not disposed to allow any more excursions of this kind with Close. 'I was banned from travelling with him ever again as a passenger,' says Illingworth.

Close must be accounted the luckiest of men to have survived in a life strewn with motoring mishaps. Travelling home from Scarborough one night he screeched round a bend; his car hurtled through a hedge and turned over. His shoes were torn from his feet and lay down the road and his shirt was ripped off his back. Yet he emerged with just a few minor scratches. He managed to obtain a lift to continue his journey home. The distress of Vivien Close, then awaiting the birth of their daughter, can be imagined when Brian returned, a dishevelled figure with his coat in shreds.

Newspapermen as well as cricketers have managed to live and tell the tales of driving with Close. One of them, so Fred Trueman related, would offer up a prayer before entering his car. He was once whisked from his London hotel in Edgware Road to The Oval in eight minutes. The same journalist drove from Old Trafford to Taunton in three hours to meet Close for dinner. He was pardonably pleased at making such good time when he arrived at their rendezvous. The smile faded when Close accused him of stopping for dinner on the way. He couldn't believe that it could take anyone three hours to drive out of Test match traffic and then another 180 miles!

Philip Sharpe, a fellow Yorkshire cricketer, emerged grimy but unscathed from what was probably his first and last journey with Close. They were travelling out of Bristol and Close turned to salute other Yorkshire players in their cars as he overtook them. The distraction caused him to go past a diversion sign indicating roadworks and plunge down a deep hole. The following convoy of Yorkshire cars – and their occupants – arrived on the scene soon afterwards. 'We saw Sharpie, his nose peering over the edge of the hole,' says Illingworth. 'He was as white as a sheet.'

Throwing caution to the winds was in Close's character, even if it did, in such circumstances, endanger others as well as him. With Illingworth at his side at cricket, he could indulge his cavalier instincts, knowing that he had a sterling man at his shoulder to resist his more extreme impulses.

Bob Platt contends that Close was the epitome of the first lieutenant in grim action on the battlefield in war. 'Brian would have led the charge, while Raymond, as the brainy army captain, would have let them go.' Platt presents a contrasting portrait of Close as Yorkshire captain. 'Brian was occasionally vague and at other times so positive. He wasn't always the man you'd turn to for technical assistance. That was Raymond's province.'

Governing all their challenges was the expedient of dangling the carrot to entice opponents. This was when Brian Close, exploiting his sense of adventure, starred as a captain. It was at the heart of his cricket philosophy. 'How long do we need to bowl them out?' was the question he would pose to his Yorkshire team-mates. The equation determined the batting time available. Out came the strokemakers who knew that their stay had to be curtailed in the quest for quick runs before the declaration.

Illingworth remembers the puzzlement of his new colleagues when he moved to captain Leicestershire. They could not understand why players' batting averages in Yorkshire often languished in the upper twenties. He explained that this was not a reflection of their talents but a product of unselfishness in pursuit of victory. It meant, said Illingworth, that wickets had to be thrown away at times, jeopardising averages. In a final telling thrust, he said: 'That is the only way to win championships.'

Solidarity and trust marked the relationship between Close and Illingworth. Their complementary assets entitled Yorkshire to claim them as the outstanding all-rounders of the age, and probably in due course the best captains to represent England as well.

Close relentlessly took the attacking option and he had a superb bowling cast to enable him to follow this route. 'We always kept our opponents in the hunt,' says Don Wilson. 'Closey's adventurous spirit meant that we could win matches in two and a half days.' The joy of the gamble is a forgotten art but it was the means by which Yorkshire so often romped to victory with the time to spare.

8

Gallantry Without Reward

'Brian never took a backward step in his cricketing life. He played
the Australian way – it's either you or me for it.'

ALAN DAVIDSON

The opportunism that startled England into submission on a
remarkable August day at Old Trafford in 1961 was brazen in its
audacity. Australia, for so long in retreat, plunged their rivals into a
crisis that should never have occurred. This was a match that veered
wildly through all its stages. Brian Close, as one of the victims of an
astonishing coup by Richie Benaud, was once again branded as an
irresponsible culprit.

Benaud himself, as the winning captain, declared that the brusque
condemnation of Close was unpardonable. He was not the only
England player whose technique was at fault in the unexpected
downfall. 'I thought the slating of Brian was one of the most unjust
things I have ever experienced.'

Twelve years after his England debut at the same venue, Close had
made the short journey across the Pennines for yet another Test
comeback. His recall by England was his fifth, after appearances in
the series against South Africa, West Indies and India. He was again
on trial after his beckoning revival as a batsman. Over three seasons
with Yorkshire, twice as a member of a championship-winning
team, he had scored over 4000 runs to demonstrate his renewed
purpose.

Through the 1950s the selectors had given Close only rare
opportunities to build upon the promise he had shown as a boy.
Fred Trueman is vehement in his criticism of the repressive attitude
adopted towards his Yorkshire colleague. He describes Close as 'an

extraordinary man with so much talent within one frame', and believes that it was a disgrace that this ability was stifled by lack of recognition. The assessors who wielded power failed to nurture the gifts that would have given Close the ranking of England's greatest modern all-rounder. 'He was treated very badly by his country and, later, his county,' says Trueman.

Close's contemporary Tom Graveney was another player withdrawn from the national spotlight until his late flowering as one of the most elegant of batting stylists. He remembers his own 'rest periods' – two three-year gaps – in the calls to the England colours. These impositions kindle his sympathy for an unlucky cricketer. Graveney, like Trueman, contends that Close was endowed with such ability as to have more than doubled his 22 Tests. 'Brian could be opinionated and outspoken. But whatever is said about his brashness, that was never vindictive. He was probably the bravest player ever to step on to the cricket field.'

Close's rehabilitation after his Australian misadventure in 1950–51 had been protracted: a succession of injuries retarded his progress, as did the confirmation of Trevor Bailey as England's mainstay and automatic choice as all-rounder. There were, however, intermittent glimpses of Close's courage and tenacity at the highest level. In 1955, he was only three wickets short of a third double. He opened the batting with another left-hander, Jack Ikin, against South Africa in a match that decided the series in England's favour at The Oval.

Close and Ikin were two of four left-handers – the others were Watson and Spooner – chosen in an attempt to counter the leg-theory attack of Trevor Goddard, the Springboks' all-rounder. There was also the knowledge that the Yorkshire-Lancashire combination possessed the steel to combat the hostility of Peter Heine and Neil Adcock, one of the most ferocious pairs of fast bowlers in Test cricket. They resisted for more than an hour, scoring 43 before one of the many vicious bouncers unleashed by Heine struck Ikin in the solar plexus and forced him to retire.

Two more years elapsed before Close, with another weight of runs to force selection, played against the West Indies at Edgbaston. He had reinforced his claim when he opened with Surrey's Tom Clark for the MCC against the tourists at Lord's. Close was rendered lame by a blow on his left foot but it did not prevent him from scoring a century. *Wisden* reported: 'Despite the handicap and needing a runner, Close drove and hooked to such effect that he made 108 out of 157, with one six and 15 fours, in a stay of two hours and 20 minutes.'

Close's opening partner in the following Test at Edgbaston was Peter Richardson. This was a match made memorable by the record fourth-wicket stand of 411 between captain Peter May and Colin Cowdrey that rescued England after the first-innings rout by Ramadhin. A similar pattern of conquest appeared certain when England lost two wickets for 65 in their second innings. Ramadhin seemed to hold the key to victory for the West Indies.

There was, in addition, the considerable threat of Roy Gilchrist, a wild man by many accounts, and a fast bowler with a dangerous throw. *Wisden,* while paying due tribute to May and Cowdrey, noted the valour of Close as a prelude to an exceptional turn of events. England were on the rack again with the early dismissals of Richardson and Insole. 'Fortunately for them,' noted the almanack, 'Close, despite a blow on the left hand, defended resolutely and he and May raised the score to 102 by the end of the third day.' Close's defiant 42 was the bulwark that helped to arrest the West Indian advance.

At Lord's in the second Test, Close was relegated to number seven in the order. Peter May had intimated that the reason for the change was to accommodate the Yorkshireman as an off-spinner as well as a batsman. As it happened, his services were not needed as a bowler. Trevor Bailey took 11 wickets in the match, including 7 for 44 in the first innings, and England won by an innings and 36 runs with more than two days to spare.

The result did indicate England's dominance, but there was another compelling footnote to demonstrate Close's part in the victory. Gilchrist had dismissed May and Graveney, both without scoring in one over, and England were uneasily placed at 34 for 3. Richardson and Cowdrey led the recovery, but it was still incomplete when Close came to the wicket. Five wickets had fallen for 134 runs.

'Not only did Cowdrey and Close add 58 for the sixth wicket,' reported *Wisden,* 'but they took the fire out of Gilchrist and Worrell and paved the way for the ensuing onslaught.' After Close's dismissal, Cowdrey and Evans were the merciless beneficiaries. They put on 174 in five minutes under two hours and England, after the early trials, totalled 424.

Close might have requested an audience with the selectors for them to explain why he was permitted only one other Test against India at Leeds before the end of the 1950s. His batting renaissance should have informed their deliberations. In 1959 Close achieved his then best aggregate of 1879 runs and was only 12 wickets short of another double. He followed this with 1699 runs in 1960 and then, in another surge which finally awakened the selectors' interest, narrowly failed to reach 2000 runs in 1961.

Cricket is a fickle game and Close, having reached the summit once again, must have shrugged in disbelief at being made the scapegoat for England's defeat by Australia at Old Trafford. 'People were always looking for Brian to fall down but he was too big a man for that,' observes Tom Graveney.

A remarkable game, in which England held the advantage until the closing stages, could not be attributed to the loss of Close at a crucial juncture. Among other factors, the absence of Colin Cowdrey, sidelined with a throat infection, was significant in at least one respect. England missed his prowess in the close catching cordon. Harvey survived slip chances off Flavell and Dexter, and Subba Row dropped Lawry, a century-maker in Australia's second innings, at 25 off Trueman. The fielding lapses, in the final analysis, exacted too high an expenditure. The cost was the victory margin of 54 runs that separated the two teams.

Ted Dexter, whose thrilling innings ignited England's hopes on the last day, refers to one contentious issue which could have affected the course of the game. At tea on the third day England led by 171 runs in their second innings, with three wickets left. Barrington had been among those criticised for slow play. He had batted for two hours and 40 minutes for his half-century. During one period in the afternoon the crawl had brought jeers from the crowd. England added only 16 runs in 50 minutes.

Dexter recalls, 'We were winning the game comfortably. At the interval there was the most unfortunate intervention by the selectors who invaded the dressing room and abused the England team for scoring so slowly. The result was that instead of batting Australia out of the game we left them with half a chance. When you do that you suffer. It was not good for the morale of the side.'

Ron Roberts, as a press observer, was also perplexed by the changed approach. He believed that the subsequent tactics were wrong. 'This view was out of step with the army of critics demanding a show of aggression with England so far out in front. A lead of around 200 with which to contemplate the weekend would have given England a moral advantage as well as a practical one. Instead the remaining wickets were carelessly surrendered, as though the batsmen were under instructions to quicken up, and thus Australia were given time to close the gap.' Simpson, with his leg-spin, took the last three wickets at the cost of two runs in 22 balls.

Lunchtime talk on the last morning did not centre on a misguided batting strategy. The consensus of opinion derived satisfaction from the prospect of an imminent England victory. Fluctuations in cricket are not uncommon but over the next few hours enough somersaults were performed to defy all predictions. One writer said that the pros and cons of the game could fill a book.

All other wagers as to the outcome appeared meaningless when David Allen, with his off-spin, took three wickets for no runs in 15 balls. Australia had been reduced to 334 for 9. England had, so it seemed, the gentlest of batting exercises. They had the rest of the day – over five and a half hours – in which to score 157 runs and win.

The match was turned on its head by a stand of 98 runs – the highest for the tenth wicket in England – between Davidson and McKenzie. Initially, as Davidson recalls, he was determined that his partner was not going to face Allen. 'I farmed the bowling as much as I could.' England were left to rue the omission of another spinner, the left-hander Tony Lock.

The gamble was taken to introduce Close, bowling his spin, at the Stretford end. According to Allen, the move was made at the instigation of Fred Trueman. 'Give Closey a bowl,' urged Trueman. 'He'll bowl any bugger out.' His faith proved to be unfounded. It was not one of Close's better days with the ball. McKenzie thereupon hit three fours – and gained much confidence – from five full tosses in Close's two overs.

Then Davidson, as if he had weighed the chances and decided that to submit to Allen's dictation was merely postponing an unsatisfactory end, took positive action. He went down the wicket and, in a single over, struck Allen with measured power for 20 runs – 6–4–4–6 – through the arc between cover and straight of the wicket. Davidson remembers his assault, which, together with the runs off Close, produced the bonus of priceless runs. 'David [Allen] had bowled very tightly – eight or nine maidens in a row. I decided now was the time to keep it going. Fortune favours the brave sometimes and it came off for me. My attack forced the issue and England were compelled to bring back their new-ball bowlers.'

He agrees with others, including England contemporaries, that Peter May erred in withdrawing Allen from the fray at this stage. 'Peter should have stayed with David. I would then have had to attack like mad as I had previously done. There was no guarantee with the footmarks as a hazard that I would have been able to get away with it two overs in a row.'

David Allen, as the affronted bowler, was well aware that Davidson considered him the chief danger. The decision by May to attempt to lure the Australian into a mistake was a like a red rag to a bull. 'Let's give him a swing ball, a little higher and little slower,' proposed the England captain. 'Perhaps we can persuade him to play a few more shots.'

Abandoning the policy of restraining pressure, which had earlier brought its rewards, was soon revealed as a futile gesture. Davidson, in an innings of great daring, feasted on the offerings. He was unbeaten on 77 and McKenzie had reached 32 before Flavell bowled him. England were set a target of 256 in three hours and 50 minutes, a rate of 66 an hour. As Ted Dexter says, this was quite a substantial challenge, which would not even have been considered by many teams.

Dexter likens himself to a 'young shaver' who was given the opportunity, without psychological pressure, to 'have a smash'. He did, in fact, play one of cricket's most majestic innings at Old Trafford. 'The initiative had been wrenched away by Australia but he magnificently and as if by divine right, stole it back,' enthused Alan Ross.

'While Subba Row went along his pawky, reassuring way,' wrote John Arlott, 'Dexter stood up commandingly. He drove Davidson with murderous intent through extra cover.' Ten runs came off an over from McKenzie. Three overs from Simpson yielded 20, and 16, including a superb long six, came from two overs by Mackay.

'England were completely in the saddle,' reported Arlott. 'In 50 minutes since three o'clock 88 runs had been made and though Benaud was economical and the Australian fielding keen, England at 150 for one seemed to be surging to a win.' Subba Row, the patient foil during the onslaught, says, 'Another hour of Ted in that vein and we would have been home and dry.' Dexter, caught at the wicket by Grout off Benaud, batted for only 84 minutes in scoring 76. It included one six and 14 fours and his stand with Subba Row had produced 110 in that time.

Dexter now wryly says that, in a sense, he 'lost the game'. 'I had scored so quickly that what had appeared an unlikely target rather committed us to keep chasing and go for the win.' For David Allen, England's ascendancy was such that 'it frightened us to lose it in the end'. The appraisal of Richie Benaud was realistic in its common sense. 'We couldn't save the match but we might possibly win it.'

Alan Ross, in a masterly essay in the *Observer*, said that the Manchester Test offered enough evidence for a profound study of the psychology of defeat. 'For four and three-quarter days England had asserted a basic all-round superiority. Yet within the space of an hour, the Ashes and the match were wantonly thrown away.'

It was impossible, concluded Ross, to over-emphasise the Australians' opportunism and Benaud's tactical courage and remarkable assessment of the match in terms of outright victory or defeat. 'Benaud, with three Test runs in four innings and not having taken a wicket in the match while conceding over a hundred, showed himself possessed of that kind of daring and faith in his own powers that is the mark of a great leader.'

Tom Graveney recalls that Benaud went into the match not 100 per cent fit. Graveney was then qualifying for Worcestershire but was permitted to play against the Australians in their opening match at New Road. 'It was a cold, miserable day and Richie bowled me a flipper and did his shoulder in.' It transpired that he had suffered a severe injury to the tendon at the top of his shoulder. Neil Harvey deputised as captain in Australia's win at Lord's but Benaud took charge again at Leeds. Trueman, at his devastating best, wrought havoc with 11 wickets in England's victory by eight wickets to level the series.

It did seem as if the fates had relented and favoured England at Old Trafford. Benaud recalled that the subsequent happenings had their origins on the previous evening. In conversation with Ray Lindwall, who was visiting England as a press observer, he proposed one possible solution if Australia ran into trouble. He asked Lindwall for his opinion on the then unusual tactic of bowling round the wicket into the footmarks to the right-handers. The answer was clearly in the affirmative, as was revealed by a remarkable spell of match-winning bowling.

During the lunch interval on the last day views were canvassed in the press box on the likely outcome of the game. John Woodcock perceptively remarked: 'We will lose three or four wickets chasing the runs and then come to grief against Richie.' His dire forecast proved correct. The series was decided in a dramatic 20 minutes before tea. Benaud took four wickets for nine runs in 19 balls.

The general view in the England camp was that Benaud's decisive bowling ploy was not only his last throw of the dice but a negative design to stop England winning the match. Arthur Milton, the former Gloucestershire and England batsman, pressed home this claim in a recent conversation with Benaud. 'Don't tell me that you were attacking. It was a defensive measure. That's why you went round the wicket,' he said. Tom Graveney adds, 'It was the right-handers' fault for losing the match. They should have kicked Richie away to embarrass him. He would then have had to revert to bowling over the wicket.'

Dexter, furiously square-cutting, was the first to fall to Benaud. May was next man in and felt compelled to follow Dexter's lead. He was dismissed off the second ball, attempting a sweep that he would not normally have contemplated. For such a superb driver, it was an unaccountable response. At first he thought he had survived the indiscretion, but a bail, dislodged by Benaud's looping delivery, had fallen silently to the ground. It lay there like a leaf disturbed by a capricious breeze.

Neil Harvey, fielding at leg slip, sported a huge grin. He turned to the baffled batsman and said, 'Sorry, mate, you're out.' May was later, in a conversation with Alf Gover, to concede an untimely rush of blood. In his haste to force quick runs he had disobeyed the cardinal principle of playing straight. 'Yes, I was guilty,' he said. 'It was a big mistake.'

The stage was now set for Brian Close to trounce his critics with a major innings. 'Play longer and play straighter,' is the mild rebuke of David Allen in his assessment of the well-intentioned aggression that led to Close's downfall. But it was in keeping with the Yorkshireman's outlook that he should look to wrest the advantage by positive means. In addition, as he says, it would have been impossible to do otherwise since his captain had not conveyed contrary directions

Alec Bedser commented that at the time of Close's arrival at the wicket it was necessary for runs to be scored quickly. 'Brian's method did not look too elegant, but with Benaud pitching into the rough, the only way open to him was either to go down the pitch and hit straight, or try to hit it away to the leg side with the spin.'

Close had watched the progress of the England innings intently; he had told Peter May that it would be inadvisable to have two left-handers together at the wicket. Logically, that should have meant the promotion of Barrington, as a right-hander, ahead of him in the order. In the circumstances, Close now had to devise a way of maintaining the offensive. 'They wouldn't have got me out in a month of Sundays if I'd played normally. I didn't have to play Richie out of the rough but we were supposedly still going for a win and I had to take a calculated risk.'

Close says that he weighed up the possibilities as the ball lifted and turned in the footmarks. 'There was no way I could play any kind of orthodox shot. You could not tell where the ball was going to go. I had to think what to do and so I elected to sweep from outside my off stump.'

The innings lasted only ten balls but it was at least a challenging riposte. Norman O'Neill, replacing Mackay who had torn a calf muscle, was now repositioned halfway back, just behind square; in some accounts he had not quite reached the place directed by his captain. 'If I hit it well,' thought Close, 'I will clear him.' The counter only narrowly failed. 'O'Neill leapt in the air to take the catch in two bloody fingers.' Close adds, 'They blamed me for losing the match. I was only the fourth man out.'

One straight drive for six had announced Close's intentions. Benaud's response was to change his first line of attack and come round the wicket to use the extensive rough outside the left-hander's off stump. The Australian captain, having witnessed the aggression of Dexter, was now aware of the comparable threat of Close. 'He could have swung the game in a matter of minutes had some of his attempted sweeps been successful. Even twenty runs at that time could have been disastrous for us.'

Raman Subba Row is sympathetic about a dismissal which once again pushed Close into the doldrums. 'The big thing as far as Closey was concerned was that they didn't repair the footholds in those days. Fred Trueman had scarred the wicket in his run up, digging increasingly bigger holes outside the off stump.' Subba Row explains that, as an opening batsman facing the quick bowlers, he had been able to establish his innings; the holes in his case did not carry a particular significance. 'Brian had to bat when Richie was bowling round the wicket into the divots. If I'd started in the same circumstances, I would have been in considerable trouble.'

He does, however, believe that more orthodox tactics might have been the safer option. 'I'm not sure that Brian was correct in trying to sweep Richie. He played across the line when he had already hit one six straight. With his strength and ability that was the way to play.' Close responds, 'I had hit the six off Benaud when he was bowling over the wicket and pitching between the wickets where it was sound.' Subba Row also expresses the view that England were not pressured by time considerations. The facts belie this statement. Benaud had pursued a good over rate even while Dexter was at the wicket. But England still needed to score at a run a minute, no mean task in a Test match.

In the end they were caught between two stools. Close expresses his verdict on the dilemma: 'We did not know whether we were going for the runs or not. We should have saved the game.'

Alan Davidson, in an intriguing postscript, remembers how he and his fellow Australians all believed that Close posed the danger to their hopes in the dramatic finale at Old Trafford. 'Ted [Dexter] had played the most incredible innings. Richie's tactical ploy of bowling round the wicket had originally served to slow the run rate but then, with the dismissals of Dexter, May and Close, it was primed as an attacking gambit.'

Davidson observes that sometimes there are issues in a Test match which can, with an ounce of luck, go one way or another. 'If Closey had got away with a couple of clubs, Richie might well have had to change his plan.' He asserts, without reservation that Close was 'playing the Australian way' and looking to regain the initiative. 'The amazing part was that the way Brian was trying to play Richie would have been my method.'

A contrast in fortunes had favoured Davidson in his assault on another spinner, David Allen. 'I backed a 100–1 shot and it came off. Closey's approach was the same but his turned out to be a 6–4 on favourite. It only needed a couple of overs from Brian achieving the success that I'd had, and the game would have gone the opposite way.' Davidson stresses that the stroke, which scandalised the purists, has to be balanced against the fact that Close was prepared to jeopardise his chances of future selection. 'It took a brave man to do what Closey tried to do at Manchester because of the simple reason he was only in the team for one game. Yet he was doing what he believed was the way to bring England victory and we believed that he was right.'

The disdain at Old Trafford turned to pride two years later when Brian Close played one of the most courageous innings in Test history against the West Indies at Lord's. It was the year of his coronation as Yorkshire captain. His 70 against the searing pace of Wes Hall and Charlie Griffith restored him in the public's esteem. Jim Kilburn, in the *Yorkshire Post*, enthused, 'England could not win at Lord's but they were greatly heartened by the late recovery in which Close played such an heroic part. Close not only augmented England's batting dignity but indicated that fast bowlers, in fast bowling conditions, can be met and contained.'

David Allen, one of Close's late partners in the unavailing quest for victory, remembers the heavy clouds which hung like a shroud over Lord's. 'It was getting dark; there was no sightscreen at the pavilion end in those days, and the dark hand of Wes Hall was not easy to locate. When he pitched short, Brian took the balls on his chest. He did not wince under the barrage but when he came off the field there wasn't much of his body that was left white.'

England were set 234 to win and rain had intervened to make it a contest against the clock as well as against the West Indies. Edrich, Stewart and Dexter were dismissed for 31 in all, and this became effectively four wickets down when Cowdrey was forced to retire with a broken wrist. Play was abandoned at 4.45 on the Monday and a combination of bad light and rain prevented a resumption until 2.30 on the final day.

Colin Cowdrey remembered an astonishing display of courage by Close on the last afternoon. 'Close batted on a flood-tide of adrenalin.' Cowdrey differed from the jury in the pavilion who thought the Yorkshireman had gone berserk in advancing down the wicket to Hall. 'He was using the logic that had been an art many years before of Frank Woolley: making room for his shot by taking a pace down the wicket as soon as the arm came over.' So what, to many, looked like 'a maniacal innings of blind courage was, in truth, a carefully premeditated assault. It was an amazing spectacle, for several times, facing Hall, he was stranded down the pitch ducking and weaving like a desperate boxer.'

The legacy of the repeated blows, said Cowdrey, was seen when he stripped off in the dressing room. Close's torso resembled a 'relief map of the Atlas Mountains'. 'There were black, blue and purple bruises from his neck down to his waist and in one or two places you could actually see where the stitching of the ball had left an impression on his skin. It had been, surely, Close's finest hour.'

The fury of the short-pitched bowling at Lord's was not a new phenomenon. Two other West Indians, Constantine and Martindale, had practised their version of 'bodyline' in 1935. It would become even more virulent when the West Indies under Clive Lloyd achieved their crushing superiority with a quartet of fast men bowling in tandem.

The testimony of Tom Graveney, who played another great innings against the West Indies at Lord's in 1966, emphasises the powers of Hall and Griffith. Griffith's bowling often placed him in the evil cast of throwers. Especially suspect was the sudden injection of pace that propelled his yorker or bouncer several yards quicker.

Graveney, then aged 39, perilously invoked Griffith's dislike at Headingley. 'Charlie thought I'd complained about him when he threw one at me.' He still retains the evidence on film of the threatening hostility of Griffith. A tell-tale red blotch on the collar of his cricket shirt reminds him, if it is necessary, of a delivery intended to wound. The incident occurred just before mid-day in the Test. 'The light was terrible,' recalls Graveney. 'Griffith pinged this ball at me.' At the end of the over one of the umpires, Charlie Elliott told him, 'I think that last delivery was unfair. I must have a word with the bowler.' Tom replied, 'I hope you do because he might get me next time.'

Simon Rae, in his book *It's Not Cricket*, provides another even more distasteful anecdote to illustrate the ferocity of Griffith. The story he relates could have had a fatal consequence for the Indian captain, Nariman Jamshedji Contractor. In an island match against Barbados, a ball from Griffith struck Contractor and fractured his skull. He did, happily, survive the blow after several weeks on the critical list but it ended his first-class career.

The hurt that Close suffered at Lord's was not in this category but it would have been sufficient to render a lesser man immobile for an extended period. His feat of strength was achieved without the protective armour of a helmet and body padding, which he would have considered unnecessary. As the principal guardian of the England fortress, Close never once rubbed an injured spot to give his assailants any satisfaction that they had disturbed him.

David Allen was Close's ally in the tumultuous finale. 'When I went in we needed 25 for victory.' As he watched the sallies down the wicket, Allen urged his partner to exercise more caution. 'If anyone is going to throw their wickets away, let it be the tail-enders. You've got to stay here, that's our best chance of winning . . . They'll be all up around the wicket. Let me see if I can have a little dabble and nick a few runs here and there.' Close listened to the entreaties but he was committed to his course. He replied soothingly, 'All right, lad. Let's do that.' Allen concedes that Close had to follow his own inclinations. 'We were second best and it was up to us to play along with him.'

Alan Ross recalled the immense fortitude displayed by Close. 'It happened, either by accident or design, he took Hall for eleven of the fourteen overs he bowled before tea, so the sickening repetitiousness of the impact can be imagined.' At five o'clock, with an hour left, England needed 48. Ten minutes later, with two boundaries by Close, including a hook off a bouncer by Hall to reach his fifty, this had been reduced to 31. 'At this stage,' continued Ross, 'recklessness having paid its way, it might have been plain sailing. Hall's shirt was stuck to his back like a second skin: his trudge back to his mark was painfully laboured.'

An epic match was nearing its conclusion. It was an absorbing television occasion, too, one of the most enthralling in the infancy of the medium. Millions watched the unfolding drama on the small screen. The news on television was abruptly cut short when viewers protested at being pulled away from Lord's with two overs to go. Workers in the City in the afternoon had deserted their desks. 'Tycoons and typists exchanged cricket bulletins more urgently than any reports on fluctuating markets,' reported Alan Ross.

Close remembers the stresses of his innings at Lord's. 'All fast bowlers wanted to play there. It was lightning quick with the ball lifting off the ridge at the far end.' Wes Hall, he recalls, was timed at 104 mph, and the back-foot no-ball rule aided him. 'The drag and long stride meant that the West Indians were bowling one and a half yards closer to you.'

Frequent delays because of drizzle and bad light also contributed to relieving rests for Hall and Griffith. 'Wes and Charlie were able to get their feet up during the breaks,' says Close. Gibbs and Sobers, the West Indian spinners, bowled only 21 overs in England's second innings. 'If they had had to bowl their full quota of overs, we would have won the game.'

A reduced over rate of 13 an hour, dropping even further at one stage to slightly above eleven, was also a factor in the need for batting haste. Bill Bowes said that Hall's long walk back and his ability to take four and a half minutes to bowl an over were deliberately used by Worrell, the West Indies captain, to try to put England against the clock. Between tea and the drawing of stumps, a period of 83 minutes, West Indies bowled only 19 overs.

At last England required 18 to win at four and a half runs an over. 'We were running out of time, so I had to try and upset Wes,' recalls Close. He made the decision to walk two or three yards down the wicket. 'My reasoning was to plant myself between him and my wickets. He couldn't bowl me out if I missed it. I would also have a chance of a free shot if he pitched it up.'

Close, as he remarked at the time, had long ceased to watch Hall through his 40-yard run. Instead he stared down the wicket, focusing only when the bowler reached the stumps. 'Suddenly, with Hall barely halfway to the crease, Close took two steps forward and seemed ready to take more,' reported Alan Ross.

The West Indian bowler was cowed by the advance and grew increasingly bewildered. 'For a moment he looked about to burst into tears,' said Ross. Worrell looked concerned as Hall clutched at his back. Quiet encouraging words from the captain coaxed Hall back into action. 'But Close, innocently expressionless, had merely started,' added Ross. 'Almost every other ball he set off down the pitch, bat raised and narrowing the distance between them until it seemed that it was Hall's person he was after.'

The duel ended when Close attempted the same tactic against Griffith, who was bowling from the nursery end. The fatal ball was a bouncer from him, which Close, looking for a boundary to ease the pressure, tried to force through mid-wicket. The ball just flicked the underside of Close's bat, snaked between his arm and body and carried through into the hands of the wicket-keeper, Deryck Murray, standing 25 yards back.

England, with nine wickets down, were just six runs short of victory when Allen played out the last two balls. Colin Cowdrey, his arm sheathed in plaster, was not required to take strike. Nine runs earlier, as Ross reported, 'Close, his bat high in acknowledgement, and his frown indelibly embedded, walked through the throng of members into the pavilion.

'Solidly, as he had earned the right to be there at the curtain, the applause that should have carried only sweetness was tinged with disappointment. It was, after all, a cruelly written script that, on the brink of triumph, ambiguously mingled regret.'

Time, said Ross, had played a key role in Worrell's strategy. 'The slow over rate meant that each batsman had always to be anxious not only about defending both body and wicket but about pressing for runs. It was not the clock that mattered; it was runs per over, an altogether harsher analogy.'

Thirty-seven years later Close and Allen were separately interviewed for a radio programme celebrating deeds rich in their memory. Some time afterwards they were reunited at a Lord's Taverners game. 'David,' said Close, 'you know what went wrong. If they'd played Statham to partner Fred Trueman instead of leaving him out at Lord's, we'd have won easily.' He was still mentally involved in the match.

A gesture which must have brought a rueful smile from the

recipient followed Close's gallantry at Lord's. It came in a letter congratulating him on a wonderful attacking innings from Lord Nugent, the MCC president. 'It was superb and we are all very proud of you. You played not only with skill but also with good sense and courage.'

Close, the indomitable gladiator, had won his spurs before an august assembly. He gleefully told one of the watching officials, 'You should see my body. I'm just like a bloody Dalmatian.' While others would have cringed in distress at the body blows, by his reckoning more than 20, he almost gloated over the punishment.

The day after his torrid contest he reappeared for Yorkshire against Glamorgan at Sheffield. The effect of his bravery was revealed in a famous picture in the morning newspapers. It showed his body to be a mass of ugly purple bruises. As one observer said, it looked as if a truck had hit him. The wounds did not prevent Close from bowling 41 overs and taking 10 wickets as well as scoring 61 in the match against Glamorgan.

Ted Lester, one of the welcoming Yorkshiremen, remembers his own feelings of amazement. 'Brian really looked a mess on the morning after the Test.' He offered his commiseration. Close smiled broadly and replied, 'You know, Ted, it's a good job we were playing with a soft ball.'

Other Yorkshire colleagues looked on admiringly as Close presented his mauled body as if on a fashion parade. 'For two hours before the start of play,' recalls Don Wilson, 'Closey marched around the dressing room without a shirt or a vest, telling us all to inspect his bruises.' The cricketing martyr was a picture of joy as he displayed what were for him the prizes of an unforgettable battle.

9

Winner and Loser in Two Acts

'We were cowed as a team by the West Indies and needed a different approach. Brian was picked as captain at The Oval, particularly for his qualities of toughness and fearlessness.'

DOUG INSOLE,
former chairman of the England selectors

The public mood at the time of his promotion to the England captaincy was distrustful of charming ambassadors in the amateur fiefdom. The arts of diplomacy were seen as an unprofitable conceit after a sequence of humiliating reverses at the hands of the West Indies. Someone more down-to-earth was needed. The baton was hurriedly passed to Brian Close for the final Test at The Oval in August 1966.

The most remarkable feature of Close's new eminence was that it came after his sixth ascent into Test cricket. He stepped up once again, this time as the next in the professional captaincy line following his distinguished Yorkshire predecessor, Len Hutton. 'It is a romantic and wonderful thing that the wonder boy of yesteryear should have trained on into the ideal leader England needs when her cricket has reached the Dunkirk of misfortunes,' observed Denzil Batchelor.

The advocates of professionals in command believed that amateurs had run the show, as they thought best – even if, very often, they were the only ones who thought that way. Over the previous three years both Close and Don Kenyon at Worcester had usurped the old order and enhanced the reputation of their counties with inspirational methods.

Throughout cricket circles there was widespread admiration for

Close's acumen and courage. His status as a likeable and straight-forward man was high with his fellow professionals. Above all, it was the unswerving honesty of a fair-minded competitor that won their plaudits. 'He always stood by his word,' says Robin Hobbs, the last of England's specialist leg-spinners, who came under Close's command.

The happiest of promotions did seem to signify that Close had at last turned the corner, but the suspicion lingered, at least in his own mind, that his tenure as captain would be short-lived. At a pre-match dinner before the Test against the West Indies, he had told his team: 'I shouldn't be here if we hadn't made such a mess of the series. What's more, neither would a few of you. You are here because you are all fighters, and we are going to keep the pressure on and keep it on for five days.'

It was at Close's insistence that Raymond Illingworth was recalled to the England colours at The Oval. Illingworth was then regarded only as a good county cricketer. 'I supported him because I knew that Raymond was a high-class all-rounder. He had previously been badly managed by other England captains.'

The West Indies came to The Oval with an unassailable 3–0 lead in the series. Majestic at the helm was Garry Sobers, peerless as an all-rounder. He established a record aggregate of 722 runs in all five Tests at an average of 103.14. It included three centuries – 161 at Old Trafford, 163 not out at Lord's and 174 at Headingley – and was supplemented with 20 wickets compelled by an adroit mixture of spin and pace. The only blemish was the duck in his last innings at The Oval, artfully contrived by the opposing captain, Brian Close.

Doug Insole was chairman of the Test selectors at the time of Close's appointment. He is unwavering in his praise of Close, the third of England's captains against the West Indies, after M.J.K. Smith and Colin Cowdrey. It had been a demoralising summer, with two innings defeats, and only partially salvaged by expectations of victory in the drawn match at Lord's. West Indies, at one stage 95 for 5 in their second innings, were rescued by Sobers and David Holford, who shared an unbroken sixth wicket partnership of 274.

'We were cowed as a team by the West Indies,' says Insole. 'A different tactical approach was needed. Brian Close was picked as captain for the last Test, particularly for his qualities of resilience, toughness and fearlessness.' He recalls that Close was called in for an 'extraordinary selection meeting' at Lord's. The Yorkshireman imbued the proceedings with a boyish glee.

Insole and his fellow selectors – Alec Bedser, Don Kenyon and Peter May – at first dwelt upon The Oval wicket as likely to be conducive to swing bowling. Their new captain thereupon announced his preferences. The subsequent recital is described by Insole. It was stamped with self-assurance and demonstrated that Close was adaptable for all contingencies.

'Well,' said Brian, 'Fred [Trueman] and Nick [Nicholson] open for us in Yorkshire but if it is a question of "swinging" I swing the ball more than either of them.' The next question – who would be a suitable spinning contender – produced another disarming response. 'Don Wilson and Raymond [Illingworth] are our main spinners but I'll often go on and spin it more than them.'

The selectors now leaned back in their chairs, not wishing, or unable, to halt the discourse. Billy Griffith, the MCC secretary, pulled on his pipe and laid his pencil and paper on the table. The actual selection was suspended. It was now just a matter of providing cues for the captain.

'What about an opener, Brian? Fancy doing that?' asked Insole. Close replied: 'It's usually Ken Taylor and Geoffrey [Boycott] but if we really mean business and need to go for the runs, I see the new ball better than either of them.' 'Suppose we need a slip,' went up the chorus. Insole says that Brian found this just as negotiable as the other queries. 'I field at short square leg because nobody else wants the job but I can catch 'em at slip just as well.'

The ebullient raconteur had a rapt audience. As Sid Field, the West End comedian, would have said in another context, 'What a performance!' Afterwards Insole summed up with a droll sally. He looked down the table and said: 'We don't really need eleven in this match.'

The conviction with which Close addressed any problem in

cricket was shown at other more serious junctures on his debut as England captain. Insole says that Close had the full confidence of the selectors at The Oval and then on his reappointment for the twin series against India and Pakistan in the following year. 'Brian captained the side sensibly and also with imagination. At times he would try something a little unorthodox and quite often it came off.'

Tactical masterstrokes energised Close's approach against the hitherto dominant West Indies. One of the keynotes of his leadership was his duel with Garry Sobers. The West Indian captain had few chinks in his batting armour but he was fallible, despite his own proficiency in the bowling guile, to leg-spin. (If this was a weakness, another great player, Wally Hammond, shared it. Tom Graveney remembers that Hammond eschewed the niceties of 'reading' spin. 'I never bothered to look,' he told Graveney. 'I just play them off the wicket.' As Graveney says, this is the best approach 'if you are in that class.')

Among Close's charges at The Oval was Lancashire's Bob Barber who rarely bowled his brand of leg-spin in county cricket at Old Trafford. The measure of Close's faith in Barber was shown when he introduced him into the attack before lunch, a highly unusual tactic in a Test match. But it was eventually rewarded, admittedly after Sobers had scored 81, by a googly that snared the West Indian maestro. 'He was obviously going to have a crack at it and he ended up hitting a catch to me at straightish mid-wicket,' recalls Tom Graveney. Sobers was not the only batsman to fall to Barber. His figures in the match bear witness to the success of Close's strategy. They included 3 for 49 runs in the first innings and 2 for 78, including the vital wicket of Seymour Nurse, in 22 overs in the second innings.

Even greater satisfaction ensued when Sobers was seduced into error in the second innings. It was yet another instance of the positive, attacking cricket that was Close's trademark. His gamble was to lay down the challenge to one of the finest hookers in the game. There was just a chance that it would work before Sobers attuned himself to the pace of the wicket. John Snow was bowling and Close directed him to try a bouncer with the first ball. 'Let him have one,' was the instruction.

It was a decisive moment on a perfect wicket. As Tom Graveney says, 'if Garry had got in on that pitch we would never have seen the end of the game'. Close, the fielding colossus, crouched expectantly in the trap. 'Closey was almost literally sitting in Sobers' pocket,' recalls Graveney. Sobers went for the hook, his bat sharply raised. The ball gently flicked his gloves and looped up to provide a simple catch. He was out for a duck.

Close did not flinch or move before the violent motion of Sobers' bat. 'It might have looked a dolly,' reported Peter West, 'but only to someone who had the guts to keep his eye on the ball rather than turn away in self-protection – as most very reasonably would have done.'

Tony Lewis, the twelfth man at The Oval, recalled an England team transformed in spirit. A sense of adventure was released by Close, who treated the job as if it had always been properly his own. Others had just kept the captain's seat warm. Close, as he recalls, had been determined to assemble a team of the 'right lads who would fight for me'. The evidence that he had chosen wisely was shown in a batting rally that set England on the winning path.

It was, for a time, a gloomy picture. The figures on the scoreboard appeared to present the dire prospect of another overwhelming West Indian triumph. England, facing a total of 268, were in the toils at 166 for 7. Graveney and Murray, both century-makers, were the saviours. Their concentration never faltered and the eighth-wicket stand of 217 runs was the turning point of the match. It was confirmed, unexpectedly, by the last-wicket alliance between Higgs and Snow.

Wisden reported: 'The West Indies bowlers must have been looking forward to an early rest but England's opening bowlers displayed their talent for batting in a highly diverting partnership of 128 in two hours. They defied all the pace and spin the West Indies could offer – and the new ball.' The resolution of Higgs and Snow, who both hit their first half-centuries in first-class cricket, narrowly failed by only two runs to overhaul the world Test last-wicket record, recorded by Reggie Foster and Wilfred Rhodes for England against Australia at Sydney in the 1903–4 series.

The magnificent supplements of the late order produced 361 runs for the last three wickets. Never before in Test cricket had the last three men scored a hundred and two fifties. John Murray, in his crucial stand with Graveney, was hardly less impressive than his senior batting partner. 'He has always *looked* a most handsome player,' commented Peter West. 'But too often in the past he had committed some indiscretion when apparently well set for a large score.' At The Oval Murray became only the third number nine batsman, following Gubby Allen and Ray Lindwall, to achieve a Test century.

The salutations for England's victory by an innings and 34 runs at The Oval gave due prominence to the heroics of the batting quartet. But it was the virtuosity of Brian Close, as captain and intrepid fieldsman, that was seen as a happy omen for English cricket. 'Heaped as he was this August with the thanks and congratulations of the nation his taste of final success must have been sweet beyond measure,' concluded Peter West.

The Establishment crusade for brighter cricket brought about what now seems the astonishing exclusion of Geoffrey Boycott after England's victory by six wickets over India at Headingley in 1967. It was implied that his unbeaten 246 was the product of wilful slow scoring. The disciplinary measure imposed on Boycott was a consequence of the monotony that was said to prevail in extended Tests over five days against weaker opposition. Norman Preston, the editor of *Wisden,* favoured a limit of four days to encourage greater batting enterprise and reduce the boredom of spectators.

Denis Compton, writing in the same edition, also expressed his disappointment at the safety-first attitudes that challenged cricket more than any other spectator sport. 'This outlook has bedevilled professional cricket for far too long and like our traffic in big cities the three-day county game has almost come to a full stop.'

Boycott, in his batting vigil at Headingley, did have the excuse that he went into the Test poorly prepared. In nine innings he had scored only 124 runs, including a pair of ducks against Kent at Bradford. Against a depleted Indian attack he scored 106 in six hours. His rate of progress was recorded: 17 in the first hour, then eight in the second, 15 in the third followed by 23, 21 and 22 in the closing sequence.

On the following day Boycott atoned by hitting 140 in three and a half hours, but the acceleration came too late to arrest the criticism. Close says his fellow selectors outvoted him in making the decision to drop Boycott. His plea was an instance of his steadfast support for members of his team: 'Anyone who has played a long innings will well understand Boycott's problem. The sheer effort makes one like an automaton. One needs to be aware of Boycott's frame of mind as an out-of-form batsman trying to prove himself good enough for England. Such tenacity, in different conditions, would have been hailed as a masterly exhibition of the bulldog spirit; but on this first day of a Test it was being viewed in a different light.'

Close's own reign was untarnished in the rest of the series against India. England were the victors by an innings and 124 runs, the match being completed in two and a half days of actual playing time. Raymond Illingworth was once again an influential aide. India lost their last six second-innings wickets in less than an hour for 35 runs. Illingworth took 5 for 12 in 10 overs and returned figures of 6 for 29 in the innings.

The series was sealed with a victory by 132 runs in the rain-affected match at Birmingham. Thirty-three wickets fell to spin; the Indian quartet of Chandrasekhar, Prasanna, Venkataraghavan and Bedi took 18, and for England, Illingworth, Hobbs and Close shared 15. India were bowled out in their first innings for 92, their lowest Test score since 1952. A lead of 206 runs did not persuade Close to enforce the follow-on. Instead England's position was bolstered by a fifth-wicket partnership of 78 between Close and Amiss.

There were many, not including Close, who thought that the buccaneering heavyweight Colin Milburn was very unlucky to be left out of the England team against the West Indies at The Oval in 1966. He had followed up his 94 at Manchester with another piece of savage strokeplay in scoring a century at Lord's. He was second in the England averages with 316 runs at an average of 52.66.

Peter West, in *Playfair Cricket Monthly*, disputed Milburn's alleged lack of mobility in the field. His Northamptonshire colleagues had said this was deceptive: he was a lot quicker than he looks, and for a man of his size his reactions close to the wicket were not exactly slothful.

Close disagreed with Milburn's selection for the first Test against Pakistan at Lord's. While respecting a 'great character', he could not respond to the carefree approach of a batsman prone to impulsive hooking. Lapses of this nature did not place his colleague in the category of authentic Test class. The indictment was not lessened when Milburn, on patrol beneath the Warner Stand, dropped a vital catch at Lord's. Hanif, the Pakistani captain, was then on 51. 'Basil D'Oliveira was bowling from the nursery end,' recalls Close. 'Hanif skied one ball from him straight to Colin and he dropped it.'

Pakistan, at this stage, had lost seven wickets for 121 and were still 248 in arrears. Asif Iqbal, then a newcomer to the Test scene, was Hanif's partner in a key stand of 130. The deficit in the end was only 15 runs. Close remembers Hanif's careful stewardship and constant urgings to Asif to rein in his aggression during the batting rally.

England, on the last day, were only 146 runs ahead with six wickets in hand. Close and D'Oliviera were associated in a stand of 104 before the declaration, which left Pakistan a target of 257 in three and a half hours. The wicket was still good and *Wisden* criticised the decision to play for a draw. 'Pakistan's lack of enterprise could not be excused.' Close recalls that he was under severe pressure to go for a win. 'I gave Pakistan a clearer chance of victory than we had. It was against my better judgement.'

The vigilance of Ken Barrington – and, as *Wisden* commented 'his inexhaustible patience' – carried England to their triumph by 10 wickets at Nottingham. His unbeaten 109 was compiled over six hours and 50 minutes. It followed his 148 in the first Test and the succeeding innings of 142 at The Oval gave the Surrey batsman an aggregate of 426 runs in the three-match series at an average of 142.

Barrington had remodelled his batting approach after his cavalier days as an apprentice at The Oval. His sheet-anchor qualities served England well, not least in his heavily criticised marathon at Trent Bridge. England, as Close recalls, had bowled out Pakistan for 140 on a good pitch on the opening day. A ferocious thunderstorm, which flooded the ground, changed the conditions. It was estimated that the city fire brigade pumped away 100,000 gallons of water. 'We had to fight like hell for every run on a transformed wicket,' says Close. He was second top scorer with 41.

His indignation in difficult circumstances grew stronger when Barrington, the pillar of England's batting, was roundly chastised by the press. The campaign to dislodge another key player did not succeed this time. 'I managed to keep Kenny in the team and he thanked me for supporting him.' An impressive new pairing from Kent took the stage in England's win by 10 wickets at Nottingham. Derek Underwood claimed five wickets in Pakistan's second innings and Alan Knott, on his Test debut, took seven catches.

Pakistan teetered on the edge of an ignominious defeat at The Oval, but in the end the August Bank Holiday crowd were able to acclaim a display of 'pure batting genius and joyous cheek' by the 24-year-old Asif Iqbal. When he entered the fray at 12.20 on the late summer morning Pakistan were 53 for 7 and still needed 167 to make England bat again. Soon it was 65 for 8.

Wisden reported: 'The next three hours and 10 minutes scarcely belonged to reality and certainly not the setting of a modern Test.' Asif hit 146 (out of 202) and his innings included two sixes and 21 fours. It was the highest score by a number nine Test batsman and his partnership of 190 with Intikhab Alam was another world record.

Asif provided his own explanation of the circumstances that provoked an exhilarating onslaught. He said that he had been displeased to learn that an exhibition match was to be held to entertain the crowd in the expectation of an early finish to the game. 'Everyone seemed to accept that it was already over. I certainly didn't. I wanted my team to be spared from taking part in an exhibition. The whole situation made me all the more anxious and determined to succeed.'

England were the winners by eight wickets, but, as *Wisden* observed, 'the stigma and sting of victory were engulfed in a wave of excitement and admiration.' For Close, unbeaten in seven Tests, almost his last act in England's cause was to dismiss Asif. 'Stumped by Knotty off my fifth ball,' he laconically relates.

The days preceding the Oval Test plunged Brian Close into yet another drama in his roller-coaster career. A highly contentious issue produced an unforgiving end to his captaincy. His appointment as captain on the forthcoming tour of the West Indies, although not actually confirmed, was widely considered a formality. Not only that but his proven outstanding leadership gave every assurance of a long reign at the helm.

According to Close, the *Daily Express* sports writer Crawford White had warned him during the season to watch his step. 'They [the MCC] are out to get you at the first opportunity they get.' The allegation was that the knives were out for Close should he ever so mildly err.

The cause of the dissension was what was perceived as time-wasting during Yorkshire's match against Warwickshire at Edgbaston. Warwickshire had been set a target of 142 to win in the last hour and 40 minutes. They failed by only nine runs. Yorkshire bowled only 24 overs and, in the last 15 minutes, during which they briefly left the field during a heavy shower, sent down two overs. One of them, from Fred Trueman, contained two no-balls and three bouncers.

Close explains the conditions at Edgbaston. 'There was a fine drizzle most of the time. I couldn't bowl my spinners.' Trueman, Richard Hutton and Tony Nicholson thus had to shoulder the bowling responsibilities. An MCC rule also obliged the fielding side to dry the ball under the observation of the umpires. Yorkshire, in fact, broke this rule, their bowlers carrying the cloth in their pockets so as to speed up the process. There was, in addition, an imperative to protect a small total. 'I had to employ deep field placings to save runs and this also ate up time,' adds Close.

Further attempts to justify his conduct were derided in some quarters. His defence, it was said, was no more than 'two wrongs don't make a right'. His critics said the fact that others had offended was not the point, which is all very well except that they were spared and Close had to suffer a drastic demotion.

The imposition of slow over rates was not a new departure, even in the 1960s. The restrictive practice, as Les Ames once told me, was beginning to develop in England towards the end of his career in the early 1950s. Ames remembered the exhortations on the county circuit. 'Come on, come on, we've got to slow the buggers down.'

It is also beyond doubt that Len Hutton, another England captain, overstepped the bounds of caution during the tour of Australia in 1954–55. 'Unfortunately, Len was the one who started the business of slow over rates,' declared Richie Benaud. Hutton was acclaimed for his series-winning strategy but Ray Robinson, the Australian writer, referred to the anger of crowds during the frequent discussions held with England's bowlers.

The briefings, coupled with the long runs taken by most of the bowlers, reduced play to below 60 eight-ball overs. Only 58 were bowled at Brisbane and Adelaide and the rate fell to 54 at Melbourne. Geoffrey Howard, the MCC manager, acknowledged that Hutton's basic objective was to keep Tyson and Statham in prime condition. 'But the slowing tactic did deprive the opposition of the chance to score more runs.'

Gamesmanship was the only true charge that could be levelled against Yorkshire at Edgbaston. As Neville Cardus wrote at the time, such tactics had a long and distinguished lineage. Cardus had once asked Jack Board, the veteran Gloucestershire wicket-keeper, if W.G. Grace had ever *really* cheated. 'Oh no,' said Jack almost indignantly, 'goodness me, the Old Man would never have cheated. But he made a large ring of the law – and then did some rum things inside it.'

Cardus added: 'Brian Close, with precious points at stake at Edgbaston, drew another capacious ring of the law. He was in a desperate and unenviable position. So he employed tactics which went to the law's extremes.'

One Warwickshire member, worthily impartial amid the general disarray, afterwards voiced his concern at Close's plight. 'On the last day it had rained in the afternoon and through the tea interval. Consequently when play resumed the ground was very wet and hazardous for the fielding side. On one side of the pitch was a very short boundary and a normal cover point was almost on the fence.' He refers to the volume of noise in this section, which meant that the Yorkshire captain had extreme difficulty in communicating with his fieldsmen. The furore built up to a climax when Trueman came on to bowl, with 11 minutes left for play. 'In my opinion, Trueman was as much to blame as Close. But had Close made any effort to walk from his position to warn Trueman he would have been attacked for wasting time. In that sense it was no fault of Close that Trueman bowled two no-balls.'

Tom Cartwright, with whom Close was later to enjoy a fruitful partnership in Somerset, was in the Warwickshire ranks at Edgbaston. He recalls: 'We were left a total that was pretty difficult. John Jameson was brilliant; he had played so well that we deserved to win. The later stages of the game were played in a fine drizzle, almost like a sea fret. The Yorkshire players threw the ball to each other and they all dried it with a towel. So it took them an age to bowl an over.'

Cartwright believes that Close, in his heart of hearts, would not have preferred this development. 'But saving the game for Yorkshire was paramount.' Like others, he maintains that the price Close paid was too costly a punishment.

Ted Lester, while in agreement with the undue severity of the censure, remembers his own embarrassment as the Yorkshire scorer at the match. 'I was genuinely upset and ashamed to be a Yorkshire-man that day.' He was prompted for the first time to go into the home dressing room and apologise to the Warwickshire captain, Mike Smith. The situation was worsened, in his view, by the fact that Tony Nicholson had maintained a reasonable over rate compared with Trueman and Hutton at the other end, who deliberately were bowling to close it down.

'You've got to blame Brian as captain but it was exploited by Fred and Richard,' Lester continues. 'Had Brian organised things properly, it wouldn't have looked so bad.' For Lester, the episode was yet another demonstration of Close's abhorrence of defeat. 'In such circumstances, he could be quite ruthless whether in the right or wrong.'

Jim Kilburn, in the *Yorkshire Post*, was also regretful that the reputation of the county was tarnished at Edgbaston. He strongly questioned the attitude adopted, exaggerated, he said, to the point of irritation, as Warwickshire made a desperate attempt to score 54 runs in the closing half-hour. 'Nobody expected Yorkshire to present Warwickshire with the match, and they were handicapped with a wet ball. But Yorkshiremen expect matches to be saved by cricketing skills rather than tactics open to question.'

One *Yorkshire Post* reader considered that the 'crowning irony' was that Yorkshire were permitted to keep their 'ill-gotten' points. 'Had the match been awarded to Warwickshire on the grounds that in their deliberate time-wasting Yorkshire had virtually "refused to play", that in itself would have been sufficient censure to Brian Close and a warning to other would-be emulators.'

There was another aspect, even more unsavoury: that of the explosion of abuse directed at the Yorkshire players. A leader writer in the *Yorkshire Post* gave this verdict: 'Warwickshire members who protest at the attitude of Yorkshire cricketers should first make sure that their own behaviour is irreproachable. They have a duty to set such an example that cricket crowds are not in danger of being likened to the more unruly elements who watch professional soccer.'

The hostility was indeed alarming in the frenzied passage of the game. The symptoms of the *cause célèbre* had been manifested in other ways. The hysterical crossfire from opposing newspaper sources rumbled on for several days. The spectacular rush into print included one malicious tabloid revelation that Close had dashed into the members' enclosure and seized a spectator by the collar to shake him angrily.

'The crowd went absolutely dilly,' recalls Don Wilson, one member of the Yorkshire team. 'They were shouting "cheats" and it became quite nasty. It just got worse and worse and we were in a lot of trouble.' One woman member brandished an umbrella as the players left the field at lunch. Close was not one to be swayed by a mob but his thoughts were preoccupied by the state of the game that was running away from Yorkshire.

One long-standing Warwickshire member remembers sitting in

front of the pavilion during the uproar. One of his neighbours had begun furiously to abuse Close. 'When they came off Close was white with anger. Meanwhile I had told the barracker to shut up and move, which he did. I rather feel by this time he had got the wind up as to what might happen.'

Close, according to the member, made a beeline for the spectator he believed to be responsible. 'Unfortunately, he had chosen the wrong individual and quite a fracas developed.' Fred Trueman, he relates, was the peacemaker, rushing his captain into the pavilion and then returning to make his apologies. He explained that Close was, at that time, highly strung following various comments on his captaincy regime. Trueman said that it had never been Close's intention to hurt anyone.

Close offers his own version of the quarrel. He remembers a remark which was more than unpleasant. 'I was hot, sticky, worried and short-tempered. I went along the empty row of seats behind the man I thought had spoken and asked: "Excuse me, was it you who said that?" I had put my hand on his shoulder. He turned and replied emphatically: "No, I did not." I replied: "I'm terribly sorry," and went in to lunch.'

Close concedes that his actions as a player in upbraiding a spectator were unusual, but there were mitigating circumstances. He recognised that he had perhaps been a little foolish and spoke to Leslie Deakins, the Warwickshire secretary. Deakins assured the Yorkshire captain that he had no need to worry and told Close to forget about the aberration.

The error in identity was later confirmed in a statement from a Staffordshire man who was the guest of the Yorkshire club at the match, also against Warwickshire, at Middlesbrough; he had been the misidentified recipient of Close's enquiry. It echoed, almost word for word, Close's interpretation of the event. The correspondent remembered his initial feelings of shock and amazement. It had been suggested that he make a complaint, but Close had apologised for the incident and it was closed as far as the spectator was concerned. 'There was nothing for me to complain about.'

Close remains unrepentant about his supposed indiscretion at

Edgbaston. He insists that his hands were clean. Had he been arraigned in a court of law, he would have been able to contest, in cricketing terms, the infringement attributed to him. Close believes that the response of Mike Smith, his opposing captain, in a conversation after the game, is evidence that he had no cause for regret. Close said, 'Bad luck, Mike, you played better than we did. But I couldn't give you the game.' Smith replied, 'I quite understand.'

Ronnie Burnet, as a member of the Yorkshire committee, recalled his satisfaction that matters had been handled properly at Edgbaston. 'On the night following the match I spoke to all the players in the side and I was convinced that there was no time-wasting.' Burnet believed that Brian Sellers, the county chairman, then made a serious misjudgement. 'Sellers wrote to the MCC president immediately apologising which put Close in a difficult position. I was with Herbert Sutcliffe when we saw the letter and we were both incensed.'

Doug Insole, as chairman of the Test selectors in 1967, is a key witness in the events that led to Close losing the England captaincy. He refers to the obstinacy of a player who was not prepared to allow people who had his best interests at heart to help him. 'I stuck my neck out for Brian and had to suffer a lot of criticism, some of it scurrilous.' He strongly disputes any Establishment prejudice against Close. 'Brian was our first choice for the tour of the West Indies and when he became unavailable we picked Colin Cowdrey as an excellent alternative. Because of what was said by me about Brian, people said, "You've done the dirty on Cowdrey."'

There was public anger, especially in Yorkshire, at the allegation that the MCC had over-ruled the selectors. A leader writer in the *Yorkshire Post* commented on an 'unprecedented step'. 'The casual observer would be confused to learn that D.B. Close was first selected as captain by a panel of experts and then thrown out by the general committee.'

Contemporary reports indicated that Close had been chosen as captain for the West Indies tour by a majority of four to two. There were only four on the actual selection committee and so this requires an explanation. Arthur Gilligan and Les Ames, the tour manager, though not on the selection committee, did take part in the discussions. They were outvoted but went along with Close's nomination.

Insole points out that no decision on Close's appointment had been made prior to the MCC ruling. He had come under fierce interrogation from a wolfish press and soon realised that it would be futile to persist with a 'No comment' reply. He therefore told reporters: 'The selectors' choice *would have been* Brian Close.' Insole now says that this was a blatant attempt on the part of the press to cause friction between Colin Cowdrey and himself. In the following season he was compelled to undertake a public relations exercise in company with Cowdrey to show the goodwill existing between them.

Cowdrey himself was horrified by the protracted discussions at Lord's, and that yet another question of the England captaincy had been thrown open to public debate. He was so concerned that his first reaction was to withdraw as a candidate. Les Ames, his manager in Kent, was his confidant. Ames told him: 'You will help no one by making yourself unavailable – that's the easy way out. You do not alter any decision that may be made over Brian Close by moving out of the picture.'

Insole is a friendly counsel and a fair-minded administrator. 'Brian was an outgoing, enterprising cricketer and what happened at Edgbaston was not his normal approach. I wish, most of all, that he had acted differently and shown some contrition.' He says that the reports of the umpires, Charlie Elliott and Laurie Gray, were very condemnatory on the match against Warwickshire. 'Brian should have said, "That's not the way I want to play the game. I realise that I made a mistake and won't do it again."'

Insole maintains that he had sympathy for Close but that he could not quarrel with the MCC decision, bearing in mind the attitudes prevailing at the time. They had taken a 'high and mighty' tone in dismissing Close. But, in their defence, it was because they thought his approach to the game was not appropriate at international level.

The crux of the matter was that the MCC feared a disastrous

outcome if Close acted in a similar way in the highly charged atmosphere of the West Indies. Tom Graveney, one of the touring party, says, 'They read all sorts of things into it if Brian had lost his rag out there. But that was not his way. At the back of their minds the MCC thought there would be a big stir up in the West Indies.' Graveney also cites the continuing amateur influence as a factor even though the distinction between the Gentlemen and Players had been abolished five years earlier. 'It took a long time before we had a cricketers' game when everyone was on the same level.'

John Murray, another England contemporary, reflected on a dark day in Close's career. 'It was said that his temperament would not allow him to carry the flag on an overseas tour, especially to the West Indies.' Murray had played under Close's captaincy for Derrick Robins' XI in South Africa. 'Having experienced his leadership on that tour when for the first time coloured cricketers were allowed to play alongside white players under Brian's command, I am convinced that he would have carried the flag with honour.'

Rex Alston, in *Playfair Cricket Monthly,* dealt with what was possibly a more exacting assignment facing Close in 1967–68. As a broadcaster, Alston had covered three series in the Caribbean. 'I know the conditions in those volatile islands, and if Close, in his zeal for victory, had behaved there as he had at Edgbaston, there would have been a riot, and irreparable harm would have been done to cricket and to England.' Alston considered that the MCC dare not take the risk and supported them in a stand that, he said, must have been thoroughly distasteful to them. 'No one likes to deprive a man of his ambition but the game is greater than any one man, and they had the courage to say so.'

It is interesting in retrospect to recall that another Yorkshireman, Len Hutton, had to withstand claims that he might be a liability on his tour of the West Indies in 1953–54. He had to be wary of not giving offence on his first tour abroad as a leader. There was strong evidence of opposition to his appointment.

The summons to Brian Close to appear before the MCC at Lord's came on the Wednesday before the Test against Pakistan at The

Oval. The executive committee consisted of Arthur Gilligan, the MCC president-elect, David Clark of Kent, Cecil Paris (Hampshire) and Eddie Gothard (Derbyshire). Brian Sellers, as the Yorkshire observer, and Doug Insole were also present. The statement communicated to Close after the meeting read: 'We have found Yorkshire guilty of wasting time and we hold you as captain responsible.'

Close was due at The Oval in the afternoon to supervise practice before the Test. Brian Sellers had to placate his distressed county captain. 'This is utterly ridiculous. We did not contravene the laws of cricket,' argued Close. In his dismay he was moved to say that he intended to withdraw from the match against Pakistan. Sellers replied, 'Put that out of your mind. Get over there and show 'em.'

There was a melancholy footnote to the rejoicing over England's victory at The Oval. Before the closing ceremony Doug Insole quietly called England's unbeaten captain to one side. 'I'm terribly sorry, Brian, to give you the sad news. But you've been replaced as captain.'

It now seems evident that Close's 'crime' was not a failure to measure up to playing standards. Instead it was considered that he had offended a code. Transgressions against the 'spirit of the game' of far worse import still occupy the attention of the game's administrators. One of the consequences of the Edgbaston episode was the decision to implement the ruling, still in existence, of a mandatory 20 overs in the last hour of a game.

Close today reflects on the craziness of the rule. 'No team bowls twenty overs unless they're bowling spinners. It takes the feet away from the captain making the declaration. In a situation on the last day, which often produces a great tussle, he wants to bowl as many overs as he can. He's only declaring to try and win the game for his team.' Close says that the imposition has created a needless dilemma. He maintains that all declarations in the third innings of a match, instead of being narrowly devised, are dictated by safety in case the result becomes tight at the end. Enterprise has been stifled by such calculations. Declarations are based on run estimates rather than on how quickly wickets can be taken.

The anxieties that beset Close were relieved by a rapturous ovation in Yorkshire's penultimate championship game against Warwickshire at Middlesbrough in August 1967. He was applauded all the way to the wicket and took his stance in another crisis to which he had the answer. Yorkshire had lost seven wickets for 125 beneath desolate skies. By his side to lighten the challenge was the best of allies, Fred Trueman.

Jim Kilburn, in the *Yorkshire Post*, wrote, 'Close could not, in a dream world, have contrived a more timely success. His supporters, warmly greeting him, were delighted that he should lead the revival with his highest score of the season.' The bruises on this day, on an unpredictable pitch, were inflicted in the line of worthy duty. An innings as earnest as any in his lifetime deserved to be sealed with a century. Close fell two runs short, having added 98 with Trueman.

'His partnership was built with a restrained Trueman,' said Kilburn. 'His dismissal at square leg from a sweep that had served so well, was a unanimous regret.' Don Wilson shared the honours, in the end, with remarkable match figures of 13 for 52, and Yorkshire were conclusive victors by 229 runs.

Rex Alston, who was also present at Middlesbrough, recalled the dignity of Close on his home soil. 'He came well out of an intolerable situation in which his immediate priority was to win a match for Yorkshire. He reacted magnificently as a player, as all who knew him thought he would, because no one has ever doubted his courage.'

A lesser man than Close would have been engulfed by torment. He had been debarred from furthering his captaincy education in the West Indies. A coveted prize had been wrenched from his grasp. Yet he was magnanimous in his exclusion. His generosity as a sportsman was shown by one of his first acts of the day at Middlesbrough. He sent a personal telegram of good wishes to his successor, Colin Cowdrey, and each member of the touring party. The message read: 'Congratulations. Have a wonderful time. Best of luck.'

10

Dishonouring a Loyalist

'It is a complete surprise. I agreed to resign at first, but decided that because I had just had a testimonial the public would think I was getting the money and packing it in.'

BRIAN CLOSE,
Bradford *Telegraph and Argus*, November 1970

Controversy continued to haunt Brian Close, this time unexpectedly on the domestic stage. His distress at being deposed as Yorkshire captain was confined in the dignified words of farewell that headed the local newspaper's front page. They cloaked the heartache of a man whose life had been devoted to Yorkshire cricket.

The abrupt decision to dispense with the services of Close after 22 years with the county was conveyed in a statement by John Nash, the Yorkshire secretary. It had been prompted, he said, by their captain's repeated public expressions of dislike for the one-day game. Close's attitude had gone against a trend. He had ignored the fact that 'this form of cricket is becoming increasingly important as the years go by'.

It was a flimsy premise to justify the dismissal of a great player and would have far-reaching repercussions. Yorkshire passed into a steep decline and a time of quarrelsome divisions over and beyond the next decade. The ultimate penalty had been imposed on one of the most loyal of their cast for voicing sentiments widely shared by other players. The advent of the shorter, 40-over version in the Sunday League in 1969 especially affronted Close as a traditionalist. It was not just the ridiculous situation of being asked to 'play like clowns' but the disturbing effect the madcap frolic had on younger players. Faults in technique emerged as a by-product of confused minds.

Close regarded himself as guiltless in his campaign. 'I hated having to encourage my team, particularly the youngsters, to think and act positively for six days of the week and then on the Sunday to have to blast them for doing the very things I'd been coaxing them to do. It went against the grain.'

The leader writer in the *Telegraph and Argus* was puzzled by the nature of Close's departure. 'It cannot surely be that a Yorkshireman is dismissed for speaking his mind. Yorkshire cricket epitomises the Yorkshire character – dogged, determined, and a thorough approach to a job of work. The present structure of professional cricket threatens to undermine these qualities and the whole county will respect Brian Close for saying so.'

Alan Ross, in another editorial in *The Cricketer*, considered the action a 'clumsy and bungled business', not least because it looked as if even Yorkshire were throwing their 'cloth bonnets at the siren call of one-day cricket'. What was not beyond dispute, he maintained, was that if three-day cricket were significantly reduced, everyone would be out of business and cricket would become merely a quaint decoration of the landscape. 'If Close's standing out against such a devaluation of county cricket was the main reason for him being shown the door, then he is a martyr of some sort.'

Observers elsewhere were confounded that Yorkshire should have opted to expel such a dedicated cricketer. Rex Alston, in *Playfair Cricket Monthly*, thought that if the objections were the sole cause of the dismissal, they should have been sorted out behind the scenes. 'As the last of the old guard, Close will be sadly missed as a player and tactician. It does seem a pity that, with all he has yet to give to cricket, Yorkshire should have discarded him when he was still "full of running".'

One West Country opponent, Bryan 'Bomber' Wells, said that Close had criticised one-day cricket with the realism of an experienced cricketer. It was wrong, he said, that Close should have been so severely treated for adhering to his principles. 'Anyone who believes that this form of cricket is adequate grounding for players is not only building castles in the air but also trying to move into them.' Wells, with enduring memories of his tussles with Yorkshire and Close, said that his adversary had acquired his skills through the guidance of wise and precise elders. 'I doubt whether he would have been half the player had he been thrust into the merry-go-round of one-day cricket as a youngster.'

The scandal of Close's exclusion occurred at a time when Yorkshire were in the throes of rebuilding their team. They were depleted by the loss of four key members. Raymond Illingworth had departed to pursue a new and illustrious career with Leicestershire and England. Fred Trueman had retired and Jimmy Binks and Ken Taylor had emigrated to take up business appointments respectively in California and South Africa. It was remarkable that Yorkshire should decide voluntarily to dismiss a trustworthy guardian at such a crucial juncture.

Even more significantly, Close had been cast aside at the behest of another Yorkshire champion, Brian Sellers, then chairman of the county's cricket committee. In more deferential days Sellers had earned respect and admiration as Yorkshire won the championship six times between 1933 and 1948, a record only challenged by Lord Hawke and Stuart Surridge, with Surrey.

In his heyday Sellers was known as 'Crackerjack' and post-war recruits referred to him, out of his hearing, as the sergeant-major. He could be as sharp as the most caustic drill instructor. Johnny Wardle related the story of one pre-match lecture by Sellers. 'You've got to concentrate on every single ball of the match,' the Yorkshire captain told the awed assembly. 'And still have enough concentration to keep an eye on me.'

These were undeniably lessons of sound cricket government, but even such an avowed admirer as Jim Kilburn conceded that Sellers exercised a harsh discipline and that sometimes he was less than tactful. 'His mistakes,' said Kilburn, 'were those of a man with the strongest sense of duty. He never courted favour nor feared unpopularity and he never shirked a task.'

Bill Bowes remembered the ruthless demands of Sellers in the 1930s and how he was quite prepared to stamp on famous feet. One pair belonged to Hedley Verity, who incurred the censure of the Yorkshire captain and was asked to answer a charge of 'unfitness' by the county committee. Verity had suffered a painful reaction, a small lump appearing under his bowling arm, to inoculations given prior to an Australian tour. Sellers always maintained that Yorkshire took priority over England. As luck would have it, a Roses match was next on the cricket calendar. Bowes, to make matters worse, also reported that he was troubled with a groin injury. Sellers insisted that both he and Verity should play against Lancashire.

At the subsequent meeting Verity was asked to explain why he had played in a match when he was obviously unfit. He said that he had advised Sellers of his problem and had expressed doubt that he would be able to bowl properly. Verity sought the corroboration of Sellers seated by his side. The Yorkshire captain looked straight ahead and did not utter a word.

A frost enveloped their relationship in the following weeks. Verity was only moved to respond when Sellers asked him a direct question. The rift was healed in time but Bowes, as the intermediary, told his captain: 'You weren't too clever, skipper. You must never threaten Hedley.'

Ted Lester, who played, sometimes uneasily, under Sellers' leadership after the Second World War, also remembers the perils of stepping out of line. While firmly in the pro-Sellers camp, he does not dispute the martinet image projected by his old captain on and off the field. In his fidelity to the Yorkshire cause Sellers demanded a subservience beyond reasonable bounds. For instance, players were not allowed to change or take a bath at the end of a cricketing day until he permitted them to do so.

Ken Taylor, as a later Yorkshire recruit, recalled that Sellers' insensitive dealings with players cut deep into their self-esteem. The flaws in his character also aroused the disdain of John Arlott. Arlott was a staunch and caring ally of professionals, as he showed in his role as president of the Professional Cricketers' Association. His career as a writer and broadcaster extended back to the resumption of first-class cricket in 1946. He had known every county player in this time. Ted Lester remembers one conversation before Arlott moved to Alderney after his retirement. Their talk dwelt upon those few people in the game who had incurred his displeasure. 'Were there any Yorkshiremen?' asked Lester. 'Yes,' said Arlott. 'Brian Sellers. He was a big bully. I could never stand him.'

Tom Graveney remembers Sellers as the worst of amateur-style captains, lacking even the basic elements of courtesy. 'I had a row with him soon after our first meeting at the Scarborough Festival.' It was the custom in those days to play a round of golf at nearby Ganton on the Sunday rest day. Graveney's then fiancée, together with the other professionals' wives and girlfriends, accompanied their menfolk to the tournament. The hospitality did not extend to the women on this social outing. 'They were totally ignored,' says Graveney. His understandable response was to turn down the golfing invitation to Yorkshire issued by Sellers for the following year.

Brian Sellers, in the end, failed to cross the generational divide. Derek Hodgson, in his *Yorkshire History*, considered that the departure of Brian Close could be likened only to the treatment of a professional captain by an amateur committee of the previous century. It did, he wrote, mark the end of an era both in the government of the club and its success on the field. 'Sellers must be remembered with both gratitude and regret, for just as he as captain enlarged and stabilised the empire founded by Hawke, he was at least partly responsible for its dismantling.'

Brian Close might well have found happier pastures as captain in Leicestershire, had he earlier agreed to succeed Tony Lock who had emigrated to Western Australia. Crawford White, the *Daily Express* cricket correspondent, who was a friend of Mike Turner, the Leicestershire secretary, had advised Close of their interest. The offer on the table was double his Yorkshire salary.

'If it ever happens you are on the wrong end of the stick,' said White, 'Leicestershire would like you to come down as captain.' Close acknowledged the invitation but his allegiance to Yorkshire was too strong to sever the connection. 'I didn't want to play for anyone else. My life was Yorkshire cricket.'

The intriguing sequel was that this opened the doors at Grace Road to Raymond Illingworth. Illingworth, then aged 36, was under challenge from a younger off-spinner in Yorkshire, Geoff Cope, who was beginning to announce his presence with useful wickets. Close was aware of his friend's increasing dissatisfaction but attempted to relax the pressure. 'Illy was much too valuable for Yorkshire to be allowed to leave.' Close assured Illingworth that his position was safe while he remained with Yorkshire.

Ronnie Burnet believed that this was when Sellers made the first of two significant misjudgements, the second involving Close, when the committee was not consulted, which had a long-term detrimental effect on Yorkshire cricket. The first was the decision to release Illingworth. The committee had agreed to a salary increase for the players with a possibility of more to come if the Sunday League should prove to be lucrative.

Illingworth, representing the players, wrote to the committee expressing their appreciation of the decision but adding his own personal request for a contract carrying identical rewards to those of players with other counties, or for his release.

Brian Close tried vainly to persuade Illingworth not to proceed with the letter. It would have been a break with the Yorkshire tradition of not offering contracts. This was made abundantly clear when John Nash, the Yorkshire secretary, passed on the letter, without reference to the committee, to Brian Sellers.

Illingworth remembers the reassurance of Nash when he sought greater security as a Yorkshire player. 'We think you are like Wilfred Rhodes. You can go on playing until you're fifty.' If the remark was intended to flatter, it did not convince. Illingworth said that he was only looking for a three-year contract. 'Sellers was trying to push Cope. I wasn't prepared to be given one more year and then put on the scrapheap when I knew there were some good contracts on offer.'

Sellers had crossed swords before with a very independent-minded player. One report indicated that Bill Bowes, then the cricket correspondent of the *Yorkshire Evening Post*, had approached Illingworth at Park Avenue, Bradford. Illingworth was aggrieved that the contents of his letter had already been leaked to the press. He wanted to know how Bowes had learned about the details. The reply was: 'Mr Nash has rung Sellers and Sellers says that you can go and any other bugger else that wants to go with you.'

Close believes that but for this intervention and the public airing of the dispute, there was a chance that the matter might have been smoothed over and that Illingworth could have remained with Yorkshire. Life is full of ironies and it seems certain that Illingworth would not have had the opportunity to prosper as England captain had it not been for his disagreement with his home county. So, as things turned out, it could be said that Sellers did Illingworth the best turn of his life.

Financially, the question of contracts had long been a bone of contention in Yorkshire. It was exacerbated, says Illingworth, by the low level of their salary terms compared to those granted to individual players in other counties. Yorkshire were the poor relations in matters of remuneration. 'What was annoying, while we were winning championships, was the fact that some members of the opposition were paid double our earnings.' Illingworth adds, 'We should at least have been given the equivalent of what the better players were getting elsewhere.'

Illingworth, like most Yorkshiremen, knew his worth and, perhaps unlike some, was not afraid to express it. He was angry that his rewards and those of other Yorkshire players, should contrast so sharply with those on offer at other counties. Yet he insists that his move to Leicestershire, however stormy its origins, was not dictated by money alone. 'That was not an issue. I fancied the job of permanently captaining a team of my own.'

It is beyond doubt that Brian Close sorely missed the all-round skills of his senior lieutenant in the two seasons preceding his own departure. Wiser counsels should have prevailed to maintain a key partnership. Continuity, for so long the bedrock of Yorkshire's success, required the influence of these two experienced campaigners.

'Our great side was breaking up,' says Close. 'We were having to start all over again. When we introduced the youngsters it was evident that they weren't quite of the same quality as those of ten years before.' It was his belief that the reason for the fall in standards stemmed from the introduction of limited overs in the Yorkshire leagues.

Don Wilson, as one of the remaining members of the championship side of the 1960s, reflected on his own waning enthusiasm. It was sad to hear a player of such infectious spirit relate the growing mood of bitterness. He believed that too many experienced players were allowed to leave the county in the late Sixties. 'Yorkshire could not afford to lose players of the quality of Illingworth, Close, Binks and others. They all disappeared within a matter of two years.' The haste to turn over to a new page was expressed by the view that 'we've had a marvellous ten years. It's time we had a sort out.' Wilson says, 'It wasn't just the committee. The public also wanted new faces.'

The young recruits in 1969 had been deprived for most of the second half of the season of the leadership of Close, absent with a persistent calf injury. He played in only 18 championship games. Jimmy Binks, in his last season, was the deputy captain and must have counted this year as the least happy in his career. Yorkshire, the champions in the previous year, subsided to thirteenth place, the lowest in its history. There were mitigating factors: Boycott, Sharpe and Hampshire all received England calls and Tony Nicholson, the bowling stalwart, was also an absentee with a broken finger.

Pride was salvaged by Yorkshire's second Gillette Cup success of the decade against Derbyshire at Lord's, which again established that Close did not allow his reservations on one-day cricket to deter him from wanting to win these games. The progress to the final included victories over Norfolk at Lakenham, where the veteran Bill Edrich was one of Close's victims, and the summary dispatch of Lancashire by seven wickets at Old Trafford. It was followed by an encore of the final triumph in 1965 against Surrey at The Oval.

Yorkshire were the victors by 138 runs and a second-wicket partnership worth 159 runs between Close and Boycott set up the platform for the success. Close began his innings in the second over of the day after the loss of Sharpe. He was not defeated until the last ball before lunch by which time he had raced to 96 at the rate of a run a ball. *Wisden* reported: 'It was a great performance, notably for his forward play on a fast true pitch.' Close also won the approval of Colin Cowdrey, the adjudicator, who named him as the man of the match.

Close missed the semi-final victory over Nottinghamshire at Scarborough but he was back in harness for the final at Lord's. The policy of taking the first innings was a way of asserting his authority. He deployed his artifice in engineering the choice of innings so that Derek Morgan, the Derbyshire captain, put Yorkshire in to bat on a rain-affected wicket. 'The coin spun up and dropped in Derek's favour. I turned away conceding the toss and, true to my intentions, he called after me: "You'll bat." ' Close had won this opening tactical round in an identical manner to one he had exercised four years earlier in the final against Surrey.

Yorkshire went into the game without Boycott, whose hand had been fractured during a withering assault by John Snow in the previous championship match against Sussex at Hove. Another Yorkshire opening batsman, Barrie Leadbeater, would also have been withdrawn at Lord's had the severity of his injury been known. Making a spectacular catch to dismiss Greig at Hove, he had broken a finger in his left hand.

Leadbeater's pursuit of runs in the final was, in the circumstances, bravely undertaken. Cajoled and coaxed by his partner Close, he earned the match award with a valiant 76. Colin Cowdrey, once again the pavilion observer, judged him the best 'by a whisker' ahead of the Yorkshire captain.

It was indeed the narrowest possible verdict in the context of Yorkshire's victory by 69 runs. Close's impact on the match was displayed with bat and ball and coupled with the leadership of a master tactician. Yorkshire's stranglehold on the Derbyshire batsmen was first exerted by Tony Nicholson who bowled his 12 overs off the reel and conceded only 14 runs. Close then proved that he was well versed in the one-day style of containment. In 10 overs he tightened the noose, giggling with pleasure at the batting famine. He could bowl like a miser as well as a millionaire. Like Nicholson, Close restricted the batsmen to 14 runs in his spell and no one could have asked for a more grudging performance.

One of the most astonishing charges against Close was the label of unfitness in his last season with Yorkshire in 1970. His feats of heroism were the stuff of legend; as one writer put it, they placed him alongside tail-gunners, free-fall parachutists and bullfighters.

His stoicism was carried almost to the point of being a fetish. He had surmounted injuries that would have tumbled most men into premature retirement. Yet the shoulder injury that curtailed his appearances in 1970 was seen as a sign of his declining resilience.

Close had started the championship campaign against Glamorgan at Middlesbrough in fine style. At the end of the first day he was 56 not out. He did not resume this innings. His next assignment was a Sunday League game at Bradford. 'I was batting with Jackie Hampshire and I turned one ball to fine leg at the bottom end of the ground. We went for two runs but the fielder down there shied the ball in like a rocket. I was going full tilt down the slope and had to dive to get in and beat the throw.'

Close regained his feet but he knew instantly from the excruciating pain that he had severely damaged his shoulder. Cortisone injections failed to ease the injury and an examination by a specialist confirmed that he had torn ligaments in the headlong dash at Park Avenue. He was out of action for over a month but such was the bedraggled state of the Yorkshire team that he had to return before he was fully restored to fitness. 'I was still badly handicapped; my guiding batting arm was merely an appendage and my bottom hand had to do all the work.' Uppermost in his thoughts was the need to improve morale and try to impose some order in his team.

Yorkshire had slumped alarmingly in his absence and were encamped in the lower half of the championship table. *Wisden* reported on the heartening effect of Close's reappearance. 'A complete change in fortune in mid-season brought a rapid rise, so much so that for a time Yorkshire were well placed to carry off the title.' A burst of three victories in July, over Derbyshire, Leicestershire and Essex, signalled the recovery and Yorkshire, after their earlier misfortunes, finished a commendable fourth.

Even this distinction did not fully show the extent of the rally. Yorkshire, in fact, failed by only a slender margin to overhaul other challengers in the title race. Five points only was the difference between them and Glamorgan, the runners-up. The absence of Chris Old and Don Wilson, selected by England against the Rest of the World XI at The Oval in August, crucially depleted the bowling resources in the drawn games at Nottingham and Worcester. It was too late to make similar headway in the Sunday League but Close's return did coincide with four victories on the trot.

Among the factors in the championship revival was the improved form of Boycott, who was soon to succeed Close as Yorkshire captain. He had scored only 353 runs in 15 first-class matches but a surge in confidence enabled him to accelerate and top 2000 runs in the season. *Wisden* pointedly paid its tribute to Close and his influence in the shape of 'inspiring leadership, good batting form and fearless fielding.'

Close could justifiably claim credit for his improving stewardship of the new arrivals on the Yorkshire scene in 1970. They included Chris Old, Trueman's successor, whose progress was acknowledged by the Cricket Writers' Club award of the Young Cricketer of the Year. Geoff Cope, installed as off-spinner, was another who made his mark under Close's leadership. Other new recruits making their first appearances for the county were Phil Carrick, the slow left-arm bowler from Armley, Leeds, and David Bairstow, the 18-year-old schoolboy wicket-keeper from Bradford.

Close's captaincy was still thought to be lacking in direction when it came to fostering the talents of young players. In this regard, it is instructive to listen to the views of one of Yorkshire's opponents, David Allen, the Gloucestershire and England spinner. Allen cites instances of Close's man-management, and his nursing of apprentices and even established, capped players in moments of crisis. 'He had a tremendous understanding of people for all his extreme ways. There was nothing crude or untoward in his manner; at all times he was a courteous cricketer.'

Allen remembers one occasion at Bristol when Don Wilson came under a fierce attack by the Gloucestershire batsmen. 'We knew what would happen after Brian and Don conferred at the end of one over.' Wilson was spared further punishment and Close replaced him in the firing line. 'Closey would always put himself in front in such situations,' adds Allen.

Close did argue that Yorkshire players with caps were those approved by the committee and he gave them preference over colts learning their trade in the second eleven. This order of priorities might have been thought to be in accord with those in authority, but it became an area of disagreement when some impatient juniors felt they were not getting a fair trial under Close's captaincy.

Bill Bowes, reflecting on the criticism, said that Close could claim quite convincingly that it was not his duty to encourage youngsters but to get the best possible results from the players chosen by the selectors. Bowes said that Close would not have wanted to destroy confidence by resting capped players to make way for juniors.

Alan Gibson remembered a similar resentment when Close moved to Somerset. 'Some members, including those on the committee, were angry with Close because they felt he was too severe a captain, particularly that he did not encourage youngsters enough.' It was a curious thing, observed Gibson, that when at last Close retired he bequeathed Somerset a legacy of as bright a bunch of youngsters, many of them locally born, as any county possessed.

One of Yorkshire's strict rules in the absence of contracts was that players had to be given notice by the end of July so that they could make arrangements for the following season. The deliberations on re-engagement were held at Sheffield at what was commonly called the 'sacking meeting'. According to Ted Lester, a less than encouraging report on a shoulder injury seemed to suggest that Close would be axed in 1970. He appeared to have been given a reprieve, but Brian Sellers later told Lester: 'I wanted to get rid of him but the committee are so weak. They have let the matter drag on.'

At the end of August, with his place apparently secure for another year, Close was unwittingly involved in a dispute with the Lancashire president, the Hon. Lionel Lister. It was an emotional occasion in every sense at Old Trafford. The gates were closed on a packed crowd of 33,000, who watched Lancashire beat Yorkshire off the penultimate ball of the match to retain the John Player League trophy.

Close was angry that victory had eluded Yorkshire. He desperately needed time to cool down and appraise where things had gone wrong. He went into the captain's room and was preparing to shower and change when the door burst open. The intruder's credentials were unknown to him. A more attentive steward would have made sure that Close was ready to receive visitors. As it was, the Yorkshire captain was subjected to a triumphal tirade. Close was in no mood to share the glee at Lancashire's victory and there was an exchange of choice words which sent Lister scurrying away.

Startled by the rebuke, Lister marched off to the Lancashire committee room and told Sellers: 'Your captain has just insulted me.' Close had, unfortunately, offended a dignitary from the highest echelons at Old Trafford, but, unaware of the repercussions of his error, had changed and was packing his car prior to driving home. His preparations were interrupted by the voice of Sellers echoing across the crowded car park. 'Close! Close!' he cried out. 'We'll sort this out tomorrow.'

Close, in his anxious journey across the Pennines, now knew that he was in the deepest hot water. That evening he wrote a letter of apology to the Lancashire president and on the following day presented a copy of the letter to John Nash, which should have been presented for examination at the subsequent committee meeting to discuss Close's position.

The first item on the agenda, produced on the day without consultation with other committee members, was the dismissal of Close. His letter was never mentioned. As he learned later, the proposal – more a command – took them all by surprise. Lancashire, says Close, were upset by their involvement; the quarrel with Lister had given Yorkshire and Sellers the excuse to carry out the intended act.

'The chairman wishes to see you,' was the message relayed to Close by Nash before the fateful meeting in November. The passage of time since the incident at Old Trafford appeared to indicate that all was well. The summons, so Close thought, was no more than an opportunity to say good luck and discuss the prospects for the following season. Close was also buoyed by the news that his testimonial fund that year had raised the not inconsiderable sum of nearly £6000.

It was quickly apparent that Sellers was not intent on friendly gestures. His first words to Close carried an ominous tone. 'Well, you've had a good innings, Brian.' The dread increased with the next announcement. 'The committee has decided to dispense with your services. We have two letters here – one of which is to accept your resignation, and the other that you will be sacked.'

Close tried in confusion to take in the shock of this sudden, unexpected and curt dismissal. In the few moments at his disposal, he struggled to reach a decision. He chose the option of resignation, believing that by doing so he would retain his dignity and create less of a row.

The meeting at the Headingley office of the club had started at eleven o'clock. By midday he was back home at Baildon. It was a fraught journey to his hilltop retreat. Driving past Kirkstall Abbey, he had to stop and get out of his car. 'I was as sick as a dog. What had happened turned me over.'

Vivien Close was just as shocked as her husband. She was adamant that he should not submit so meekly to the Yorkshire committee. 'You're playing into their hands,' she said. Urgent measures were needed and legal minds involved in a response. Telephone calls were made to two friends, Jack Mewies, the Skipton solicitor, and Roy Parsons, the JP. Both unhesitatingly said: 'Don't resign, Brian. You're doing the dirty work for them.' Close thereupon telephoned the Yorkshire office to withdraw his resignation. 'I'm sorry,' he told Nash. 'I'm not going to resign; you will have to sack me.'

Nash, in a press statement, said that Sellers, the chairman of the cricket committee, had suggested to Close that he might resign, to which he had agreed. 'But about one and a half hours later, at 12.30, he rang back to say that he did not wish to resign. This meant that we had to tell him he would be requested to leave.'

The leave-taking was swifter than anticipated. It had been intimated to Close that one or other of the letters would be released to the press at two o'clock in the afternoon. Close had barely made his phone call of retraction when he learned that the news had already reached London. The action must have been implemented soon after his departure from the meeting. The news had electrified

Fleet Street. Reg Hayter, the sports agency proprietor, now made a call to Close. He knew that reporters would soon be converging on Yorkshire. 'Get out [of your home] as quickly as possible. Grab a toothbrush and your pyjamas and come down here,' urged Hayter.

Close hurriedly made his escape, leaving his wife to cope as best she could with the imminent siege of their home. Hayter had made provision for an overnight hotel stay in London and he advised Close to travel directly to Wembley where England were engaged in a soccer international that evening. Close watched the match and was then interviewed by David Coleman on his *Sportsnight* programme. He had sufficiently recovered his wits to adopt a measured response to his dismissal on the broadcast. 'I was employed by the Yorkshire County Cricket Club. It is their prerogative. I am just disappointed,' he said.

The blow of Brian's dismissal by Yorkshire, five years after his marriage, led to an enforced separation. His summers when he later moved to Somerset would be largely spent at Taunton, only 30 miles from Vivien's former home in Devon.

Vivien had other responsibilities. She remained in Yorkshire with their two young children, Lynn and Lance, near Brian's relatives and his roots. It was a testing time for their relationship. Vivien was often called upon to repel intrusive telephone calls from the press whenever reporters scented a headline story concerning her husband. Very rarely was the telephone silent for long. 'We conducted most of our life over the wires between April and September. Never have Viv's great qualities of adaptability been so valuable,' says Close.

Gordon Ross, editor of *Playfair Cricket Monthly,* commented that the departure of Close would have been sad in the normal circumstances of reaching the age of retirement. It was even less fitting that he should be leaving Yorkshire cricket in a way that many regarded as nothing less than tragic. 'He will always be Yorkshire, flesh and blood, and his contribution to the county's cricket will rank with the great Yorkshiremen, of this or any other age . . . Controversy has surrounded him; a mantle he is so well used to wearing, but you know he is fighting for you every minute he is on the field.

Cricketers from the Mendips to the Pennines may not agree with all that he has done. But they cannot fail to admire him, as do we all.'

Men ill-deserving of his loyalty had ousted a fearless champion. The injustice rankled with Brian Close for a long time. He would later share the company at a dinner of members of the Yorkshire committee who had authorised his dismissal, where he was informed that the decision had been unanimous. Close replied: 'I will tell you this. Whatever you were thinking about at the time, it couldn't have been Yorkshire cricket.

'In the next ten years you will realise your mistake. And you'll know then who *was* thinking about Yorkshire.'

11

Firing Young Guns in the West

'There was a genuine enthusiasm for cricket which rubbed off on all those playing alongside him. You couldn't help but get excited about the game.'

IAN BOTHAM

A rare accord conveying the wisdom of many summers delivered a daily masterclass for the young pupils at Taunton. It was a timely rendezvous in the Somerset market town for two old campaigners, Brian Close and Tom Cartwright. 'It was a revelation to me,' recalls Cartwright. 'The rapport with Brian was instant. We thought the same way and he was as close as anyone I've been with on a cricket field.'

The united veterans would guide Somerset from lowly estate into an era of unprecedented success. Their measured counsel helped to nurture the talents of another generation, notably the greatest English all-rounder of modern times, Ian Botham, and the West Indian Vivian Richards whose early sequence of monumental scores brought comparisons with the young Don Bradman.

Sharing cricket knowledge with the apprentices in Somerset was the common cause for Close and Cartwright. Both brought a yield of different experiences and philosophy from other parts of the country. The glow of his association with Close lingers in Cartwright's memory. 'He was a special person, a fine cricketer and captain. He was always a good man to have around.' Few cricket companions could have earned his signal tribute: 'If I could play for another twenty years and play with Closey, I would be very happy.'

Their mutual respect is affirmed by Close. 'I had the great pleasure of fielding close to the wicket to Tom. He was a genius.

Under English conditions there was nobody better. His ability to bowl line and length and move the ball both ways off the wicket was absolutely fantastic.'

In 1971 Close, spurned by Yorkshire, embarked at the age of 40 on an unexpected reign at Taunton. He had had offers from other counties, including Lancashire, Glamorgan, Middlesex and Leicestershire, but each was discounted as likely to create difficulties and place undue demands on the incumbent captains. It was an inquiry, pressed with unceasing fervour, from another quarter that propelled Close into an invigorating new role in Somerset.

The caller was another forthright veteran, Bill Andrews, who was no stranger to dismissals himself at Taunton. Andrews was stunned by the news from Yorkshire; he was determined that a great personality and natural leader should not be lost to the game.

'I sat down immediately and wrote a long letter to Brian. I followed up with two more letters and a pleading phone call. Never have I been more persistent. Suddenly, I could visualise him taking my county to the top.' Close remembers the reassuring messages and how Andrews, with the backing of the Somerset chairman Colin Atkinson, also a Yorkshireman, persuaded him to step back into the first-class spotlight. 'You can do our county the world of good,' said Andrews. 'I was amazed and surprised that Somerset wanted me to join them,' recalls Close.

Close would, in time, achieve folk hero status in Somerset. But the appointment of a cricketer with the strictest work ethic was not universally welcomed. Some committeemen at Taunton voiced grave doubts. Their fears were overcome by the new direction Close gave to cricket in the west. They soon discovered the paradox at the heart of his personality. He was on the one hand tough, dour and unrelenting, and on the other a 'lovely bloke', sensitive and disarmingly sentimental.

One onlooker remembered how Close, as a guest at village club dinners, was all affability and brimming with anecdotes. There was not a hint of rancour. 'Old Closey isn't such a bad bugger after all,' was the verdict. Brian Langford, who captained Close in his first season in Somerset, considers that it was the perfect move for the

Yorkshireman at that stage in his career. 'Brian had to make a new mark and that was the challenge he needed. It was a good base for him, too, and he was not subject to the same demanding pressures, as had been the case in Yorkshire. He was very popular and loved his time down here.'

Close remembered, in a conversation with Peter Walker, the former Glamorgan and England cricketer, how being a single cog in the Somerset team gave him the chance to have a fresh look at the game. He did not expect his appointment to last more than two or three years. Above all, he was intent on relinquishing the chains of captaincy. 'Few people, even those closely connected with cricket,' he told Walker, 'fully appreciate the strain of leading a county side seven days a week in the various competitions we play these days.'

Close confessed that he had been overcome by nervous tension. 'I can't begin to think of how many cups of tea I've made when I haven't been able to sleep because of an aspect of the game which was worrying me; either the way it was going, or perhaps an emotional concern about one of my players.'

Close's appetite was sharpened and after only one season in the Somerset ranks he was installed as captain. The tensions had been released in an exceptional first summer in 1971. He did not miss a match as he hit 1389 runs, including five centuries, to head the averages of his adopted county. 'Many people, I suspect, expected a great upheaval when he arrived,' commented a writer in the *Somerset County Gazette*. 'The only upheaval, however, has been on the cricket field where he has leapt into the national averages and amazed supporters with nerve-tingling, close-to-the-wicket fielding. Even at 40, there are few cricketers in the land able to make a bigger impact on the game.'

One of Close's centuries in 1971 was, almost inevitably, against Yorkshire at Taunton in June. 'Patiently, head grimly over the line of delivery, Close took 102 off his former colleagues,' wrote Tony Lewis in *The Cricketer*. 'Close rarely lost concentration and reminded Yorkshire most emphatically of their loss during what proved to be a match-winning third wicket partnership,' reported the *Somerset County Gazette*. Close and Graham Burgess put on 142

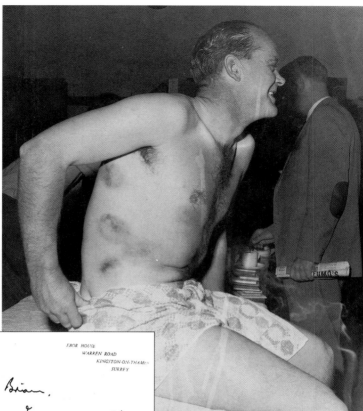

MALDEN 0604

EBOR HOUSE
WARREN ROAD
KINGSTON-ON-THAMES
SURREY

My Dear Brian,

I would like to congratulate you on the magnificent innings which you played at Lord's on Tuesday.

It was one of the best innings I have seen, & I want you to know how much I enjoyed seeing you do it.

All good wishes for the remainder of the season.

Yours sincerely
Len Hutton.

Badges of courage: Close displays his mauled body after his heroism against the West Indian pace men, Wes Hall and Charlie Griffith, at Lord's in 1963. Left: 'A congratulatory message from Sir Leonard Hutton.'

The first toss of the coin as England captain with his West Indian rival, Garry Sobers, at The Oval in August 1966. Below (left and right): A telegram of good wishes from his former Aireborough Grammar School headteacher, John MacDonald. The Oval scorecard recording England's victory by an innings and 34 runs (Surrey CCC).

Surrey County Cricket Club   6d.

ENGLAND v. WEST INDIES

at Kennington Oval, Thurs., Fri., Sat., Mon., Tues., Aug. 18th, 19th, 20th, 22nd & 23rd 1966

WEST INDIES

		First innings		Second innings	
1 C. C. Hunte	Barbados	b Higgs	1	c Murray, b Snow	7
2 E. D. McMorris	Jamaica	b Snow	14	c Murray, b Snow	1
3 R. Kanhai	Guyana	c Graveney, b Illingworth	104	b D'Oliveira	0
4 B. F. Butcher	Guyana	c Illingworth, b Close	12	c Barber, b Illingworth	60
5 S. M. Nurse	Barbados	c Graveney, b D'Oliveira	0	c Edrich, b Barber	70
*6 G. S. Sobers	Barbados	c Graveney, b Barber	81	c Close, b Snow	0
7 D. Holford	Barbados	c D'Oliveira, b Illingworth	5	run out	7
‡8 J. L. Hendriks	Jamaica	b Barber	0	b Higgs	0
9 C. C. Griffith	Barbados	c Higgs, b Barber	4	not out	29
10 W. W. Hall	Barbados	not out	30	c D'Oliveira, b Illingworth	17
11 L. R. Gibbs	Guyana	c Murray, b Snow	12	c & b Barber	3
		B 1, l-b5, w , n-b1	5	B1, l-b14, w , n-b1	16
		Total	**268**	**Total**	**225**

Fall of the wickets 1—1 2—56 3—73 4—74 5—196 6—218 7—218 8—223 9—268 10—268
1—5 2—12 3—50 4—107 5—137 6—137 7—142 8—168 9—204 10—225

Bowling Analysis 1st Ins.	O.	M.	R.	W.	Wd.	N.b.	2nd Ins.	O.	M.	R.	W.	Wd.	N.b.
Snow	20.5	1	66	2				13	5	40	3		
Higgs	17	4	52	1				15	6	18	1		
D'Oliveira	21	7	35	1		1		17	4	44	1		1
Close	9	2	21	1		1		3	1	7	0		
Barber	15	2	49	3				22.1	2	78	2		
Illingworth	13	7	40	2				15	9	22	2		

TROLLOPES   *Builders of the Surrey Tavern*
BUILT FOR TRADITION, BY TRADITION
TROLLOPE & SONS [Construction] Ltd.
Radnor House, Norbury, S.W.16.
POLLARDS 9491.

ENGLAND

		First innings		Second innings
1 R. W. Barber	Warwickshire	c Nurse, b Sobers	36	
2 G. Boycott	Yorkshire	b Hall	4	
3 J. H. Edrich	Surrey	c Hendriks, b Sobers	35	
4 T. W. Graveney	Worcestershire	run out	165	
5 D. L. Amiss	Warwickshire	lbw b Hall	17	
6 B. D'Oliveira	Worcestershire	b Hall	4	
*7 D. B. Close	Yorkshire	run out	4	
8 R. Illingworth	Yorkshire	c Hendriks, b Griffith	3	
‡9 J. T. Murray	Middlesex	lbw b Sobers	112	
10 K. Higgs	Lancashire	c & b Holford	63	
11 J. A. Snow	Sussex	not out	59	
		B8, l-b14, w , n-b 3	25	B , l-b , w , n-b
		Total	**527**	**Total**

Fall of the wickets 1—6 2—72 3—85 4—126 5—130 6—150 7—166 8—383 9—399 10—527
1— 2— 3— 4— 5— 6— 7— 8— 9— 10—

Bowling Analysis 1st Ins.	O.	M.	R.	W.	Wd.	N.b.	2nd Ins.	O.	M.	R.	W.	Wd	N.b.
Hall	31	8	85	3		3							
Griffith	32	7	78	1									
Sobers	54	23	104	3									
Holford	25.5	1	79	1									
Gibbs	44	16	115	0									
Hunte	13	2	41	0									

*Captain   ‡ wkt.-keeper

Umpires—J. S. Buller & C. S. Elliott   Toss won by—WEST INDIES   Result—ENGLAND won by an innings and 34 runs.

Hours of play—1st, 2nd, 3rd & 4th days 11.30—6.30.   5th day 11.0—5.30 or 6.0   Lunch 1.30 all days

NEW BALL may be taken by the fielding captain after 85 overs.

SUPPORTERS' ASSOC. URGENTLY NEED AGENTS.   Apply at the Office by Press Entrance

Top: The England team against India in the first Test at Headingley in 1967. Back row (left to right): John Edrich, Robin Hobbs, John Snow, Ken Higgs, Basil D'Oliveira, Geoffrey Boycott. Front row: John Murray, Ken Barrington, Close (captain), Tom Graveney, Raymond Illingworth. Below: Meeting the Queen during the second Test against India at Lord's. Graveney is presented to the royal guest and others in the line-up are Edrich, Hobbs, Illingworth, Murray and Snow.

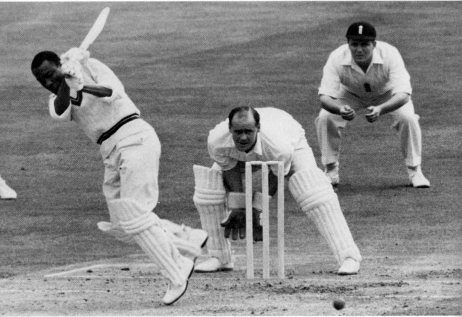

Above and below: The intimidating presence as a fieldsman. Crouched in his familiar station (Somerset Cricket Museum) and deputising as wicket-keeper for the injured Jim Parks against the West Indies at The Oval in 1963.

A buoyant Close displays his CBE, awarded for his services to cricket, in 1975. With his wife, Vivien, after the investiture at Buckingham Palace. Below: Another engagement for Vivien, in uniform as a BOAC air hostess, and her fiancé in January 1965.

All-round sportsman: (Left and below): The ambidextrous golfer, who played off low handicaps with either hand in his younger days. The expert on the snooker table. His successes included a victory over Joe Davis, the world professional champion.

Top: The Somerset 'father figure' enjoys a celebratory drink with Ian Botham (left) and Philip Slocombe (right). Above (left and right): Tom Cartwright, bowling ally and wise tutor, and Vivian Richards, the star recruit from Antigua. (Somerset Cricket Museum Limited).

The sprightly old campaigner remains in the spotlight at a charity event.

---

*All the illustrations are from the private collection of Brian Close except where indicated otherwise.

runs for the wicket. Tom Cartwright was again the immaculate bowling tormentor, hounding Yorkshire near to an innings defeat. He took nine wickets in the match, including a spell of 4 for 13 in 19 overs. Somerset required only seven runs to win by 10 wickets.

There was another unassailably heroic feat by Close against Surrey, the eventual champions, in this season. It happened the day after he had suffered a severe facial injury in the intervening Sunday League game. The venue was Torquay, a tiny club ground, only 100 yards wide with inviting short boundaries. Brian Langford had been appraised of Close's aggressive intentions. 'You're in charge,' he said. 'You played for England. I'm not going to tell you what to do.'

The first two balls from John Hooper, the Surrey bowler, were pulled contemptuously for sixes into the adjoining gardens. 'Off the next ball I got a top edge and knocked my bloody teeth out,' recalls Close. The sickening impact of the crack had uprooted four teeth, which were scattered on the ground. Back in the dressing room wet towels were produced to staunch the flow of blood and Close was liberally plied with whiskies to deaden the pain. On the following morning Langford took his team-mate to see George Ledgard, the cricketers' dentist in Taunton. The roots had to be cut out and as many as 30 stitches inserted in Close's gums.

Peter Roebuck, one of Close's young charges, remembers the stubborn self-belief of the Yorkshireman and his ability to survive all manner of conflicts. To bat with him, he says, was to witness a player 'steaming with determination'. That Close was 'hewn out of granite' was demonstrated when he reappeared at Taunton to insist on resuming his championship innings against Surrey.

While he needed to convalesce, Maurice Hill also reported sick. Hill, who had not played in the Sunday match, bore a doleful look. 'Skipper,' he told Langford, 'I don't think I can play today.' 'What's up, my boy?' inquired Langford. Hill replied: 'I've got toothache.' Close was in his usual corner, his face almost hidden by a huge plaster to ward off the wind. The other players glanced at him and then at Hill. Amid general laughter, they said, 'What about Closey then? He's got half his head knocked off.' Roebuck later said, 'Bette Davis never matched Close's anguished stare at Hill.'

The wounded Close was deaf to entreaties not to risk further injury by going out to bat. As he recalls, he buckled on his pads and went out to the wicket as if in a dream. He was hardly able to focus his attention; a combination of the sedating whiskies and the extractions of teeth had given him a giant-sized hangover. Robin Jackman unceremoniously greeted Close with a bouncer as an opening gambit. 'I went, not really in earnest, for a hook and the ball took the top edge and went for six. That really woke me up.'

What followed was a miracle of resolution. Before he left the field for more dental surgery he responded to Jackman's impertinence by scoring a hundred. It countered a magnificent century by John Edrich for Surrey. *Wisden* reported on a 'remarkable 114 in four hours by Close, who had lost several teeth in a painful accident the previous day'. The innings included five sixes and 10 fours and Close shared a second-wicket partnership worth 147 runs with Mervyn Kitchen.

Brian Langford remembers one typical rejoinder by Close at the lunch interval during the innings. 'He had not had a good night after that vicious smack on the mouth and his face was painfully swollen.' Close was 38 not out and he sat slumped in his chair in the dressing room with a pot of tea by his side. Langford inquired how he was feeling. Close's response demonstrated why he was regarded as one of the best competitors in the game. 'I shall be glad when I get my hundred. I'm a little tired.'

Alec Bedser, the chairman of the Test selectors, was another who welcomed the zeal of Close as the new Somerset captain in 1972. It was at Bedser's request that Close was recalled to lead England in the Prudential Trophy series against Australia. The emergency call-up came in a neat exchange of Yorkshire batons when Raymond Illingworth had to stand down with an ankle injury. Close did not betray the faith of the selectors. He maintained his unbeaten record as England captain with a 2–1 series win over Australia.

Close's rivals, hitherto unknown to him, included Bob Massie whose disconcerting swing bowling had rocked England at Lord's in the preceding Test series. Massie was one of those transient figures in cricket. His star shone and just as quickly waned. But he had an analysis to cherish – 16 wickets for 137 runs in his first Test at Lord's. Massie was aided in his tremendous feat by the hostility of his partner, Dennis Lillee, a major discovery for Australia on this tour. Lillee and Massie shared 54 wickets in the drawn series as England retained the Ashes.

All three of the Prudential Trophy games in late August were won, unusually, by the side batting second – at Lord's and Edgbaston by choice. Ian Chappell, the Australian captain, won the toss and batted at Old Trafford where England won by six wickets. At Lord's he chose to field on the reckoning that his team could not do worse.

In the event, as John Thicknesse reported in *Playfair Cricket Monthly*, the inability of Snow and Arnold to control a freakish new ball meant that Australia surged to 83 for 1 – 12 of them in wides – and cruised to victory by five wickets. Close, with a respectable total of 236 to defend, believes that the match turned on an umpiring decision that went in favour of Keith Stackpole. Stackpole, top scorer with 54 in the match, was adjudged not out when Snow 'had him absolutely plumb lbw on the back foot'.

Close was twice run out, once fortuitously for Australia, backing up at Old Trafford, and again in a mix-up with his partner, Dennis Amiss, at Lord's. Amiss had been the unwitting culprit at Manchester but in the next dismissal he either misheard or slipped when Close called out, 'Look for two'. 'I touched down and was halfway back for the second run when I realised that Dennis hadn't come back.'

A fine innings was nipped in the bud at Lord's. It was, as one writer said, of such excellence that not even Sobers could have bettered the cleanness of Close's strokes. *Wisden* enthused, 'Close rolled back the years with a splendid innings of 43 in 12 overs. His crisp hitting included one six and seven fours. He looked a matchwinner until he was run out after a misunderstanding with Amiss.'

England kept their supporters on tenterhooks in the deciding match at Edgbaston. Australia, at one stage 136 for 8, added 43 runs for their last two wickets. They could have been costly, for after

Boycott and Amiss had scored 76 in the opening counter a tumble of wickets produced a scramble for the winning runs. It was left to the ninth-wicket pair, the Sussex combination of Greig and Snow, to arrest the decline. Close was able to rest content as the successful captain once again.

The conversation at the Crown and Sceptre, just down the road from the county ground, rarely strayed from cricket. It was reinforced when Brian Close took up lodgings there. His feats soon placed him in the roll-call of Somerset luminaries. They gave a renewed vigour to the gossip, which paid homage to an exceptional man.

The 'bald blighter', as he was amusingly dubbed by Alan Gibson, had a regular pattern to his day. Each morning, after a hearty breakfast, he would enter the Somerset dressing room with the *Sporting Life* tucked under his arm. The smoke-rings of a glowing cigarette curled over the assembled players. The lyric of the old song might have been especially written for Close. 'I like a nice cup of tea in the morning,' ran the refrain,

> '. . . And when it's time for bed,
> There's a lot to be said
> For a nice cup of tea.'

No one at Taunton can remember Close disturbing the ritual of nourishment with sandwiches at the lunch and tea intervals. What was paramount – and this was one of the most important duties of the twelfth man – was the organisation of mugs of hot tea throughout the cricketing day. Close's idea of refreshments was copious amounts of this favourite beverage. Tom Cartwright recalls one moment of trepidation at Bristol when the essential big teapot did, for some reason, fail to appear. Peter Robinson, as the twelfth man that day, was dispatched on an urgent shopping expedition in the city to procure another receptacle.

There were, as Tom Cartwright said, some 'interesting times' with Allan Jones. Jones was both antagonised and charmed by his captain. They were companionable off the field, changing alongside each other for five seasons. But their tempers could become frayed in exchanges on the field. The insistence on complete obedience by his captain often placed Jones in violent disagreement with Close. A particular area of conflict involved defensive field placings, especially in the final stages of one-day games.

In one Sunday League match against Nottinghamshire at Trent Bridge in 1973 Jones was reprimanded by Close for lack of attention and narrowly escaped the indignity of being sent off the field. On this occasion the entire playing area was in use, with the boundaries stretching to the perimeters of the field. 'I was fielding at fine leg under the pavilion. Closey was about 250 yards away at long on beneath the scoreboard,' remembers Jones.

A blazing quarrel ensued when Jones committed the folly – in Close's eyes – of conceding a boundary. Jones protested that it was a trivial and innocent mistake. Derek Randall also incurred Close's wrath in the tight finish to the game. Jones was bowling the last few overs, during which time Randall was persistently backing up before each delivery. He was so eager for runs that he ignored the threat of being run out. On one occasion Jones whipped off the bails when Randall had actually reached the batting end. The umpire, without an appeal, gave him out. 'Derek was cheating by trying to gain ground,' says Close. 'But I asked the umpire to reverse his decision and allow him to continue his innings.'

One of the most bizarre episodes concerning Jones and Close occurred in the Gillette Cup second round match against Leicestershire at Taunton. Somerset had totalled 212 and Leicestershire, in their reply, were toiling at 58 for 5 at tea. The decline continued with two more wickets falling after the interval. The total had advanced to 127 but the pursuit of a target of 86 runs now seemed such a forlorn quest that Mike Turner, the Leicestershire secretary, got in his car and drove home.

Wisden reported on the ensuing somersault in fortunes: 'Having apparently played Leicestershire completely out of the game, Somerset lost control in a shattering fashion.' An injury to Jim Parks led to Close replacing him as wicket-keeper and becoming embroiled in a furious duel with Jones. The result of the match now became secondary to a contest between bowler and keeper. 'They were not getting on at all well,' remembers Brian Langford. Two wide-eyed juniors, Ian Botham and Vic Marks, watched the commotion in the middle from the scorebox.

The developing feud was exacerbated by the fact that Jones had dropped a catch offered by Balderstone off Close's bowling. He would go on to make a century. Mervyn Kitchen darkly declared, 'We're going to lose it.' Peter Robinson replied, 'It will be the eighth wonder if we do.'

An incensed Jones glowered down the pitch in a duel moving towards an absurd climax. His disquiet was not lessened when Close abruptly dispensed with his gloves because they were too small. They were an encumbrance as he sought to prevent byes being run to him behind the wicket. Barehanded he stood sentinel against a menacing bombardment. 'Jones instead of bouncing the batsmen was trying to bounce Closey,' recalls Robinson. The winning four runs came off a leg-side wide which eluded the desperate dive of Close. Leicestershire, hardly able to believe their luck, won by two wickets. Afterwards there was a grim silence in the Somerset dressing room. There was not even the solace of dignity in defeat.

The perfectionist that was Brian Close as a batsman was reflected in an aggregate of over 7500 runs with Somerset. His sojourn in the West Country enabled him to become the seventh all-rounder to complete the tally of 30,000 runs and 1000 wickets. The distinction was shared with W.G. Grace, Wilfred Rhodes, George Hirst, Frank Woolley, J.W. Hearne and James Langridge. Close's record in Somerset also included 13 centuries and an additional 2658 runs in one-day competitions. It was, all in all, a handsome performance for a player in his fourth decade in first-class cricket.

Wisden observed, 'Some of his innings, played usually in adversity, were classics of attentive concentration and power. It is small wonder that occasionally he had a bang in the Sunday games to relieve his feelings.' Brian Langford remembers the cussedness of Close on bad wickets. 'He was good and watchful and really enjoyed the challenge of the turning ball.'

In 1974 Close hit his fiftieth century against Leicestershire at Weston, and with 19 sixes in the season in the John Player League he beat Stuart Leary's 17 for Kent in 1970. In a remarkable one-day game against Yorkshire at Bath, Somerset won by four runs with three balls to spare. It was a match strewn with spectacular six-hits. Close smote eight of them – and 12 fours – in his 131 out of a total of 224. Chris Old, in Yorkshire's reply, was not far behind with five sixes and eight fours in his 82, which briefly aroused the promise of a dramatic victory.

This was a season of distinctive advancement by Somerset. They rose to fifth place in the championship and their challenges in the Benson and Hedges and Gillette Cup competitions only faltered at the semi-final hurdles. In the John Player League they finished second to Leicestershire. Somerset had a late chance of lifting the trophy, for when Leicestershire had only one match left they were eight points behind with two outstanding games. The decider was at Grace Road but an intriguing struggle was wrecked by rain. Somerset had completed their innings with a total of 161 for 9 before play was abandoned and the points were shared between the two leading counties.

Close had to brush aside the indignity of his first pair in 26 seasons in first-class cricket in 1974. It was inflicted by Middlesex at Taunton in July and swiftly countered by a record fourth-wicket partnership for Somerset against Glamorgan at Swansea. Close's stand of 226 with Derek Taylor in just over three and a half hours surpassed that of Gimblett and Woodhouse, who had put on 200 against Middlesex at Taunton in 1946. Taylor opened the innings for Somerset at Swansea but he was also an accomplished wicket-keeper, formerly with Surrey. He had moved to the West Country on the recommendation of Arthur McIntyre, his distinguished counterpart at The Oval.

In his first season as Somerset captain in 1972, Close won a tactical argument with Wilf Wooller, the Glamorgan secretary, in another championship fixture at Swansea. Wooller's displeasure was incurred by a delayed declaration lasting until three o'clock on the second day. It prompted him to announce over the tannoy that any spectator could have a refund of his entrance money on application. Wooller imperiously told his audience, 'Somerset are ruining this game.'

Close explains his predicament. 'Play had been restricted by rain to two or three hours on the first day. On the second day we had to score heavily to hopefully gain a result and so we batted on for another hour after lunch.'

Somerset had made snail's-pace progress on the first day, scoring only 113 for 2 in 72 overs. Close then hastened the run rate with a century in two and three-quarter hours. Despite Wooller's public address intervention, he relentlessly pursued his course. Cartwright, with substantial support from Langford and O'Keefe, took eight wickets in the match. Somerset were able to enforce the follow-on and won by an innings. Throughout the controversial proceedings Close maintained that his only concern was to win the match – and the scoreboard ultimately proved him right. Wooller's defence was that he had acted in the interests of the cricketing public.

Alan Gibson, writing in *The Cricketer*, took the side of Close, expressing the view that a captain's first responsibility was to win a match by what seemed to him the best method, even if it meant batting on and trying to bowl the other side out again. 'It is not always entertaining for spectators but it is a perfectly legitimate way of winning a three-day match.'

Any criticism of Close, he believed, stemmed from a tendency to regard the three-day game as a sanctified version of the one-day game. 'If bunfight finishes could save three-day cricket, they would have done so long ago, for we have had more of them in the last 20 years than ever before, and they have done nothing to arrest the decline in support.'

The explosive affair at Swansea was defused in a manner typical of two charitable opponents. The central figures in the dispute were reconciled. Each had made his stand and the matter was consigned to history. The furore attracted the attention of television on which Close dutifully explained his mission to a Welsh audience. He then dipped into the proceeds of the interviews to mollify the redoubtable Wooller with a round or two of drinks at the club bar. 'Wilf did not bear grudges. He was a grand chap,' says Close. 'We had a good laugh about the way things had turned out.'

Close had ample runs to his credit to compensate for those days when, as Peter Roebuck puts it, 'he lost his wicket, sometimes infuriatingly in pursuit of an idea'. As other Somerset colleagues recall, Close rarely believed that he was actually out. The conviction in his indestructibility was also paraded off the field. He had watched the epic fight – 'the rumble in the jungle' – between Mohammed Ali and George Foreman in Zaire on television. 'When I was young,' he cheerily told one Somerset player, 'I would have taken either of them on.'

Tom Cartwright remembers the seriousness with which Close excused his cricket setbacks. 'Brian always had a reason; before walking in he might have a row with a spectator who had vexed him at the wicket by strolling across to the refreshments tent.' It was a sensible practice for the rest of the team to scatter while their captain recovered his composure. 'As he came through the door, I would hand him a calming cigarette and let him take stock of the situation,' says Cartwright.

In any assessment of Close's Somerset years, attention has to be strictly paid to his partnership with Cartwright. Peter Roebuck believes that the secret of a great combination lay in the fact that they were opposites in personality. 'Closey was instinctive, always going forward, whereas Cartwright was the craftsman, left-leaning and individualistic in outlook and character.'

The alliance closely paralleled the one Close enjoyed with Illingworth in Yorkshire. 'We had a mutual respect for each other and enjoyed a terrific relationship with the kids at Taunton,' observes Cartwright. 'I could say things to him which he probably would not have wanted to hear from anyone else.'

There was, however, a division of responsibilities between them when Close took over as captain in 1972. 'Our understanding from the start was that from 11.30 to 6.30 he was in charge. After that time it was over to me as coach. If ever I felt he was encroaching on my duties – and he could be a little overbearing as captain – I would gently rebuke him.' Close would acknowledge the admonishment with an 'All right, lad.'

The flair and decisiveness that Close displayed on his best days leaves Cartwright in no doubt that he was unquestionably the finest captain in his experience. For others, including Brian Langford, Close was brilliant on the attack and when his team was on top. But there were stalemate situations when Close tried to make things happen and then lost interest when his efforts failed. Cartwright was the 'brain' who aroused Close from his torpor. 'Tom would then bowl a great session and get us back in the game.'

Incredibly, Cartwright played only five times for England despite the unyielding accuracy with which he claimed over 1500 wickets at an average of just over 19 runs each. In 1973, at the age of 38, he headed the national averages, bowling 772 overs and taking 88 wickets. *Wisden* described him as a superb and indispensable player. 'His wonderful skill and energy through dozens of long spells – several during tropical August weather – were monuments of true professional application.'

Close endorses the powers of concentration displayed by Cartwright. 'Tom was injury-prone and if he could have stayed fit there is nothing we could not have won. He perhaps bowled one half-volley on the first day of the season and did not bowl another one.'

Mike Selvey, in an article in the *Guardian*, paid his own eloquent tribute to the prince of medium-pace bowlers. He remembered inspecting the wicket at Park Avenue, Bradford, after Cartwright had taken 12 wickets for 55 runs for Warwickshire against Yorkshire in May 1969. 'For the most part it was lush and emerald like the Centre Court on the opening day at Wimbledon. The exception, however, was a strip about five paces from the crease, no more than one pace long and six inches wide, and centred on the line of the off-stump. It was totally devoid of grass as if it had been removed by a mechanical scoop. I had never seen the like before and have not done so since.'

The bare expanse was the result of precise bowling. Each one of Cartwright's deliveries, estimated Selvey, must have landed on that length and line. For this to happen, it demanded that the seam was 'bang upright and rotating backwards like a buzz saw.' Selvey added,

'It was the result of strong fingers and the flick of a wrist like a whiplash. The grass had no more chance than the batsman.'

Selvey remembered that Cartwright did not 'bluster or blast, or twirl and tease'. 'I doubt whether he bowled a bouncer in his life. Instead he nagged and niggled like a rotten tooth, swung the ball both ways, and moved it in and out off the seam. The keeper stood up and he employed a claustrophobic field of slips and short-legs. Few knew how or where to hit him. I thought he was fantastic.'

Cartwright's disciples in Somerset join in the chorus of praise. Peter Robinson recalls: 'Tom would take over one end. He wasn't the sort of bowler you took off. He knew himself when the time had come to take his sweater.' In an apparent contradiction in terms, even in a defensive situation Cartwright was always on the attack. He would still have an encircling field preying on opponents. All the while he was steadily bowling wicket to wicket, with lbws a certainty should a batsman err in judgement.

Robinson says that Cartwright was a model for a young bowler, not especially on the field, but in the studious manner of his preparations away from match play. There was an insistence on proper behaviour in the nets. If someone was free and easy at practice, Cartwright would turn away and bowl in another net.

Close also subscribed to this earnest regime. He is remembered as a captain who led by example. There was a mellow ring to his leadership. 'He did not rant or rave in the dressing room,' recalls Peter Roebuck. 'He was never personal or pointed in his remarks to his team'. Close was fair-minded in his discipline. 'If something displeased him,' adds Brian Langford, 'he would have his say and there the matter ended. We were a very happy side.'

Even in these twilight years Close still presented a physical, intruding presence in his familiar perch beneath the batsman's gaze. 'I always wanted him to get the obligatory body blow so that we could get on with the game,' says Cartwright. If a bowler erred in length, and the hit was duly registered, Close would wag his finger and simply say, 'Pitch it up, lad.' The reflexes of the veteran were still sharp enough for Close to claim 140 catches with Somerset and enter the fielding lists as the fifth highest catcher (813) behind Grace, Woolley, Hammond and Lock.

His rule was still impervious in the short leg terrain. Over the years he would often reminisce about the brilliance of Surrey's Tony Lock. Neville Cardus recalled Lock holding 'quite sinful catches, catches which were not there until his rapid, hungry eyesight created them'. Micky Stewart considered that the spectacular catches, brought about by sudden, full-length dives, were the easiest taken by his Surrey colleague. 'His best were when he took rockets, close in, without anyone noticing.'

The nonchalance of Lock was cited by Close in his exhortations to his Somerset pupils not to exaggerate the difficulty of catches. 'Lockie,' he told them, 'would have caught them in the cheeks of his arse'. He then proceeded in a match against Middlesex to confirm the probability of this exercise.

Clive Radley was the batsman and bowling to him was Brian Langford. 'I was crouched down at forward short leg, about one and a half yards away,' recalls Close. 'Clive got an edge and the ball flicked his pad and spun upwards above me at forward short leg. I leapt up and managed to knock it up into the air. As I jumped up, being heavier than the ball, I fell sooner. All the time I was keeping my eye on the ball. As I was falling, I realised that it would fall on top of me. So I arched my back and put my hands there where the ball came to rest.' Ian Botham was among the astonished throng. 'We never believed you when you told us about Lockie,' he told his captain. 'But we've seen it happen and believe you now.'

Peter Robinson, like others in a joyous time, has his stock of stories about an irrepressible exile. 'Closey was never one for names; as long as he had eleven lads in the dressing room, that was fine.' By 1975, Robinson, a slow left-arm bowler and adaptable batsman, had taken up duties as coach at Taunton, but he also had to be on standby for recalls to the first eleven.

One Saturday morning he was rolling the wicket at Bath. It was a very hot day and he had been hard at work since seven o'clock. Close appeared and said that he had only 10 players for the match against

Surrey. 'Have you got your kit in the car?' he asked. Encouragingly he added, 'I think this wicket will turn today'.

Robinson only bowled 12 overs in the match but he was quickly involved as a fieldsman, taking a catch off Moseley to dismiss Edrich for a duck. Moseley later reciprocated this aid by taking a stunning catch off Robinson's bowling at long on to claim the wicket of Intikhab Alam. 'It was an absolute screamer heading for the girders of the stand,' says Robinson. Close beamed with delight and said: 'I knew you'd get him out there, lad.'

Peter Roebuck ranks Close high among those provocative, unpredictable men who have enriched Somerset cricket. 'We missed him when he left and realised how much we had enjoyed his personality, for all its impulsiveness.' The originality of the Yorkshireman ensured that life was never dull under his leadership. Close, deeply scheming, always kept his team on their toes. His field placings had to be minutely observed. 'You'd always stay put, just in case the Old Blighter was right.' There was a sense of unease about making a personal adjustment, moving a little nearer or deeper.

Roebuck remembers how in the field he tried not to look at his captain because this could prompt a swift repositioning. When this happened it was advisable to scrape a mark to define your place so as not to upset him. It was an escape option in the event of a disastrous missed catch.

Close, as Brian Langford also recalls, was exacting in his precise orders. 'I had played for Somerset five hundred times and was fielding at mid-off in one match.' Langford thought he was safe there. He made his little mark. Close was undeterred by the seniority of his colleague. 'He moved me six times in one over.' As Langford and Roebuck both say, you could end up with a series of crosses resembling a pools coupon.

The talismanic qualities of Brian Close reached their apogee when Ian Botham and Vivian Richards were recruited to sprinkle their stardust at Taunton. Richards, the 'shy, timid boy' – as described by Tom Cartwright – from Antigua, was almost unknown, but he had influential advocates when Graeme Watson, the Australian all-rounder and Somerset's original overseas choice, withdrew with an ankle injury.

Tom Cartwright remembers that, as coach, he had been allocated £6000 to bring six good young players on to the Somerset staff. His chosen boys included Peter Denning, a butcher's son from Chewton Mendip, the immensely talented Phil Slocombe from Weston, Peter Roebuck, and three other local products, Vic Marks from Middle Chinnock, Colin Dredge from Frome and Keith Jennings from Wellington. 'I had all these kids but I wanted a young black player. It would be a big plus for him in life if he could grow up laughing and crying with the other boys.'

Len Creed, the Somerset bookmaker, is generally credited with the discovery of Richards during a winter tour as manager of the Mendip Acorns side. In Antigua he had spotted on a piece of waste ground two young enthusiasts, both batsmen. One of the boys hit a handsome 50 but the other, Richards, made only a modest contribution. Creed initially favoured the first boy, but another Antigua cricketer dissuaded him from this verdict. He was Danny Livingstone, the Hampshire batsman, who had also watched the two youngsters and told Creed that Richards was the better prospect. The subsequent fateful toss of the coin decreed that the latter would make his home in Taunton.

Before the return of the Mendip Acorns party from the West Indies, Tom Cartwright had attended a Players' Association meeting at Edgbaston. Among his companions was Mike Brearley, who had been a guest player with Kent on a club tour of Antigua. Brearley's recommendation carried authority when he recalled Richards 'smashing Bob Woolmer (the Kent bowler) all over the field'. Rohan Kanhai, a senior West Indian and former Warwickshire colleague, added his voice of endorsement at the meeting.

Cartwright, on his return to Taunton, immediately followed up his quest. He went to see R.K. (Jimmy) James, the Somerset secretary. James told him that he had received a call from a friend in the Immigration Department. They had earlier been associates on Foreign Service in Kenya. 'Have you got a Mr Creed?' asked the caller. 'We've got someone by the name of Vivian Richards locked up in the back room.' Richards had travelled on a separate flight from Antigua via New York and was met at London airport by Creed.

It transpired that Creed, in the rush of events, had failed to get the necessary documentation to allow Richards to enter England. The omission was highly indiscreet and a punishable offence. The course of the West Indian's career might have been jeopardised but for the friendship between James and the immigration official, who was coincidentally a Somerset supporter. Creed was given 48 hours' notice in which to obtain a work permit for the cricketing apprentice.

This hurdle was duly surmounted but Creed and Cartwright then had to persuade the Somerset committee of the worthiness of the young candidate. 'We brought Vivian down to the ground for a trial,' says Cartwright. 'He batted for around half an hour and never got the ball off the square. He was trying too hard.' But amid the nervousness the observers had noted one telling image: the boy's head was so still that one could almost have rested a pint of beer on it and not spilled a drop. The hunger for runs, which was to become Richards' trademark, was next fostered at the Lansdown Club. 'I would like you to score as many runs as you can there,' was Cartwright's instruction.

Richards, at the age of 22, made his debut for Somerset in 1974. Such was the excitement that he engendered that the cricket world greeted a 'wonderful phenomenon'. In Somerset he made the biggest impact of any player since Harold Gimblett in 1935. *Wisden* reported, 'Fresh from club cricket, he glowed with good humour and glorious batting adventure, his broad grin belying the withering force of his exquisitely timed strokes.'

Richards' first appearance was against Glamorgan at Swansea at the end of April in the Benson and Hedges Cup competition. Close put him in number four and he scored 81 not out. David Foot recalled, 'At the captain's insistence, the players lined up to applaud him in. Creed, the hardened turf accountant, was in tears. Charles Barnett gave Richards the gold award. Afterwards he said to everyone within earshot: "Today we have seen a truly great player of the future."'

Tom Cartwright remembers Richards in the following match against Gloucestershire. The opening flurry of the duel with Mike Procter produced for Cartwright 'just about the best five minutes of cricket I've ever seen'. 'Viv hit the first ball off the front foot through extra cover and the second ball also went for four. We all knew where the third ball would pitch. It was a bouncer and Viv hit it into the local organ works. You could hear the ball rolling around in the machinery.' Somerset were the victors by 81 runs and Richards hit 71, including one six and eight fours. *Wisden* reported: 'The newcomer played superbly. He struck Procter for 15 runs in his first over.'

Brian Close and Tom Cartwright inherited a host of talents. They broadened the horizons of Somerset youth at an impressionable age. Brian Rose, who was to succeed Close as captain in 1978, referred to this time as an educational stepping-stone. Peter Denning said, 'It is Brian's determination that impresses me. He does chase the young pros – but it's right that he should. Brian is very much part of the team, socially after the game. He has a real sense of humour and we have a good atmosphere in the dressing room.' Close himself was touched with star quality and one of the few players that the fans came specifically to watch.

The camaraderie at Taunton was bolstered by team discussions on days of rain. Cartwright sought to thaw the shyness of the more introverted by asking them to express their views on the game. Close, half-listening behind the pages of the *Sporting Life*, would intervene and disclaim one or other of the pronouncements as tosh. He would stand up and address the team for several minutes. After he had finished, Cartwright smiled in agreement. 'I know the boy is talking nonsense. He has got it wrong, but let's get them *all* talking about cricket.'

The advent of Ian Botham brought another dimension to Somerset cricket. Almost from the start he exuded an aura that informed everyone that he was a great cricketer in the making. Botham always had a great respect for Close, with whom he had much in common. 'Closey kept me in order,' he once said. 'We were always a better side when he was there.' Cartwright believes that

Close had a physical presence that helped to keep Botham in check at times. 'As a boyhood prodigy himself, he recognised the same merits in Ian.'

Among the lessons that Close instilled in Botham and Richards was the absolute importance of imposing your will on opponents, either a batsman or a bowler. It was an essential part of the Yorkshireman's doctrine. Significantly, he was able to communicate this attitude to other players. 'Ian and Viv were naturals in this aggressive approach,' says Cartwright. 'Everyone around the ground knew they were coming out to make an impression.'

Cheshire-born Botham, whose family moved to Yeovil when he was two, had been hailed as an outstanding prospect in the county youth team. As soon as he left school at 16 in the spring of 1972 he took a job on the Lord's ground staff under the supervision of Harry Sharp and Len Muncer. A likeable young man, in the words of his contemporaries, he was considered at Lord's to be too much of a gambler in cricketing terms and did not fit the mould expected of him. Muncer reported, 'He is an outstanding cricketer who does everything his own way.' Botham, it seems, returned home under a cloud. Close had been told that he was unlikely to make his mark in the game, but he preferred the evidence of his own eyes. 'Bring him down,' he told the Somerset committee. 'Let's have a look at him.'

At the end of August 1973 Botham returned to Taunton and two days later he played in his first match for Somerset in the John Player League at Hove. The folly of his critics was made apparent in the following season. He was still only 18 when he produced an indomitable display in the Benson and Hedges quarter-final against Hampshire at Taunton.

This was a foretaste of the zestful aggression of the young champion. John Arlott later enthused, 'He has most of the cricketing strokes but he – like those who watch him – most enjoys his athletically free cover driving; with, by way of variety, those fearless and violently spectacular hooks.'

Somerset, chasing a target of 183 against Hampshire, had declined to 113 for 8 after 40 overs. They seemed doomed to defeat. A bouncer from Roberts struck Botham full on the mouth. He was bleeding profusely and eventually lost four teeth. He later admitted that he had been foolish to carry on, but at the time he was stung into a reprisal. He bludgeoned two sixes in his eighth-wicket stand of 63 with Moseley, who was lbw with seven runs still required. Botham's valour did not go unrewarded. He was unbeaten at the end with 45 and Somerset, against the odds, were victors by one wicket.

Botham's first meeting with Close, who would become a father figure, occurred when they shared digs at the Crown and Sceptre. It was soon after he had been brought down from Lord's to renew his association with Somerset. 'It didn't take long for me to realise that Closey was a special person,' Botham says. It was the coming together of two strong personalities. They both could be explosive in disagreement; Close remembers an exuberant lad with whom it was necessary at times to have a few words.

Len Creed recalled one car journey during a match at Worcester when Close was driver and Botham the passenger. Suddenly, Close took his hands off the steering wheel and asked Botham whether he could see any blood on them. The young man was puzzled by the question. 'Well, there should be,' stormed Close. 'I saw you out on the field sliding on your arse. Back in the dressing room, I picked up your bloody boots and rubbed my hands along where your studs should have been.' It amounted to a stern order for Botham to improve his footwear on the following day.

The estrangements on this and other occasions were always fleeting. 'If we had a bust-up you would make your point and he would make his,' says Botham. 'I think he respected you more if you objected and said "that's not fair".' Afterwards there were no grudges and Close would be the first to buy a drink at the end of the day's play.

One discipline for which Botham will always be grateful was that his captain taught him how to win. 'You've got talent. Don't waste it,' was the command. As a junior professional, Botham did enjoy the patronage of the Yorkshireman but this did not extend to favouritism. 'He was there to help everyone. There was such a vast amount of experience to tap. You would have been a pretty dumb person not to take advantage of his wisdom.'

Botham also had the ideal bowling tutor in Tom Cartwright. He agrees that the Somerset coach encouraged him to believe that he could bowl. Cartwright observes, 'I allowed Ian to develop in a completely natural manner. For his part he had the most receptive ability to absorb quickly. He was physically strong and virile, and it was like dealing with an adult. I didn't try to curb or over-coach him. He took criticism and didn't answer back.'

As an outstanding fieldsman, Botham fielded at first slip to the bowling of his coach. This was at variance with the usual duties of a young professional, who was generally stationed in a bat-pad position or on the boundary. 'Closey did not believe in this regime. If you were a good catcher you went in the slips. It didn't matter whether you were in your third game or three hundredth.'

Botham remembers the surge of enthusiasm that ran through the Somerset team. 'Closey led from the front and expected the same level of commitment within his team. Everyone was expected to give it his best shot and no one was carried.' Defending was not part of Close's captaincy strategy; his sense of adventure would have carried appeal for a like-minded player such as Botham. 'His theory was that the best form of defence is attack – and in many instances he was proved right.' There were also elements of vision in Close's leadership. 'He was often two steps ahead of us.'

Brian Close remembers his cricketing travels with his young apprentice and the opportunities they gave him to formulate Botham's thinking. Their talks, after Close had made his racing calls, would range widely over the merits of the opposition on the county circuit. The hazards bedevilling Close's driving companions still persisted in Somerset. 'It wasn't a car in which you closed your eyes and went to sleep,' recalls Botham.

There was one occasion during a match at Guildford when Botham fortuitously refused a nightcap and returned to the team hotel with two other team-mates. Close, meanwhile, was involved in a crash in his car. The door on the passenger side was demolished but the driver emerged without a scratch. In another driving mishap, Close headed a convoy of team cars taking a route down the back lanes on a journey back from Bath. They moved on to a long ribbon of straight road. Close was trying to listen to the racing results when his radio slipped across the dashboard. He caught it before it hit the floor. Unfortunately, in doing so, he moved the steering wheel just at the point of a sharp bend in the road. The car slewed 25 yards, ran up a bank, and came to rest on the top of a hedge.

Undeterred, Close scrambled clear, unhurt, and obtained a lift from a couple of Somerset members travelling into Taunton. They told him, 'You've done a good parking job there.' Tom Cartwright was another who saw the damaged car on its lofty perch. He and his fellow passengers were surprised to find on their arrival that Close had preceded them to the ground.

'Closey was sitting in the corner smoking and reading the *Sporting Life*,' says Cartwright. The players told him that they seen his vehicle astride the hedge. Close sported a sheepish smile. 'Oh, is it still there, lads?' he said.

There was another episode, unconnected with driving, which could have had fatal consequences for Close when Somerset came to play Essex at Westcliff. Close, blinded by bright sunshine, collided with the sliding glass doors of the team's hotel. Botham and other team-mates were about 30 yards away and opening their car doors. There were immediate expressions of horror. 'It was just like a bomb going off,' recalls Botham. (This was around the time of a spate of IRA bombings in England.) 'Closey had walked straight through a plate glass door.' Happily, instead of suffering a serious injury, Close tottered out with just a graze on his hand. 'That's the only time I've seen him physically shaken,' says Botham. 'He was all right initially until he realised how lucky he had been.' It was one moment in his charmed life when Close bore a near-catastrophe with less than his usual equanimity. He was recorded as 'absent ill' and took no further part in the match against Essex.

The degrees of velocity attained by opposing bowlers were always registered by the responses of a brave man. Close did, admittedly, have a higher pain threshold than most batsmen, but for his watching Somerset colleagues he served as the ultimate yardstick of pace. Ian Botham recalls that the fearless veteran used to test the speed of rival bowlers by confronting the ball with his massive chest.

'Our theory in the dressing room was based on an ascending scale of difficulties. First, if he didn't even flinch, then the bowler was not that quick; second, if he rubbed his body, the delivery was quick; and third, if he actually called for the physio, then the bowler was extremely fast.'

Brian Close would soon have reason to examine his grades of resilience anew in a bombardment that exceeded in ferocity all he had known before. In 1976, at the age of 45, he was again called to the England colours. The field of heroism was Old Trafford, where he had made his Test debut in 1949. Waiting to challenge him were a band of unrelenting marauders from the West Indies.

12

Holding up the Bowling Bruisers

'A succession of deliveries pounded his body. It was like watching
a Hitchcock horror movie.'

PETER ROEBUCK

A terrific barrage, cruel in its intensity, raged for over an hour at Old
Trafford on a Saturday evening in July 1976. Besieged in combat on
a 'cracked, unpredictable wicket' in poor light were the two English
batting martyrs, Brian Close and John Edrich. With a combined age
of 84 years, they were the oldest opening pair since 1930 when
George Gunn and Andrew Sandham had represented England in the
West Indies.

English cricket had seen nothing as intemperate as the onslaught
of bouncers unleashed by the West Indian trio of pacemen, Michael
Holding, Andy Roberts and Wayne Daniel, at Manchester. *Wisden*
reported on a disquieting passage of play: 'Close and Edrich
defended their wickets and themselves against fast bowling, which
was frequently too wild and hostile to be acceptable.'

On the night before the Test the England captain, Tony Greig,
had asked Close if he would open the innings. Close reminded Greig
that it had been several years since he had occupied this role.
Moreover, he believed, as he proved earlier in the series, that he
could best serve England in the middle order. He pointed out that
Bob Woolmer, the Kent opener, was in the selected eleven. Greig
replied, 'We think that he has a lot of Test cricket in him and we
don't want to destroy his confidence.'

Close had faced, as a chastened boy in Australia, the might of
Lindwall and Miller. In his maturity he had won acclaim against the
West Indian fast bowlers, Wes Hall and Charlie Griffith, at Lord's

in 1963. He was now called upon, 13 years later, to weather an assault of frightening intimidation. 'It must have been the worst wicket I experienced in Test cricket,' says Close. 'The faster the West Indians bowled the worse it got because the balls broke through the surface of the wicket. They exploded and flew at you.'

There had been a warning of the troubles ahead on a crumbling wicket when England lost their last eight first-innings wickets for 25 runs inside an hour. Holding, who took five wickets for nine runs in nine overs, spearheaded the downfall as England tumbled to 102 all out. *Wisden* related, 'Some balls lifted at frightening speed and Greig and Underwood both had narrow escapes from what could have been serious injury. Even the greatest of batting sides would have been severely taxed.'

Close recalls the pandemonium in the second innings and the state of high excitement among the West Indian spectators. Each of the ugly bowling thrusts was greeted with renewed fervour. 'They were making a hell of a din. We saw Roberts off and then came Daniel. He was even more threatening, a hulking fellow who bowled bloody quick, even if he didn't always know where the ball was going.'

One delivery from Daniel careered over the head of Edrich as he ducked in evasive action. It almost lifted wicket-keeper Deryck Murray off his feet as it crashed into his gloves. At the end of the over Edrich walked down the wicket and asked Close, 'How near was that?' Close wryly replied, 'If it had been any nearer you would have felt it.'

The banter continued between the batsmen. Humour was a required commodity in the prevailing madness. Close and Edrich were engaged in a delaying operation. England's target of 552 in 13 and a quarter hours was such an impossible quest as to induce a kind of hysteria. 'What the hell are we doing out here?' inquired Edrich. 'Hang on,' answered his partner. 'Remember where we are. This is Old Trafford. It might rain on Monday and Tuesday.' Eventually, after yet another jarring blow, Edrich had the solution to their plight: 'Let us both walk off. We can sell our story to the *People*.'

During the bombardment Bill Alley, the umpire, had sternly

warned Holding after he had bowled three successive bouncers at Close. He was ordered to pitch the ball up. Clive Lloyd, the West Indian captain, would later concede an excessive ration of bouncers. 'Our fellows got carried away. They knew that they had only 80 minutes that night and went flat out, sacrificing accuracy for speed. They bowled badly.'

Close remembers that his opponents had 'lost their rag' because they could not make a breakthrough. 'The bouncers were flying and it was like being in a coconut shy. You were dodging balls whistling past your head.' The courage of Close and Edrich yielded 54 runs, the highest opening partnership by England in the series. Runs were not a great consideration before they nursed their wounds over the weekend. Twenty-one, including 11 off the bat, were eked out in the ordeal which lasted 17 overs on the Saturday evening. As a contest, says Close, 'it was great fun, a trying time, but you enjoy those battles'.

It was clearly even more trying for those waiting to enter the fray. Not one of the England players was padded up when Close and Edrich, having survived the duel, entered the dressing room. 'It was just like walking into a morgue except that the bodies were upright,' says Close. The grimness of the situation had even affected David Steele, usually a keen competitor, who was next in the order. He had made a diplomatic withdrawal. 'Where is he?' asked the veterans. 'He's on the medical couch in the back room,' was the response. 'He's got a migraine.'

Edrich, a doughty campaigner in the tradition of his family, was more impressed with the qualities of his resolute partner. Compliments did not flow easily from his lips. But as he watched the bruised and battered Close depart for a soothing shower, he remarked, 'Watching him play out there this evening made you proud to be an Englishman.'

The torrid encounter had been watched on television by Peter Roebuck and two other Somerset colleagues, Graham Burgess and Mervyn Kitchen, in their hotel room. They had squirmingly observed the succession of devastating deliveries pounding their captain's chest. 'We were diving under the sheets as if it was a

Hitchcock horror movie. And we were a hundred miles away!'

The sequel to the heroics at Old Trafford was enacted a few days later. Close returned to the Somerset team for the Gillette Cup second round match against Warwickshire at Edgbaston. The scars still disfigured his body. Versions differ as to which of the opposing bowlers first caused him to buckle in pain. Ian Botham says it was Steve Rouse, a left-arm medium-pacer. 'He bowled Closey one that popped and hit his bruises.' There was a frown of disdain as Close leaned heavily on his bat. But it was a symptom of the damage that had already been done.

As Peter Roebuck recalls, another bowler, Bob Willis struck Close on his ravaged body. 'It's the only time that I saw him near to collapse. He didn't go right down to the ground but he went perilously close.' If Close pardonably flagged, it did not prevent him from top-scoring for Somerset with 69 (out of a total of 140) and winning the man of the match award.

Wisden reported: 'Close played a fine aggressive innings, although plainly in pain after a blow on the body from Willis.' The meagre resistance of the fit and well among his colleagues must have irritated Close. Somerset, from 130 for 4, lost their last six wickets for 10 runs in 23 balls.

The West Indies, notwithstanding the inglorious chapter at Old Trafford, were imperious masters in 1976. Supplementing the bowling strengths was the majesty of Vivian Richards, who scored 829 runs, including two double centuries at Nottingham and The Oval. His century at Manchester was the sixth in Tests that year. These gargantuan feats gave him an average of 118.42 in seven innings against England.

Richards, as a key witness at county and Test level, was warm in his praise of Close's endurance in another remarkable season for the Yorkshire veteran. 'Viv had great respect for Closey,' says Peter Roebuck. 'He set much store by honesty and courage and Closey had these qualities in abundance. Viv had played against him for the West Indies. He recognised and appreciated the vital fire of a lion-hearted cricketer.'

Close exhibited boyish elation at yet another recall by England in 1976. Only one other English player, Gubby Allen, in the West Indies in his last Test in 1947–48, had outdone him as the oldest to represent his country since the Second World War. The valiance of Close at Old Trafford had been preceded by an innings that commended him to the selectors, against the tourists at Taunton in May. Close was associated, in an anchor role, with Botham in a superb counter-attack. Somerset were in the toils at 70 for 5. Botham, hooking and driving magnificently, had begun the rally with two sixes and five fours. Close was top scorer, with 88 and 40, in both Somerset innings. In the first innings, as *Wisden* reported: 'the dogged, watchful and courageous Close kept vigil for four hours and 35 minutes.'

Botham recalls that this was the first time they had witnessed the aggressive pace of the West Indians. Andy Roberts and Wayne Daniel were two of Somerset's rivals at Taunton. One delivery from Roberts struck Close in the most vulnerable area of his anatomy. 'He bowled a short one and I laid back to pull it. It didn't bounce as high as I expected and cracked me right in the box. I gritted my teeth and played on.' At lunch it was thought wise to call in the doctor to check on any damage. 'The plastic box was splintered into pieces and there was I *stuck* in the *middle* of it.'

Close's exploits in 1976 elicited widespread admiration. He again topped 1000 runs and was third in the England batting averages behind David Steele and John Edrich. In two of his three Tests against the West Indies he made substantial contributions. His exclusion from the team at Leeds and The Oval was regarded by many, not just in Somerset, as a shabby act.

Wisden commented, 'Close always took a full part for Somerset, and drove his team as hard as ever. In fact, there were times when his drive for efficiency, notably at the height of the John Player League excitements, seemed to add to, rather than subtract from, the pressures on young men.' Close did take pride in the gains in confidence, believing rightly that he had advanced their progress beyond their own expectations. 'I had to be strict with the boys but I think I made a few of them play a little better.'

Ian Botham says that there were times when Close ruffled a few feathers in the Somerset ranks. 'But he was always doing something he believed in. Once you realised this – and accepted it – he was easy to get on with.' *Wisden* agreed with these assessments: 'The overall team achievements of an unfancied side suggested that Close's fiercely demanded requirements might have provoked some players beyond their normal capabilities.'

Bill Andrews, who was largely responsible for recruiting Close, remembered his unwavering dedication. 'He played for us as hard as he ever did for Yorkshire and that's the best compliment I can pay him.' From a collection of individuals Close had knitted Somerset into a combined unit. The unremitting command deserved to be crowned with success. The margin of one run off the final ball of the competition in September deprived Somerset of the John Player League title.

Peter Robinson recalls the disappointing outcome of the match against Glamorgan at Cardiff. The interest in this decisive encounter attracted a crowd of 7000, exceeding the expected demand. Unprepared for such an invasion, Glamorgan had to allow many spectators in free and then go round with honesty buckets and make collections.

Close remembered the enthusiasm among Somerset supporters in the challenge for the title. 'We had trouble at home matches trying to get everyone into the ground and even on marathon away trips we had more than our share of loyal supporters. Tension was at fever pitch as everyone in Somerset, so it seemed, made his or her way to Cardiff. Glamorgan missed out on a bumper pay day when our thousands of spectators – fearful of not getting a seat or even entrance to the game – came early, and were well and truly entrenched before any officials came along to man the gates.'

Kent were the winners for the third time in five years after a hair's-breadth finish on a thrilling Sunday. The issue was in such doubt that Peter Walker, the BBC2 programme presenter, had to decide to which ground he should direct the helicopter delivering the trophy. His choice of Canterbury proved correct but it might so easily have been Cardiff. Even a tie would have been sufficient for Somerset.

From the last ball of the match they needed three to tie and four to win. Graham Burgess went for a big hit off Nash that would have sealed victory. The ball soared over the bowler's head. Two runs were scampered but, as Colin Dredge looked for the vital third run, Alan Jones threw the ball to Nash, who then relayed it to wicket-keeper Eifion Jones. Dredge failed by inches to make his ground.

Peter Roebuck said that the only time that Close conceded he was in error occurred at Cardiff. Alan Jones, the Glamorgan captain, who went on to make a match-winning 70, was dropped by Close. As he admits, his lapse did affect the result of the game. Jones pulled a ball from Moseley to square leg. 'I caught the ball in front of my chin and Alan, seeing this, started walking towards the pavilion. A second or so later, as I was walking in to the wicket, I brought my hands to my waist and the ball slipped out of my fingers to the ground. I was horrified and could have dug my grave and gladly fallen into it.'

So Brian Close moved into his last season in first-class cricket still looking to reward his adopted county. 'I wanted so badly to win something for Somerset, to repay a little to the county which had given me such a warm and sincere welcome when my cricket world seemed shattered.'

The stresses of his years of undeviating commitment were now beginning to take their toll. There was a recurrence of a shoulder injury and attacks of bronchitis and influenza to inform him that the time was drawing near when he should at last depart from the game. 'I had built a team of good young players. Now I was keeping one of them out of a place in the team and from further experience. No longer did they want "Dad" around to look after them when things got tough.'

Close's Test recall in 1976 had been followed only a few weeks later by the entry of Ian Botham into the international ranks. Botham played in two Prudential Trophy matches against the West Indies at Scarborough and Birmingham. Botham's father had given him two aims: 'to play for your county at 18 and your country before 25'. He achieved one of these targets and surpassed the other when, at the age of 21, he represented England against Australia in the

Queen's Silver Jubilee Year in 1977. Watched by Her Majesty at
Trent Bridge, Botham took five wickets on his first day of Test
cricket. He followed this remarkable debut with even more stunning
figures at Leeds. Australia were bowled out for 103 and he took five
wickets for 21 runs in 11 overs.

The young guard was superseding the old, as Close perceived
when he announced his retirement, coincidentally on the day of his
Somerset pupil's debut at Nottingham. His decision was made 28
years after his own first England appearance as an 18-year-old. It
was, in a way, a link that preserved the unity of their friendship, on
and off the field. They were both fiercely independent men, alike in
character in their dislike of autocratic rule.

Through the reminiscences of his wife's family, long-established
friends of the Closes, Botham had learned of the career traumas of
his Somerset captain. The brushes with authority had cast an unforgiving pall over Close's career in a time when a lack of deference
could exact punishing retribution. Botham was able, in due course,
to appreciate the inner strength that had enabled Close to weather so
many setbacks. He was also in thrall to a kind and generous person
whose loyalty brought commendation from all who knew Close. He
was not subject to the damaging neglect that had halted the advance
of his senior as a boy.

Botham undoubtedly was indebted to the discipline exerted at an
early age. His extrovert personality, coupled with an awesome will
and determination to succeed at the top level designated him as a
player who would reach the high plateau of fame.

The hero-worship that Ian Botham attracted in a more media-
conscious age had also been directed at Brian Close in another era.
Audacity was the keynote of his cricket. Even in his venerable years,
Close was a magnet for legions of excited schoolboys as well as adults
of celebrated stature in other walks of life. One of these, as David
Foot recalls, was the actor, Peter O'Toole. On a sunny afternoon
O'Toole had travelled to Bath to watch his hero and fellow
Yorkshireman. Their resulting meeting was the first since wild
teenage years in Leeds, when O'Toole had worked as a copy boy on
the local evening paper. Foot had known the actor, then a jobbing

thespian, while he was a raw young drama critic in Bristol. All these years later, at Bath, he was brought to a halt as he rushed in search of the nearest call box to send his early edition report of the game to the *Sunday Express*.

The voice from the beer tent was that of O'Toole. 'What's the chance of meeting Brian again? Can you manage it for me?' It was, says Foot, a scene of touching humility. 'Here he was, an international film star, anonymously tucked away in the corner of the marquee asking, in effect, whether it was all right to have a natter with Closey.'

The meeting was arranged and before the ice was broken it was Close who was initially the more awe-struck of two personalities. It did not take him long to delight in the old memories of their friendship in Yorkshire. They talked animatedly for over an hour. O'Toole, says Foot, had almost as much affection for sport as for Shakespeare. It is a matter for conjecture whether he would have liked to exchange brooding nightly on the boards as Hamlet, the prince of Elsinore, for the role of an 'intermittent fast bowler of ferocious intent' in action at Lord's.

Peter Roebuck says that Close left first-class cricket 'not with a whimper but with a bang'. The expletives must have rung out even louder than usual when rain reduced Somerset's Gillette Cup semi-final against Middlesex in 1977 to a 15-over farce. In painful self-rebuke, he harshly reflected on the subsequent defeat. His last dream was extinguished, and he felt that his life had been 'a series of cock-ups'.

Close recalls that they had hung around at Lord's for three days while heavy rain turned the ground into a quagmire. The appalling weather in London meant that the players spent six days trying to start the game. It resulted in the unprecedented step of postponing a championship match between the sides to accommodate the semi-final.

A start was finally achieved on the Friday morning when the skies cleared and the umpires were compelled because of the conditions to limit the game to 15 overs for each team. 'In the short innings, we hurried,' says Close, 'and only succeeded in making mistake after mistake.' Illustrating the rush was the manner of the dismissals. Four batsmen were out to full tosses, two dragged wide balls on to their wickets and two were run out. Two West Indians – Joel Garner, Somerset's new fast bowling giant who would soon take centre stage at Taunton, and Wayne Daniel, for Middlesex – each took four wickets.

Wisden commented on the unnecessary panic by Somerset. 'Richards, with a vast off-driven six, and Close and Burgess with a boundary each off powerful drives, showed what might have been achieved.' Middlesex only needed to score at four runs an over and won by six wickets with an over to spare. 'It was unsatisfactory to lose in that way on such an important occasion, and whichever side had lost would have had cause for complaint,' lamented Close.

Close's sense of occasion did not desert him in his final home appearance for Somerset. The fires were rekindled and he bowed out in the grand manner. He was exuberantly back at the helm in the headlong pursuit of runs against Gloucestershire at Taunton. Somerset, set a target of 272 in three hours, won by five wickets with eleven balls to spare. Peter Denning, a batsman overlooked by England, hit two centuries in the match. By his side in a thrilling finale was the old master. Close struck one six and 13 fours and he and Denning added 144 in 90 minutes to seal the result of an enthralling contest.

Close recalls how he caught the enthusiasm of Denning and went on to his highest score of an ill-fated season. 'As we needed only 18 to win, with wickets and time in hand, I could allow myself the luxury of thinking that it would be nice to go out with a century in my last innings in Somerset.'

Thirteen runs separated him from a coveted goal. 'I struck the ball hard, but unfortunately not high enough. Zaheer, standing deep at mid-off, leaped up, stopped the ball with his outstretched fingers and caught it as it came down.' He walked off the Taunton ground for the last time, ruefully reflecting that nothing seemed to turn out right. 'But we had won well and that's what it's all about.'

For a happy spirit and extraordinary guide in the Cider County, things had in truth turned out very well indeed. Somerset would go on to win five one-day trophies in the next few years. Ian Botham pays tribute: 'The glory days ahead were part of his inheritance. Closey pulled that young side together and produced a team that would dominate limited-overs cricket for a long time.'

13

The Master at the Academy Class

'Closey batted in the nets against the pace of young lads like Hoggard, Sidebotham and Silverwood. He did not wear a box or thigh pad. They must have hit him about a dozen times.'

FRANK TYSON

The happy discipline of the tutorial was one to astound and charm the assembled boys of the Yorkshire Academy. They would have been even more awe-struck to know that their teacher and captain had forged links with other county stalwarts going back for almost a century. At 63, Brian Close was still as engrossed in cricket as he had been at their age. The sage veteran was now invested with a status that had belonged to one of his own tutors, George Hirst, who had begun his distinguished reign before the turn of the twentieth century.

Yorkshire had always had a priceless sense of continuity. Close, who now once again reached across the generations, had garnered his skills in the company of older men. He was in his most beguiling mood as he addressed his group of young pupils, many of whom would later step up into the senior ranks.

Sidney Fielden, a Yorkshire committee associate, eavesdropped on an intriguing cameo at Close's invitation. Close mapped out the campaign with his usual precision. The pre-match talk began with the announcement that he had won the toss and elected to field. 'I want you to remember one thing, lads. Cricket matches are won or lost in the field. I want none of this clapping and shouting "Well bowled" when the ball is pitched well outside the off stump. That's a wasted ball.'

The attentive boys were next asked to define a maiden over. One of them ventured, 'Well, Mr Close, it's when you bowl six balls and the batter doesn't score any runs.' It was a reasonable answer, one might have surmised, except that, as their captain explained, the proper function of a maiden over was to make sure that a batsman played every ball and did not score any runs.

In front of the Academy captain on the dressing-room table was a helmet with a cage in front. 'What's this bloody thing?' he asked. It was, chorused the boys, for the short-leg fieldsman. Close brusquely told them to leave the offensive guard on the table. It would not be needed because that was his position and he would be posted there without a helmet that afternoon.

Watching her husband that day was Vivien Close, who suffered tremors of fright at the spectacle of the ageless cricketer crouched in the danger zone. Close – down on his haunches with his bottom in the air – was completely unruffled, displaying all his well-remembered aggression. 'We nearly had to send for an ambulance, not for Closey, who was quite unstressed, but for Vivien,' recalls Fielden.

As Fielden also remembers, Close had in this match rallied his team as a batsman when they got into a 'spot of bother'. He had come in at number eight and scored 37 not out. The preparations for the game had been conducted with the utmost seriousness. They had included a session in the Headingley nets where one of the bowlers was Craig White, the England all-rounder. Close would not have wanted a gentle exercise and did not get one. One delivery from White broke through his guard. There was the familiar glare down the wicket as Close picked up the ball. 'That would have hurt,' he said, 'if the ball had been hard.'

Two years later, Frank Tyson was another observer of the veteran in combat with the younger generation. Tyson had travelled from his home in Australia to fulfil a coaching engagement at the Woodhouse Grove School, near Leeds. Close, at 65, was then chairman of the Yorkshire cricket committee. Tyson remembers visiting the county's winter practice shed at Headingley. 'Closey batted in the nets against the pace of young lads like Hoggard, Sidebotham and Silverwood. He did not wear a box or thigh pad. They must have hit him about a dozen times.'

Ryan Sidebotham, one of the Academy boys, was sternly rebuked by Close in one Yorkshire League game at Headingley. Sidebotham thought it was safe to take a rest between overs. He leaned contentedly on the boundary wall. A soft breeze ruffled his mop of unruly hair. But Close, peering backwards through his legs as he squatted by the wickets, had spotted the reclining boy. 'Ryan,' he called out, 'Get off that bloody wall – and get your bloody hair cut as well.'

Afterwards at home, Ryan's father Arnie, the former Yorkshire cricketer, asked him how he had got on with Close. 'He's a wonderful man, Dad, but he does swear a lot.' He reflected for a moment and inquired, 'Was Mr Close a good player?' Arnie indignantly replied, 'Wash your mouth out and go and look at his record.' Ryan then turned to his mother and said, 'Mr Close says you've got to sew my trouser pockets up because I can't have my hands in them on the field.'

Brian Close bridged the generations in yet another phase in his remarkable life. The rescue of the historic sporting citadel at Park Avenue, Bradford, was especially pleasing to him. He remembers it as an exciting ground upon which to play cricket. In this spartan hilltop retreat he had flourished mightily as a boy. One renowned Bradfordian, J.B. Priestley, memorably tugged at the imagination in evoking the atmosphere at Park Avenue. Recalling his own boyhood fervour, he wrote, 'A shilling entrance fee, even when ill-afforded, enabled you, like half the town, to push your way through a turnstile into another and altogether more splendid kind of life, hurtling with conflict.'

The establishment of the Yorkshire Academy at Park Avenue in 1989 revived the joys of olden times. Legions of boys, curious and enchanted, began to besiege the restored ground in the summer holidays. Close, along with his former Yorkshire colleagues Bob Appleyard and Bryan Stott, was among the instigators of the development. It was a major success story that would produce inestimable rewards for Yorkshire cricket.

Close recalls, 'League cricket, with its emphasis on limited overs, wasn't doing its job as a nursery. It was essential for us to get together young kids at sixteen or seventeen and teach them the proper way to play the game and develop their skills as cricketers.' The value of the scheme now ensured that anyone with promise or talent was brought to the attention of the county coaches. It had also contributed, in 2001, to Yorkshire's first championship for 33 years, an occasion of much rejoicing. 'One of the reasons for our success was that we had reserves available to take the places of those lads chosen to represent England.'

Appleyard, at the launch of the project, had described the project as a way of testing the mettle of aspiring boys. It had been instituted by the Friends of Park Avenue to remedy the lack of progression from under-17 and under-19 ranks through to first team and Test levels. The concept was designed to give boys an extra dimension to enable them to make the transition. 'We aim to discover whether they have got the heart to combat the pain threshold, a vitally important factor in the making of a cricketer. These boys are the seedcorn for the future.'

The yield of outstanding Academy recruits has amply justified a visionary venture. Darren Gough was the first of its products to achieve international recognition and Ryan Sidebotham, Chris Silverwood and Matthew Hoggard have followed him as Test players. Others who have moved up into the Yorkshire first team include Gary Fellows, Matthew Wood and Anthony McGrath.

The arcane world of cricket committee manoeuvres did not come naturally to a man who thrives on instant decisions. On his return to Yorkshire, Close joined the county's general committee as a member for Bradford. He was cricket chairman when the pro-Boycott faction took over, and resigned in protest at Boycott's dual role as a player and committeeman. He resumed office at the next series of elections.

During this time the Yorkshire committee was reshaped, with the 23 members reduced to 12, and three in each case were allocated to the four districts. It was ruled that only one ex-player could be elected as a member for one or other of the areas. Close, Appleyard and Stott were all members in the Central District (an amalgamation of the Bradford and Leeds districts). Appleyard had other business commitments that took priority and Stott also stood down when Close was elected as cricket chairman.

It led to a sad exodus, an occurrence that could have been prevented, when Close was ousted from the committee at a subsequent annual meeting at Harrogate. Sidney Fielden remembers his anger – and the depression of Close – after the meeting. 'Brian was very distressed and sitting in the corner of the bar, just looking at the floor.' Fielden says that the meeting ended without any recognition of the immense contribution made by Close to the club over 50 years. It was remedied with handsome tributes in the press on the following day. 'I thought it was a bit late then,' adds Fielden.

In committee as chairman, observes Stott, Close acted in the same manner as on other occasions. The minutiae of procedures wearied him. He was too honest in debate to win points as a politician. Stott says: 'Brian was not organised. He is an intelligent man who thinks on his feet. He deals with matters as they arise and then comes up with a solution.' Appleyard believes that any criticism of Close in this role was unwarranted. 'It was up to the club to maximise his knowledge of the game.'

Close was happier in an ambassadorial role. Selfless, unpublicised acts demonstrated his devotion to the Yorkshire cause. Fielden remembers a members' meeting at Denaby in South Yorkshire. It was a bleak winter evening and Close, earlier in the day, had had an injection for some medical complaint. He had travelled to Newcastle for a business appointment, then returned home to Baildon before travelling on to the meeting. 'Brian was unwell. He should have been resting at home. Yet he spoke for about an hour, without notes, to entertain our audience.' It was a reciprocal gesture, acknowledging the support he had received in the past from Fielden. Close was then, as always, a dutiful member of the team.

Two excited boys also had reason to treasure Close's kindness during a coaching assignment at a leisure centre at Prestatyn in North Wales. They were on a family holiday and their father relates how Close made it one to linger in the memory. 'In the nets my two cricket-mad sons learnt a great deal and loved every minute. Brian declined to wear batting gloves and pads, his technique coping with all the bowling, some of it really fast.'

After his years of exile in Somerset Brian Close had returned home to resume his cricket round with Todmorden, Scarborough (in the Yorkshire League) and his home club at Baildon. The association with Scarborough continued when he was invited to assemble and lead celebrity elevens at the annual festival at the Yorkshire resort. His last first-class appearance, at the age of 55, was at Scarborough in September 1986. The honesty that Close displayed as a batsman was shown in the match againt the New Zealand tourists. Close required only six runs to reach an aggregate of 35,000 in first-class cricket. He recalls, 'The Kiwi quickie, Willie Watson, bowled one down the leg side. It lifted a little and actually brushed my glove. I turned round and saw the wicket-keeper take the catch. They didn't know I had touched it but I did. I walked off as that was the way I played the game.'

The New Zealanders were effusive in their apologies when they learned that Close had just fallen short of a career milestone. 'Why didn't you tell us?' they asked. Close replied that the target was immaterial; he knew he was out and always walked in such circumstances. He told his rueful opponents, 'It is an honourable game and I was brought up that way.'

The final at Scarborough ought to have been marked by one last triumphant hurrah against the New Zealanders whose predecessors had provided the opposition on his Test debut 37 years earlier. Instead the festival stage belonged to Ken Rutherford, New Zealand's opening batsman. His batting revel has rarely been matched. In an astonishing innings, Rutherford hit 317 off 245 balls in ten minutes short of four hours. It included eight sixes and 45 fours. He scored 101 before lunch, 199 between lunch and tea, during which he hit Doshi for four consecutive sixes, and a third hundred off 33 balls in 35 minutes in the final session.

Rutherford achieved the highest score by a New Zealander abroad. Bert Sutcliffe (355 in 1949–50) and R.C. Blunt (338 in 1931–32) are his only fellow countrymen, both with Otago, to exceed this feat. In addition, it was the highest innings played at Scarborough, passing Hobbs's 266 in 1925.

The years have rolled by since Close's official retirement, but this unflagging entertainer continues to play on. 'I'm thinking of burning my boots so that they can't ask me to turn out again,' he says. He still accepts invitations to play in charity events. It is an indication of his loyal support of deserving causes. His namesake, the Reverend Brian Close at Alconbury, near Huntingdon, first initiated one of them which has become a long-standing engagement. The cricketing Close was sufficiently intrigued by a letter from the clergyman to telephone and confirm the name of the correspondent, who was asking him to appear in a match to raise funds for church repairs. The Rev. Close has since moved to another part of the country but the fixture is still played annually, with the other Close now captaining Norma Major's XI in games in aid of the Mencap charity.

Close has also been in regular demand as a captain of teams abroad. One assignment three years ago placed him at the helm of a Rest of the World eleven in a charity match against Australia at Melbourne. In his own ranks were Richard Hadlee and Graeme Pollock and others with their best Test days behind them. The Australian opposition was of more recent vintage but Close – aided by his band of veterans – was wily enough to defeat the younger rivals. There was another bonus for Close, the golfer; he was able to fulfil an ambition to play on the Royal Melbourne course.

Close's competitive streak was strong in other areas too, as in his soccer confrontation with England and Wolves defender Billy Wright. It occurred in a charity match between a Yorkshire XI and the Television All Stars before a crowd of 22,000 at Odsal Stadium, Bradford. Bob Platt recalls: 'In the last minute, Closey, at centre-forward, challenged Billy and flattened him. The ball ran loose and Sharpie [Phil Sharpe] tapped it in. We won 1–0. Wright came into the showers afterwards and said: "I've played a hundred games for England and I don't think any player ever treated me like Closey did."'

Another great England footballer, Tom Finney, was in action at

Elland Road, Leeds. Facing him at left back in this charity match was the Yorkshire bowler Don Wilson. Not surprisingly, Wilson had spent most of the first half in vain pursuit of Finney. At the interval, the hapless defender was given a fierce ticking off by Close, his captain. 'I had been given the run-around, like many far better than me, by one of the best players of his time,' says Wilson. Close was not prepared to accept this as a reasonable excuse for what he considered a lamentable performance. Wilson was replaced and did not take any further part in the game.

Don Mosey, the former cricket reporter and commentator, gave another example of Close in this competitive vein. He recalled one rare victory over his friend at table football in a Worksop pub. Mosey was partnered by Len Shackleton. 'Brian – noble as ever in defeat! – snarlingly pointed out that I had to get an international forward to *partner* me.'

Brian Close still exudes the buoyancy of a schoolboy. Broad guffaws punctuate his disclosures of a fulfilling life in cricket. It was a Gloucestershire man, Bomber Wells, who once explained why Yorkshire were the county with a special quality for their rivals. 'At the end of the most demanding day you'd split up into parties to learn all about cricket, Fred at one end of the bar, Closey at the other. When you'd got fed up of listening to Fred, you moved down for a chat with Closey.'

The cornucopia of knowledge that whiled away the evening hours was fixed in Close's mind like a card index. Don Mosey observed, 'It is so detailed that he can trot out, as a throwaway line, the way to get a batsman out, or the way to deal with a bowler, which would stagger the most erudite critic.' He has, as the Bradford writer David Swallow said, an unmatched ability to 'read' the game and an uncanny instinct in arriving at the root of any problem.

The late Peter Smith, an esteemed cricket writer, was one recipient of Close's wisdom during their association in the press box on England's tour of the West Indies in 1967–68. With Close by his side, he was able to enlarge his understanding of the game. Smith recalled one instance of Brian's acumen in the Test in Trinidad after

John Edrich had survived a slip chance off the bowling of Charlie Griffith. There was whole-hearted condemnation from Smith and his fellow scribes for Edrich's moment of wildness. Close was not among the critics. 'Don't have a go at Edrich,' he said. 'Congratulate Garry Sobers on his captaincy.'

Smith was puzzled as to how Sobers could have had anything to do with the incident. Close explained that Sobers had started that over with one short leg, three slips and a gully. All the way through, Griffith had been tempting Edrich with a ball outside the off stump, thought by many to be a weakness of his. He had refused to bite.

After the first ball, Close continued, Sobers had a chat with Griffith, moved himself across and became a second short leg, widening the gaps between the slip fielders. For the next few deliveries Griffith bowled down the leg side, tempting Edrich to have a go. Rightly, he refused. The next ball was the shortish one outside the off stump. With the number of slips reduced and his concentration momentarily focused on the leg side and less on the restraint on the off side, he went for it and as a result nearly lost his wicket. It was a sudden inspiration by Sobers to make Edrich think he was changing the line of his attack to the leg side and then asking Griffith to work in a tempting delivery outside the off stump. It almost worked.

The reason for the switching of position by Sobers had eluded all the press corps, but not Close in his intent scrutiny of the over. 'Brian had spotted it. The cool professional mind was at work,' recalled Smith. As a postscript to the story, Smith remembered the joy and pleasure of working with Close throughout three months in the Caribbean. He was filled with gratitude for the experience and knowledge he had gained.

Bob Appleyard looks back across the years at his first meeting with Close, the 'brash young schoolboy with tremendous talent'. He marvelled, like others, at the stylish vigour of Close in one match between his club, Bowling Old Lane, and Yeadon. 'Brian had a backlift to match his golf swing and he also bowled really fast. He was quite extraordinary for his age.'

Appleyard echoes the lament of many devotees that woeful man-management arrested the progress of a supremely gifted boy. Therein lies a lesson for others charged with the task of encouraging those youngsters with prodigious ability. Close had to shoulder the burden of high expectations. 'Brian had so much talent,' says Appleyard, 'that he would inevitably attract criticism if he failed. And there were people who should have known better only too ready to knock him down.'

Bob Platt, the current Yorkshire cricket chairman, says that Brian has had enough setbacks to 'sink the *Titanic*'. Vivien Close, a strong personality in her own right, has helped to keep him afloat with the assurance of the most skilled navigator. She has learned over the years to sympathise with the highly complex individual who is her husband.

Behind the forbidding façade lies a sensitive and emotional man, who can all too easily be knocked off his pedestal. The fatalism of his nature does, though, mean that worries are soon dispelled. 'He is easy-going to a fault,' says Vivien, 'but he is also a strong character who can be hard when needed. Up to the time we married I generally got my own way. With Brian, there is no way that I can win.'

Above all, the couple display a pride in each other, and a generosity and sense of fun, sometimes unwittingly revealed, as when Brian introduced Vivien to his Somerset colleague, Vivian Richards. 'Viv, lad,' he said to the West Indian, 'I'd like you to meet Viv, lad.' It was a cue for peals of merriment and still evokes smiles in remembrance of the salutations.

It was always likely that Close would have a bumpy ride because of his temperament. However, despite all the cruel blows he counts himself lucky to have played the game when he did. His own happy days contrast with the fortunes of the modern game. Old campaigners are entitled to their opinions, particularly when they project a passion and conviction born of long experience. Close does not hide his disdain for certain aspects of the modern game. The downgrading of the county championship is one of his particular concerns. 'This has been the lifeblood of English cricket. It was the best domestic competition in the world, providing an education in differing conditions.' Proposals to reduce county staffs, he contends, seem certain to reduce the education. 'If this is the intention, who will teach young players coming into the game? I learnt my cricket through playing with older men all the time. They were my guides.'

Close considers the introduction of four-day cricket, supposedly designed to encourage spin bowling, has instead diminished the art. In the 1950s and 1960s England could field 10 of the top 15 spinners in the world and now there is not one to merit attention. He wistfully looks back at Yorkshire's own left-arm spinning tradition, remembering how it dominated their cricketing outlook until it almost became an act of faith. He speculates now on the breed of batsmen captains whose lack of understanding of the attitudes needed to deploy spin has contributed to a sad impoverishment.

Close maintains that despite all the modifications over the past 20 years, cricket has gone steadily downhill. The proliferation of limited-overs cricket, a mentally unrewarding exercise, is another undermining factor. Even more distasteful for Close, the astute gambler, has been the loss of adventure. 'We now have a situation where fielding sides go on the defensive from the start of a game.'

The approach of the millennium prompted Robert Mills, the *Yorkshire Post* cricket correspondent, to nominate Brian Close as the outstanding Yorkshire sportsman of the twentieth century. It could be argued that the Yorkshire side has never been the same since his dismissal, and certainly the team he captained can stand comparison with any in the history of the county. Michael Parkinson has reflected on the attributes of his fellow Yorkshireman: 'There was more to Brian than guts and willpower. He was a subtle psychologist on the field of play. He didn't go in for the ugly, abusive sledging we see and hear nowadays. He chose a more artful approach.'

Close's winning ways found accord with a legion of followers. Amid the jumble of precious memorabilia at his home lies a portfolio of impressive correspondence. It is a harvest of acclamation on his accession to the England captaincy and also contains deeply felt lament at his downfall only 12 months later. The letters, some hastily penned and others more purposefully expressed, are a reminder of the impact he made as a cricketer. They testify to the immense reservoir of good will and the admiration that his sportsmanship aroused among his devotees throughout the country. One correspondent observed that he had never before written to a cricketer but felt compelled to add his voice to the chorus of praise.

An extraordinary man, he has a phenomenal recall of the passages of his eventful life. 'It is an education to listen to him,' says Sidney Fielden. Brian Close, provocative in all his seasons, is in his element as a persuasive raconteur. Every visitor to Headingley, if he has an hour or two to spare, can be assured of a pleasurable interlude of cricket talk. It will, as they must be warned, take the form of a lecture. But a treasure trove of memories is waiting to be revealed. His guests will depart enlightened and grateful, as we all are, to have been entertained by the best of companions.

Statistical Appendix

Compiled by Paul Dyson

BRIEF CHRONOLOGY

Birth: February 24, 1931, Rawdon, Leeds

First day in first-class cricket: May 11, 1949, Yorkshire v Cambridge University, Fenner's

First day in Test cricket: July 23, 1949, England v New Zealand, Old Trafford

Awarded county cap: August 15, 1949, Yorkshire v Derbyshire, Bradford

Appointed Yorkshire captain and led county to Championship, 1963

One of the Five Cricketers of the Year, *Wisden Cricketers' Almanack*, 1964

First day as England Test captain: August 18, 1966, v West Indies, The Oval

First one-day international: August 24, 1972, England v Australia, Old Trafford (captain)

Final day in Test cricket: July 13, 1976, England v West Indies, Old Trafford

Final day in first-class cricket: September 2, 1986, D.B. Close's XI v New Zealanders, Scarborough

FIRST-CLASS CRICKET

BATTING AND FIELDING

In each season

	M	I	NO	Runs	HS	Avge.	100	50	Ct
1949	31	50	10	1098	88*	27.45	–	4	19
1950	4	7	1	202	92*	33.66	–	2	5
1950/51	9	13	3	231	108*	23.10	1	–	9
1951	6	12	1	384	135*	34.91	1	2	5
1952	33	45	9	1192	87*	33.11	–	8	27
1953	2	2	1	14	10	14.00	–	–	1
1954	31	43	7	1320	164	36.66	2	7	25
1955	32	53	5	1330	143	27.71	2	5	38
1955/56	12	20	1	684	92	36.00	–	5	12
1956	27	37	5	802	88	25.06	–	3	23
1957	34	56	4	1666	120	32.04	4	6	37
1958	34	53	5	1497	120	31.19	2	7	33
1959	33	56	3	1879	154	35.45	5	8	37
1959/60	3	5	1	111	78	27.75	–	1	1
1960	36	51	3	1699	198	35.40	3	8	44
1961	37	64	8	1985	132	35.45	5	9	47
1962	29	46	6	1447	142	36.18	3	7	30
1963	31	50	3	1529	161	32.53	1	10	27
1964	36	55	7	1455	100*	30.31	1	8	48
1964/65	1	2	0	52	52	26.00	–	1	2
1965	30	46	7	1127	117*	28.90	3	2	31
1966	34	56	11	1331	115*	29.58	3	6	46
1967	23	32	4	884	98	31.57	–	8	29
1968	27	34	8	660	77*	25.38	–	3	34
1969	20	27	4	812	146	35.30	1	4	10
1970	20	28	2	949	128	36.50	1	6	20
1971	26	42	10	1389	116*	43.41	5	6	34
1972	20	33	6	1396	135	51.70	3	7	17
1972/73	2	4	0	59	27	14.75	–	–	6
1973	21	32	5	1096	153	40.59	3	3	21
1973/74	7	11	3	200	50	25.00	–	1	8
1974	24	40	9	1153	114*	37.19	1	5	25
1974/75	7	13	4	332	102	36.88	1	–	7
1975	22	38	6	1284	138*	40.13	1	8	14
1976	20	34	5	1137	88	39.21	–	8	17
1977	16	25	2	438	87	19.04	–	2	19
1978	1	2	0	9	8	4.50	–	–	2
1982	1	1	1	26	26*	–	–	–	1
1983	1	2	0	52	51	26.00	–	1	–
1984	1	1	1	15	15*	–	–	–	–
1985	1	2	2	42	22*	–	–	–	2
1986	1	2	0	26	22	13.00	–	–	–
Totals	786	1225	173	34994	198	33.26	52	171	813

For each team

	M	I	NO	Runs	HS	Avge.	100	50	Ct
Yorkshire									
County									
matches	448	683	83	18241	198	30.70	24	95	492
other matches	88	128	19	4229	164	38.80	9	15	72
Somerset									
County									
matches	132	216	36	6955	153	38.64	12	34	133
other matches	10	15	3	612	103*	51.00	1	3	7
England XI	6	10	2	250	102	31.25	1	–	6
MCC (in UK)	6	9	2	269	108*	38.43	1	1	5
MCC (overseas)	8	11	3	230	108*	28.75	1	–	8
MCC 'A'	12	20	1	684	92	36.00	–	5	12
Players	6	10	1	440	112	48.88	1	4	4
North	4	7	2	98	36	19.60	–	–	3
Combined	7	13	2	483	135*	43.91	1	4	10
Services									
T.N. Pearce's XI	9	17	3	423	51*	30.21	–	2	7
D.H Robins' XI	13	23	9	453	50	32.36	–	1	14
D.B. Close's XI	5	8	4	161	51	40.25	–	1	3
Under Thirty	1	2	0	36	19	18.00	–	–	1
International	4	7	0	192	102	27.43	1	–	9
Wanderers									
Commonwealth	4	7	1	163	78	27.17	–	2	3
XI									
International XI	1	2	0	8	8	4.00	–	–	–

Summary

	M	I	NO	Runs	HS	Avge.	100	50	Ct
Yorkshire	536	811	102	22650	198	31.95	33	110	564
Somerset	142	231	39	7567	153	39.41	13	27	140
Others	86	146	30	3890	135*	33.25	6	20	85
England (Tests)	22	37	2	887	70	25.34	–	4	24
Totals	786	1225	173	34994	198	33.26	52	171	813

Against each opponent

	M	I	NO	Runs	HS	Avge.	100	50	Ct
Derbyshire	33	52	7	1533	120	34.07	2	9	36
Essex	36	60	12	1852	142*	38.58	2	10	47
Glamorgan	36	56	4	1547	120	29.75	4	7	38
Gloucestershire	45	73	10	1759	138*	27.92	3	7	59
Hampshire	33	57	5	1447	102	27.83	1	9	28
Kent	32	46	7	1243	77	31.87	–	8	33
Lancashire	45	65	12	1696	128	32.00	2	12	43
Leicestershire	28	40	7	1531	114*	46.39	2	11	30
Middlesex	39	58	2	1332	153	23.79	1	7	39
Northants	33	55	5	1673	161	33.46	3	7	37
Nottinghamshire	39	53	9	1796	184	40.82	3	8	41
Somerset	33	49	6	1493	143	34.72	4	5	23
Surrey	39	69	10	1869	198	31.68	5	5	41
Sussex	36	53	9	1381	103	31.39	1	6	34
Warwickshire	42	64	7	1788	140	31.37	2	10	62
Worcestershire	37	58	7	1549	93	30.37	–	11	42
Yorkshire	6	11	2	394	102	43.77	1	2	4
Cambridge U.	13	17	2	740	114	49.33	3	2	12
Oxford U.	13	15	4	476	144	43.27	1	1	10
MCC	34	55	9	1343	88*	29.20	–	6	25
Gentlemen	6	10	1	440	112	48.88	1	4	4
South	4	7	2	98	36	19.60	–	–	3
Scotland	2	3	0	49	20	16.33	–	–	2
Rest of England	2	3	0	199	86	66.33	–	2	2
England U-25	1	1	1	29	29*	–	–	–	1
Young England	1	2	0	30	30	15.00	–	–	–
Over Thirty	1	2	0	36	19	18.00	–	–	1
Combined Services	1	1	0	164	164	164.00	1	–	3
Australians	10	17	2	559	59	37.27	–	3	5
Canadians	1	2	0	66	45	33.00	–	–	2
Indians	7	9	5	352	103*	88.00	1	1	6
New Zealanders	8	12	0	437	146	36.42	2	2	5
Pakistanis	6	8	3	254	123*	50.80	1	–	5
South Africans	6	11	2	448	135*	49.77	2	1	8
Sri Lankans	1	1	1	15	15*	–	–	–	–
West Indians	10	18	3	588	108*	39.20	1	3	7
Rest of World XI	3	6	2	88	32	22.00	–	–	4
Commonwealth XI	1	2	1	116	102	58.00	1	–	3

	M	I	NO	Runs	HS	Avge.	100	50	Ct
Sir Frank Worrell's XI	1	1	0	29	29	29.00	–	–	–
Combined XI (Aust)	1	2	1	9	5*	9.00	–	–	–
New South Wales	1	1	0	18	18	18.00	–	–	–
Queensland	1	1	0	21	21	21.00	–	–	–
South Australia	2	3	0	22	14	7.33	–	–	2
Victoria	2	3	1	52	30	26.00	–	–	4
Western Australia	1	1	1	108	108*	–	1	–	2
Bengal Chief Minister's XI	1	2	0	52	52	26.00	–	1	2
Amir of Bahawalpur's XI	1	1	0	92	92	92.00	–	1	1
Combined XI (Pak)	1	1	0	82	82	82.00	–	1	1
Combined Universities (Pak)	1	2	1	65	52*	65.00	–	1	2
East Pakistan	1	1	0	32	32	32.00	–	–	–
Governor–General's XI (Pak)	1	2	0	19	16	9.50	–	–	2
Karachi C.A.	1	2	0	114	66	57.00	–	1	1
Pakistan (non-Test)	4	8	0	240	71	30.00	–	1	4
Pakistan Services XI	1	2	0	26	25	13.00	–	–	2
Punjab C.A.	1	1	0	14	14	14.00	–	–	1
Combined XI (S.A.)	1	2	1	17	9	17.00	–	–	–
Eastern Province	2	3	1	78	35*	39.00	–	–	2
Inv/Int XI (SA)	4	7	1	208	78	34.66	–	2	3
Natal	2	4	1	45	15	15.00	–	–	2
President's XI (S.A.)	1	2	0	7	7	3.50	–	–	–
Rhodesia	3	5	0	161	102	32.20	1	–	8
Transvaal	4	7	3	134	36*	33.50	–	–	4
Western Province	2	3	1	52	29	26.00	–	–	3

Summary

	M	I	NO	Runs	HS	Avge.	100	50	Ct
British Teams	670	1035	140	29487	198	32.95	42	149	700
Overseas Teams	94	153	31	4620	135*	37.87	10	18	89
Test matches	22	37	2	887	70	25.34	–	4	24
Totals	786	1225	173	34994	198	33.26	52	171	813

On each ground (including Test matches)

a)   in United Kingdom, listed by county

	M	I	NO	Runs	HS	Avge.	100	50	Ct
Chesterfield	14	23	3	662	120	33.10	1	3	19
Derby	2	2	0	1	1	0.50	–	–	1
In Derbyshire	16	25	3	663	120	30.14	1	3	20
Chelmsford	3	4	0	44	23	11.00	–	–	6
Clacton-on-Sea	1	1	0	38	38	38.00	–	–	–
Colchester	4	7	1	165	88	27.50	–	1	7
Leyton	4	8	3	178	62*	35.60	–	2	9
Romford	2	2	0	61	31	30.50	–	–	1
Southend-on-Sea	2	4	1	65	46*	21.66	–	–	3
Westcliff-on-Sea	2	4	1	38	18	12.66	–	–	2
In Essex	18	30	6	589	88	24.54	–	3	28
Cardiff									
Arms Park	3	6	0	73	36	12.17	–	–	3
Sophia									
Gardens	4	7	0	171	81	24.43	–	2	6
Neath	1	2	0	119	108	59.50	1	–	1
Newport	1	2	0	19	19	9.50	–	–	–
Pontypridd	1	2	0	28	20	14.00	–	–	2
Swansea	10	16	1	481	120	32.07	2	2	14
In Glamorgan	20	35	1	891	120	26.21	3	4	26
Bristol	20	34	5	827	138*	28.52	2	3	22
Cheltenham	1	2	0	17	10	8.50	–	–	1
Gloucester	2	3	1	119	78	59.50	–	1	2
Lydney	1	1	0	0	0	0.00	–	–	1
In Gloucestershire	24	40	6	963	138*	28.32	2	4	26
Bournemouth	10	20	3	509	78	29.94	–	3	8
Portsmouth	4	6	1	331	135*	66.20	2	1	6
Southampton	2	4	1	139	86*	46.33	–	1	1
In Hampshire	16	30	5	979	135*	39.16	2	5	15
Canterbury	3	2	0	3	2	1.50	–	–	2
Dover	5	7	2	129	36	25.80	–	–	7
Folkestone	1	2	0	59	48	29.50	–	–	–
Gillingham	2	4	2	153	47	76.50	–	–	4
Gravesend	2	3	0	109	44	36.33	–	–	3
Maidstone	3	6	1	246	62	49.20	–	3	3
Tunbridge Wells	1	1	0	8	8	8.00	–	–	–
In Kent	17	25	5	707	62	35.35	–	3	19

	M	I	NO	Runs	HS	Avge.	100	50	Ct
Blackpool	1	2	0	15	15	7.50	–	–	1
Liverpool	1	2	0	28	25	14.00	–	–	1
Old Trafford	26	39	6	985	111	29.85	1	8	29
Southport	1	2	0	33	31	16.50	–	–	1
In Lancashire	29	45	6	1061	111	27.21	1	8	32
Leicester	15	23	4	759	104*	39.95	1	5	20
Lord's	52	77	6	2050	153	28.87	3	9	38
Northampton	14	25	4	953	161	45.38	3	3	12
Wellingborough	2	3	0	58	36	19.33	–	–	2
In Northants	16	28	4	1011	161	42.13	3	3	14
Trent Bridge	20	28	4	825	154	34.38	1	4	20
Worksop	2	2	1	211	115*	211.00	1	1	7
In Notts	22	30	5	1036	151	41.44	2	5	27
Bath	17	29	5	876	128	36.50	1	4	19
Bristol	1	1	0	26	26	26.00	–	–	1
Glastonbury	2	1	0	34	34	34.00	–	–	6
Taunton	52	83	15	3157	143	46.43	7	16	49
Wells	1	2	0	5	5	2.50	–	–	–
Weston-super-Mare	17	25	4	955	114*	45.48	2	5	16
In Somerset	90	141	24	5053	143	43.19	10	25	91
Guildford	1	2	0	22	20	11.00	–	–	–
The Oval	25	44	3	1157	198	28.22	2	3	22
In Surrey	26	46	3	1179	198	27.42	2	3	22
Eastbourne	2	4	2	117	41	58.50	–	–	2
Hastings	1	2	0	36	19	18.00	–	–	1
Hove	15	23	4	623	103	32.79	1	1	12
Worthing	1	2	0	77	77	38.50	–	1	–
In Sussex	19	31	6	853	103	34.12	1	2	15
Coventry	1	1	0	57	57	57.00	–	1	1
Edgbaston	23	37	5	911	82	28.47	–	5	22
In Warwickshire	24	38	5	968	82	29.33	–	6	23

	M	I	NO	Runs	HS	Avge.	100	50	Ct
Kidderminster	2	3	1	62	41	31.00	–	–	4
Worcester	17	29	5	775	92*	32.29	–	5	14
In Worcestershire	19	32	6	837	92*	32.19	–	5	18
Bradford	59	82	7	2346	146	31.28	5	12	61
Harrogate	16	21	1	611	164	30.55	1	3	27
Headingley	48	69	7	1769	103	28.53	1	10	42
Huddersfield	4	5	1	38	17*	9.50	–	–	4
Hull	20	32	3	998	103	34.41	1	8	23
Middlesbrough	19	27	3	693	98	28.88	–	6	30
Scarborough	65	108	20	2854	184	32.43	1	14	53
Sheffield	62	99	17	2999	142*	36.57	5	14	66
In Yorkshire	293	443	59	12308	184	32.05	14	67	306
Fenner's	13	17	2	740	114	49.33	3	2	12
The Parks	13	15	4	476	144	43.27	1	1	10
Torquay	2	4	1	162	102	54.00	1	–	3
Glasgow	1	2	0	40	20	20.00	–	–	2

NOTE: All Close's Sheffield games were at Bramall Lane (this also applies to limited-overs matches, dealt with later).

b) Overseas, listed by country

	M	I	NO	Runs	HS	Avge.	100	50	Ct
Adelaide	2	3	0	22	14	7.33	–	–	2
Brisbane	1	1	0	21	21	21.00	–	–	–
Launceston	1	2	1	9	5*	9.00	–	–	–
Melbourne	3	5	1	53	30	13.25	–	–	5
Perth	1	1	1	108	108*	–	1	–	2
Sydney	1	1	0	18	18	18.00	–	–	–
In Australia	9	13	3	231	108*	23.10	1	–	9
Calcutta (India)	1	2	0	52	52	26.00	–	1	2
Bahawalpur	1	1	0	92	92	92.00	–	1	1
Chittagong	1	1	0	32	32	32.00	–	–	–
Dacca	1	2	0	31	31	15.50	–	–	–
Karachi	3	6	0	234	71	39.00	–	2	4
Lahore	2	4	1	132	52*	44.00	–	1	2
Layallpur	1	1	0	14	14	14.00	–	–	1
Peshawar	1	2	0	41	39	20.50	–	–	1
Sargodha	1	2	0	26	25	13.00	–	–	2
Sialkot	1	1	0	82	82	82.00	–	1	1
In Pakistan	12	20	1	684	92	36.00	–	5	12

	M	I	NO	Runs	HS	Avge.	100	50	Ct
Bulawayo	1	2	0	33	27	16.50	–	–	2
Cape Town	4	7	2	106	38	21.20	–	–	5
Durban	3	5	1	95	50	23.75	–	1	3
Johannesburg	6	11	3	245	78	30.63	–	1	4
Port Elizabeth	2	3	1	78	35*	39.00	–	–	2
Pretoria	1	2	1	17	9	17.00	–	–	–
Salisbury	2	3	0	128	102	42.66	1	–	6
In Rhodesia and South Africa	19	33	8	702	102	28.08	1	2	22

Summary

	M	I	NO	Runs	HS	Avge.	100	50	Ct
United Kingdom	745	1157	161	33325	198	35.13	50	163	768
Overseas	41	68	12	1669	108*	29.80	2	8	45
Totals	786	1225	173	34994	198	33.26	52	171	813

Bowlers with most dismissals of Close

13	B. Langford (Somerset), D.J. Shepherd (Glamorgan)
12	P.J. Sainsbury (Hampshire), F.J. Titmus (Middlesex)
11	T.E. Bailey (Essex), J.B. Statham (Lancashire)
10	T.W. Cartwright (Warwickshire & Somerset), G.A.R. Lock (Surrey & Leicestershire), J.B. Mortimore (Gloucestershire), N.I. Thomson (Sussex)
9	B.D. Wells (Nottinghamshire)
8	A.S. Brown (Gloucestershire) J.A. Flavell (Worcestershire), C.C. Griffith (West Indies), R.N.S. Hobbs (Essex), D.C. Morgan, E. Smith (Derbyshire), C.T. Spencer (Leicestershire)

How out

Caught	611	(58.1%)
Bowled	284	(27.0%)
Lbw	81	(7.7%)
Stumped	38	(3.6%)
Run out	36	(3.4%)
Hit wicket	2	(0.2%)
Total	1052	(100.0%)

Scores of over 150

198	Yorkshire v Surrey	The Oval	1960
184	Yorkshire v Nottinghamshire	Scarborough	1960
164	Yorkshire v Combined Services	Harrogate	1954
161	Yorkshire v Northamptonshire	Northampton	1963
154	Yorkshire v Nottinghamshire	Trent Bridge	1959
153	Somerset v Middlesex	Lord's	1973

A century and a half-century in the same match

66 & 135*	Combined Services v South Africans	Portsmouth	1951
59 & 114*	Somerset v Leicestershire	Weston-super-Mare	1974

Two consecutive centuries
(47 &) 114* v Essex (at Taunton) and 153 v Middlesex (Lord's) for Somerset in 1973

Pair
Somerset v Middlesex, Taunton, 1974

10,000th run
41 (out of 82) Yorkshire v Warwickshire, Edgbaston, 20 August 1958

20,000th run
5 (out of 17) Yorkshire v Lancashire, Headingley, 1 August 1964

30,000th run
94 (out of 108) Somerset v Glamorgan, Neath, 21 July 1973

Double-century partnerships

252	3rd	D.E.V. Padgett	Yorkshire v Nottinghamshire	Trent Bridge	1959
249	3rd	D.E.V. Padgett	Yorkshire v Nottinghamshire	Scarborough	1960
244	3rd	D.E.V. Padgett	Yorkshire v Oxford University	The Parks	1959
227	5th	I.V.A. Richards	Somerset v Yorkshire	Harrogate	1975
226	3rd	D.E.V. Padgett	Yorkshire v Surrey	The Oval	1960
226	4th	D.J.S. Taylor	Somerset v Glamorgan	Swansea	1974
224	3rd	J.V. Wilson	Yorkshire v Cambridge University	Fenner's	1955
220	3rd	P.A. Slocombe	Somerset v Gloucestershire	Bristol	1975
217	5th	R. Illingworth	Yorkshire v Warwickshire	Sheffield	1962
205	3rd	D.E.V. Padgett	Yorkshire v Somerset	Bath	1959
201*	4th	J.H. Hampshire	Yorkshire v Surrey	Bradford	1965

Summary of Century Partnerships (93)

For each wicket

1st – 3   2nd – 10   3rd – 36   4th – 15   5th – 18   6th – 8   7th – 3

For each team

61	Yorkshire
22	Somerset
2	England, MCC, Players
1	Commonwealth XI, England XI, MCC 'A', D.H. Robins' XI

With each partner

17	D.E.V. Padgett
9	R. Illingworth
7	J.V. Wilson
5	M.J. Kitchen, P.J. Sharpe
3	J.B. Bolus, G. Boycott, P.W. Denning, J.H. Hampshire, B.C. Rose, W.B. Stott, W. Watson
2	G.I. Burgess, J.H. Edrich, T.W. Graveney, R.A. Hutton, J.M. Parks, I.V.A. Richards, P.A. Slocombe, F.S. Trueman, N.W.D. Yardley
1	J.C. Balderstone, K.F. Barrington, A. Clarkson, A. Coxon, R.A. Gale, J.T. Ikin, C. Johnson, P.E. Richardson, W.H.H. Sutcliffe, D.J.S. Taylor, S.G. Wilkinson

Against each team

7	Lancashire
6	Leicestershire, Nottinghamshire, Warwickshire
5	Northamptonshire, Somerset, Surrey
4	Glamorgan, Gloucestershire, Sussex, New Zealanders
3	Derbyshire, Essex, Hampshire, Middlesex, Worcestershire
2	Kent, Yorkshire, Cambridge University, MCC, Gentlemen, The Rest, South African Invitation XI, West Indies
1	Oxford University, Combined Services, Australians, West Indians, Commonwealth XI, Pakistan (non-Test)

On each ground

11	Taunton
7	Bradford
5	Hull, The Oval, Sheffield
4	Lord's, Scarborough, Weston-super-Mare
3	Bristol, Edgbaston, Harrogate, Headingley, Leicester, Northampton, Trent Bridge
2	Bath, Fenner's, Hove, Middlesbrough, Old Trafford, Swansea
1	Cardiff, Chesterfield, Dover, The Parks, Portsmouth, Southend-on-Sea, Southport, Torquay, Worcester, Worksop, Durban, Lahore

BOWLING

In each season

	O	M	R	W	Avge.	5wi	10wm	Best
1949	1245	324	3150	113	27.88	6	–	6-47
1950	153.1	46	386	20	19.30	1	1	6-61
1950/51	+ 98	9	475	13	36.54	–	–	3-81
1951	101.4	37	246	4	61.50	–	–	1-22
1952	1106.4	330	2746	114	24.09	6	–	6-69
1953	45	19	105	3	35.00	–	–	2-61
1954	534	138	1474	66	22.33	4	–	6-38
1955	871.4	257	2274	97	23.44	5	–	7-62
1955/56	145	58	313	11	28.45	–	–	2-40
1956	266.5	75	674	24	28.08	–	–	4-27
1957	289	93	787	32	24.59	1	–	5-29
1958	342.1	85	921	34	27.09	–	–	4-30
1959	757.2	210	2162	88	24.57	5	–	8-41
1959/60	125	28	442	9	49.11	–	–	4-100
1960	611.3	207	1493	64	23.33	3	–	8-43
1961	615	220	1716	67	25.61	3	–	6-49
1962	413.5	164	929	32	29.03	–	–	3-4
1963	425.2	134	1176	43	27.35	1	1	6-55
1964	563.5	199	1360	52	26.15	1	–	6-29
1964/65	30.1	4	170	4	42.50	–	–	2-55
1965	527.2	202	1217	58	20.98	4	1	6-49
1966	563.3	201	1362	60	22.70	2	–	6-27
1967	372.1	134	870	29	30.00	–	–	4-68
1968	340	139	772	32	24.13	–	–	4-87
1969	115	47	282	7	40.29	–	–	1-4
1970	34	10	95	2	47.50	–	–	1-15
1971	39	11	160	5	32.00	–	–	3-20
1972	35	10	128	3	42.66	–	–	2-77
1972/73	40	6	218	6	36.33	–	–	3-59
1973	159.5	29	560	10	56.00	–	–	2-3
1973/74	47	9	184	2	92.00	–	–	1-0
1974	104	30	287	14	20.50	1	–	5-70
1974/75	27.5	1	129	4	32.25	–	–	4-36
1975	294.1	87	931	29	32.10	–	–	4-22
1976	163.1	36	605	15	40.33	–	–	3-35
1977	0.2	0	8	0	–	–	–	–
1978	8	1	31	1	31.00	–	–	1-31
1983	1.4	0	5	1	5.00	–	–	1-5
1984	1.1	0	2	0	–	–	–	–
1985	6	1	33	2	16.50	–	–	2-33
1986	10	1	71	1	71.00	–	–	1-71
Totals	11531.2	3583	30949	1171	26.43	43	3	8-41
	+ 98	9						

+ 8-ball overs

For each team

	O	M	R	W	Avge.	5wi	10wm	Best
Yorkshire County matches	7932	2608	19501	817	23.87	35	2	8-41
Other matches	1545.1	463	3988	150	26.59	5	–	5-29
Somerset County matches	745.3	195	2458	69	35.62	1	–	5-70
Other matches	32	5	128	5	25.60	–	–	3-35
England XI	53	10	183	4	45.75	–	–	2-28
MCC (in UK)	82.2	18	272	2	136.00	–	–	1-48
MCC (overseas)	+ 91	8	447	12	37.25	–	–	3-81
MCC 'A'	145	58	313	11	28.45	–	–	2-40
Players	100.4	29	298	14	21.29	1	–	5-23
North	102.4	14	484	7	69.14	–	–	4-160
Combined Services	165.3	53	426	15	28.40	1	1	6-61
T.N. Pearce's XI	107	19	497	14	35.50	–	–	3-58
D.H. Robins' XI	63	10	269	3	89.66	–	–	1-0
D.B. Close's XI	18.5	2	111	4	27.75	–	–	2-33
Under Thirty	28	5	111	3	37.00	–	–	2-47
International Wanderers	58.5	7	294	10	29.40	–	–	4-36
Commonwealth XI	155.1	32	612	13	47.08	–	–	4-100
International XI	4	0	25	0	–	–	–	–

Summary

	O	M	R	W	Avge.	5wi	10wm	Best
Yorkshire	9477.1	3071	23489	967	24.29	40	2	8-41
Somerset	777.3	200	2586	74	34.95	1	–	5-70
Others	1084	257	4342	112	38.77	2	1	6-61
+	91	8						
Test matches	192.4	55	532	18	29.55	–	–	4-35
+	7	1						
Totals	11531.2	3583	30949	1171	26.43	43	3	8-41
+	98	9						

Against each opponent

	O	M	R	W	Avge.	5wi	10wm	Best
Derbyshire	540.2	161	1342	55	24.40	2	–	6-59
Essex	556	185	1378	68	20.26	4	1	8-43
Glamorgan	509.5	170	1261	55	22.93	2	1	6-52
Gloucestershire	639.5	200	1755	60	29.25	3	–	6-45
Hampshire	486.2	152	1371	52	26.37	2	–	6-94
Kent	540.1	199	1364	67	20.36	6	1	8-41
Lancashire	583.4	176	1473	63	23.38	3	–	6-130
Leicestershire	418	134	987	42	23.50	1	–	5-24
Middlesex	563.5	168	1458	47	31.02	1	–	5-75
Northamptonshire	420.2	131	1032	40	25.80	2	–	6-38
Nottinghamshire	698	216	1761	74	23.80	2	–	6-69
Somerset	512	171	1292	53	24.38	2	–	6-87
Surrey	504.4	138	1499	52	28.83	3	–	6-27
Sussex	610.5	211	1497	50	29.94	2	–	5-64
Warwickshire	581.5	196	1395	56	24.91	1	–	5-12
Worcestershire	707.2	256	1670	69	24.20	1	–	6-47
Yorkshire	17	2	78	1	78.00	–	–	1-43
Cambridge U.	318.1	101	714	34	21.00	1	–	5-29
Oxford U.	247.3	85	531	25	21.24	1	–	5-40
MCC	387	74	1240	43	28.84	1	–	5-64
Gentlemen	100.4	29	298	14	21.29	1	–	5-23
South	102.4	14	484	7	69.14	–	–	4-160
Scotland	55	24	91	2	45.50	–	–	2-65
Rest of England	27.4	2	139	6	23.17	1	–	5-47
England U-25	16	0	70	2	35.00	–	–	2-28
Young England	6	1	17	0	–	–	–	–
Over Thirty	28	5	111	3	37.00	–	–	2-47
Combined Services	18.1	3	55	2	27.50	–	–	2-55
Australians	103	22	345	5	69.00	–	–	3-80
Canadians	25.4	8	68	5	13.60	–	–	3-35
Indians	43.2	15	133	3	44.33	–	–	1-20
New Zealanders	119.4	43	303	12	25.25	1	–	5-69
Pakistanis	129	52	318	7	45.43	–	–	4-54
South Africans	171	50	463	12	38.58	–	–	3-58
Sri Lankans	1.1	0	2	0	–	–	–	–
West Indians	97	18	390	15	26.00	–	–	3-35
Rest of World XI	37	10	129	4	32.25	–	–	2-33
New South Wales	+ 12	0	68	0	–	–	–	–
Queensland	+ 7	0	30	1	30.00	–	–	1-30
South Australia	+ 5	1	19	1	19.00	–	–	1-8
Victoria	+ 48	6	226	6	37.66	–	–	3-103
Western Australia	+ 19	1	104	4	26.00	–	–	3-81

	O	M	R	W	Avge.	5wi	10wm	Best
Bengal Chief Minister's XI	30.1	4	170	4	42.50	–	–	2-55
Amir of Bahawalpur's XI	10	3	18	1	18.00	–	–	1-9
Combined XI (Pak)	6	1	25	1	25.00	–	–	1-25
Combined Universities (Pak)	33	12	84	2	42.00	–	–	1-16
East Pakistan	5	1	9	0	–	–	–	–
Governor-General's XI (Pak)	8	5	4	0	–	–	–	–
Karachi C.A.	12	6	17	0	–	–	–	–
Pakistan (non-Test)	32	16	61	3	20.33	–	–	2-40
Pakistan Services XI	39	14	95	4	23.75	–	–	2-46
Combined XI (S.A.)	55	14	192	4	48.00	–	–	4-100
Inv/Int XI (S.A.)	63	11	249	3	83.00	–	–	2-122
Natal	6	0	35	0	–	–	–	–
President's XI (S.A.)	3	0	18	0	–	–	–	–
Rhodesia	46	7	243	6	40.50	–	–	3-59
Transvaal	55.5	10	179	7	25.57	–	–	4-36
Western Province	11	2	57	1	57.00	–	–	1-57

Summary

	O	M	R	W	Avge.	5wi	10wm	Best
British Teams	10196.5	3204	26363	1042	25.30	42	3	8-41
Overseas Teams	1141.5 + 91	324 8	4054	111	36.52	1	–	5-69
Test Matches	192.4 + 7	55 1	532	18	29.55	–	–	4-35
Totals	11531.2 + 98	3583 9	30949	1171	26.43	43	3	8-41

On each ground (including Test matches)

a) in United Kingdom, listed by county

	O	M	R	W	Avge.	5wi	10wm	Best
Chesterfield	302.1	95	677	32	21.16	1	–	6-59
Derby	2	1	1	0	–	–	–	–
In Derbyshire	304.1	96	678	32	21.19	1	–	6-59
Chelmsford	40.5	8	114	10	11.40	1	1	6-61
Clacton-on-Sea	5	1	12	0	–	–	–	–
Colchester	18	6	60	0	–	–	–	–
Leyton	75.5	30	173	11	15.73	–	–	4-43
Romford	37	7	126	5	25.20	–	–	2-27
Southend-on-Sea	12	4	27	2	13.50	–	–	1-10
Westcliff-on-Sea	5	1	12	0	–	–	–	–
In Essex	193.4	57	524	28	18.71	1	1	6-61
Cardiff								
Arms Park	39	9	139	0	–	–	–	–
Sophia Gardens	38	17	76	1	76.00	–	–	1-41
Newport	9	1	38	1	38.00	–	–	1-10
Pontypridd	11	2	30	1	30.00	–	–	1-23
Swansea	162.1	53	332	24	13.83	1	–	6-52
In Glamorgan	259.1	82	615	27	22.77	1	–	6-52
Bristol	256	72	712	21	33.90	1	–	6-68
Cheltenham	9	2	22	1	22.00	–	–	1-22
Gloucester	51	24	102	3	34.00	–	–	1-8
In Gloucestershire	316	98	836	25	33.44	1	–	6-68
Bournemouth	141.1	37	396	18	22.00	1	–	5-32
Portsmouth	77	20	220	4	55.00	–	–	2-45
In Hampshire	218.1	57	616	22	28.00	1	–	5-32
Canterbury	34	10	85	4	21.25	–	–	3-64
Dover	109	37	286	12	23.83	1	–	6-49
Folkestone	17	4	73	0	–	–	–	–
Gillingham	69	28	177	13	13.62	2	1	6-49
Gravesend	57	24	122	5	24.40	–	–	2-44
Maidstone	11	1	64	1	64.00	–	–	1-24
Tunbridge Wells	6	3	27	0	–	–	–	–
In Kent	303	107	834	35	23.83	3	1	6-49

	O	M	R	W	Avge.	5wi	10wm	Best
Blackpool	27.4	2	234	4	58.50	–	–	4-160
Liverpool	11	2	35	0	–	–	–	–
Old Trafford	267.2	84	681	20	34.05	–	–	4-53
In Lancashire	306	88	950	24	39.58	–	–	4-53
Leicester	267.3	89	643	26	24.73	1	–	5-24
Lord's	643	150	1849	60	30.82	2	–	5-23
Northampton	202.1	64	535	18	29.72	1	–	5-88
Wellingborough	52	17	108	3	36.00	–	–	3-77
In Northants	254.1	81	643	21	30.62	1	–	5-88
Trent Bridge	392.2	124	978	40	24.18	2	–	6-69
Worksop	10	2	28	0	–	–	–	–
In Nottinghamshire	402.2	126	1006	40	24.88	2	–	6-69
Bath	127.4	42	298	13	22.92	1	–	6-87
Taunton	489.1	143	1536	46	33.39	1	–	5-70
Wells	38	7	105	5	21.00	–	–	4-58
Weston-super-Mare	101.5	23	344	13	26.46	–	–	4-22
In Somerset	756.4	215	2283	77	29.65	2	–	6-87
The Oval	299.1	71	1000	31	32.26	2	–	6-27
Eastbourne	7	1	32	1	32.00	–	–	1-20
Hastings	28	5	111	3	37.00	–	–	2-47
Hove	286	89	742	20	37.10	–	–	4-57
Worthing	26	9	57	4	14.25	–	–	4-30
In Sussex	347	104	942	28	33.64	–	–	4-30
Coventry	12	6	17	2	8.50	–	–	2-17
Edgbaston	359.1	120	900	30	30.00	–	–	4-68
In Warwickshire	371.1	126	917	32	28.66	–	–	4-68
Kidderminster	45.5	20	110	5	22.00	–	–	3-48
Worcester	362.1	116	956	37	25.84	1	–	6-47
In Worcestershire	408	136	1066	42	25.38	1	–	6-47

	O	M	R	W	Avge.	5wi	10wm	Best
Bradford	920.5	331	2217	119	18.63	7	–	7-62
Harrogate	279.3	83	810	26	31.15	–	–	4-46
Headingley	890.3	303	2151	92	23.38	6	–	8-41
Huddersfield	100	28	270	11	24.55	1	–	6-105
Hull	348	120	822	34	24.18	2	–	5-36
Middlesbrough	129	39	345	19	18.16	1	–	5-64
Scarborough	972.1	274	2946	101	29.17	2	–	6-94
Sheffield	1197.3	404	2678	107	25.03	3	1	6-45
In Yorkshire	4837.3	1582	12239	509	24.05	22	1	8-41
Fenner's	318.1	101	714	34	21.00	1	–	5-29
The Parks	247.3	85	531	25	21.24	1	–	5-40
Torquay	18	3	65	2	32.50	–	–	2-46
Glasgow	46	23	67	2	33.50	–	–	2-65

b)   Overseas, listed by country

	O	M	R	W	Avge.	5wi	10wm	Best
Adelaide	+ 5	1	19	1	19.00	–	–	1-8
Brisbane	+ 7	0	30	1	30.00	–	–	1-30
Melbourne	+ 55	7	254	7	36.29	–	–	3-103
Perth	+ 19	1	104	4	26.00	–	–	3-81
Sydney	+ 12	0	68	0	–	–	–	–
In Australia	+ 98	9	475	13	36.54	–	–	3-81
Calcutta (India)	30.1	4	170	4	42.50	–	–	2-55
Bahawalpur	10	3	18	1	18.00	–	–	1-9
Chittagong	5	1	9	0	–	–	–	–
Karachi	49	27	69	3	23.00	–	–	2-40
Lahore	36	12	97	2	48.50	–	–	1-16
Sargodha	39	14	95	4	23.75	–	–	2-46
Sialkot	6	1	25	1	25.00	–	–	1-25
In Pakistan	145	58	313	11	28.45	–	–	2-40
Bulawayo	26	2	144	4	36.00	–	–	3-59
Cape Town	26	4	106	2	53.00	–	–	1-0
Durban	18	3	79	0	–	–	–	–
Johannesburg	94.5	16	353	9	39.22	–	–	4-36
Pretoria	55	14	192	4	48.00	–	–	4-100
Salisbury	20	5	99	2	49.50	–	–	1-15
In Rhodesia and South Africa	239.5	44	973	21	46.33	–	–	4-36

Summary

	O	M	R	W	Avge.	5wi	10wm	Best
In United Kingdom	11116.2	3477	29018	1122	25.86	43	3	8-41
Overseas	415	106	1931	49	39.41	–	–	4-36
	+ 98	9						
Totals	11531.2	3583	30949	1171	26.43	43	3	8-41
	+ 98	9						

Seven wickets or more in an innings

8-41	Yorkshire v Kent	Headingley	1959
8-43	Yorkshire v Essex	Headingley	1960
7-62	Yorkshire v Essex	Bradford	1955

Ten wickets or more in a match

11-116	Yorkshire v Kent	Gillingham	1965
10-74	Yorkshire v Glamorgan	Sheffield	1963
10-94	Combined Services v Essex	Chelmsford	1950

Batsmen most frequently dismissed

10   R.M. Prideaux (Kent, Northamptonshire & Sussex)

9   A.S.M. Oakman (Sussex), R.C. Wilson (Kent)

8   H.L. Johnson (Derbyshire), P.E. Richardson (Worcestershire & Kent), O.S. Wheatley (Glamorgan)

7   A.C.D. Ingleby-Mackenzie (Hampshire), D.J. Insole (Essex), C.A. Milton (Gloucestershire)

6   T.E. Bailey (Essex), E.R. Dexter (Sussex), R.A. Gale (Middlesex), H. Horton (Hampshire), D. Kenyon (Worcestershire), Khalid Ibadulla (Warwickshire)

How out

Caught	745	(63.3%)
Bowled	276	(23.6%0
Lbw	108	(9.2%)
Stumped	39	(3.3%)
Hit wicket	3	(0.3%)
Total	1171	(100.0%)

Most fielding dismissals off Close's bowling (all Yorkshire)

79	Caught and bowled
75 (50 ct 25 st)	J.G. Binks
59	J.V. Wilson
44	P.J. Sharpe
38	F.S. Trueman
33	R. Illingworth
24	D. Wilson
20	J.H. Hampshire, D.E.V. Padgett

500th wicket

J.B. Mortimore c J.V. Wilson b D.B. Close 2, Yorkshire v Gloucestershire, Bristol,
    19 May 1958

1,000th wicket

M.J. Stewart c D.E.V. Padgett b D.B. Close 0, Yorkshire v Surrey, The Oval,
    29 August 1966

FIELDING

Four catches in an innings

Yorkshire v Essex	Harrogate	1961
Yorkshire v Essex	Leyton	1966
Yorkshire v Warwickshire	Middlesbrough	1968
Somerset v Worcestershire	Taunton	1971
Somerset v Warwickshire	Glastonbury	1971

Five catches in a match

Yorkshire v Essex	Harrogate	1961
Yorkshire v Nottinghamshire	Worksop	1966
Somerset v Warwickshire	Glastonbury	1971
Somerset v Glamorgan	Swansea	1974

Players from whose bowling Close took most of his catches (all Yorkshire, unless stated)

101	R. Illingworth
79	D.B. Close, own bowling
79	D. Wilson
75	F.S. Trueman
46	J.H. Wardle
33	T.W. Cartwright (Somerset)
31	A.G. Nicholson

NOTE: In September 1964, playing for T.N. Pearce's XI against Australia, Close deputised as wicket-keeper when Keith Andrew was injured. In the Australians' innings, Close stumped Neil Hawke off the bowling of R. Hobbs for 23.

ALL-ROUND FEATS

A century and five wickets in an innings in the same match (all for Yorkshire)

128 & 6-87	v Somerset	Bath	1959
103 & 5-36	v Somerset	Hull	1961
115 & 5-69	v New Zealanders	Bradford 1965

Two half-centuries and five wickets in an innings in the same match
91 & 58 and 6-38   Yorkshire v Northamptonshire Bradford 1954

A half-century and ten wickets in the same match
61 and 6-55 & 4-19   Yorkshire v Glamorgan   Sheffield 1963

1,000 runs and 100 wickets in the same season

	Runs	Avge	Wkts	Avge
1949	1098	27.45	113	27.87
1952	1192	33.11	114	24.08

TEST CRICKET
BATTING AND FIELDING

In each series

		M	I	NO	Runs	HS	Avge.	50	Ct
1949	New Zealand	1	1	0	0	0	0.00	–	–
1950/51	Australia	1	2	0	1	1	0.50	–	1
1955	South Africa	1	2	0	47	32	23.50	–	–
1957	West Indies	2	3	0	89	42	29.66	–	2
1959	India	1	1	0	27	27	27.00	–	4
1961	Australia	1	2	0	41	33	20.50	–	2
1963	West Indies	5	10	0	315	70	31.50	3	2
1966	West Indies	1	1	0	4	4	4.00	–	1
1967	India	3	4	1	102	47	34.00	–	2
1967	Pakistan	3	5	0	95	41	19.00	–	6
1976	West Indies	3	6	1	166	60	33.20	1	4
	Totals	22	37	2	887	70	25.34	4	24

Against each opponent

	M	I	NO	Runs	HS	Avge.	50	Ct
Australia	2	4	0	42	33	10.50	–	3
India	4	5	1	129	47	32.25	–	6
New Zealand	1	1	0	0	0	0.00	–	–
Pakistan	3	5	0	95	41	19.00	–	6
South Africa	1	2	0	47	32	23.50	–	–
West Indies	11	20	1	574	70	30.21	4	9
Totals	22	37	2	887	70	25.34	4	24

On each ground

	M	I	NO	Runs	HS	Avge.	50	Ct
Birmingham	3	6	0	198	55	33.00	1	1
Leeds	3	4	1	105	56	35.00	1	7
Lord's	5	8	0	264	70	33.00	2	6
Manchester	4	7	0	125	33	17.86	–	3
Nottingham	2	3	1	79	41	39.50	–	4
The Oval	4	7	0	115	46	16.43	–	2
Melbourne	1	2	0	1	1	0.50	–	1
Totals	22	37	2	887	70	25.34	4	24

By batting position

	I	NO	Runs	HS	Avge.	50
2	8	0	140	42	17.50	–
4	4	1	111	60	37.00	1
5	8	0	248	56	31.00	2
6	12	1	319	70	29.00	1
7	4	0	69	32	17.25	–
9	1	0	0	0	0.00	–
Totals	37	2	887	70	25.34	4

Half-centuries

70	v West Indies	Lord's	1963
60	v West Indies	Lord's	1976
56	v West Indies	Leeds	1963
55	v West Indies	Birmingham	1963

Century partnerships

101*	3rd	J.H. Edrich	v West Indies	Nottingham	1976
101	5th	P.J. Sharpe	v West Indies	The Oval	1963

Bowlers with most dismissals of Close

6   C.C. Griffith (West Indies)   3   E.A.S. Prasanna (India)

How out

Caught	23	65.7%
Bowled	5	14.3%
Lbw	5	14.3%
Run Out	1	2.9%
Stumped	1	2.9%
Totals	35	100.0%

BOWLING
In each series

		O	M	R	W	Avge.	Best
1949	New Zealand	42	14	85	1	85.00	1-39
1950/51	Australia	+ 7	1	28	1	28.00	1-20
1957	West Indies	2	1	8	0	–	–
1959	India	16	1	53	5	10.60	4-35
1961	Australia	8	1	33	0	–	–
1963	West Indies	25	5	88	0	–	–
1966	West Indies	12	3	28	1	28.00	1-21
1967	India	60.4	20	144	8	18.00	4-68
1967	Pakistan	27	10	65	2	30.50	1-4
Totals		192.4	55	532	18	29.55	4-35
		+ 7		1			

Against each opponent

	O	M	R	W	Avge.	Best
Australia	8	1	61	1	61.00	1-20
+	7	1				
India	76.4	21.	197	13	15.15	4-35
New Zealand	42	14	85	1	85.00	1-39
Pakistan	27	10	65	2	30.50	1-4
West Indies	39	9	124	1	124.00	1-21
Totals	192.4	55	532	18	29.55	4-35
+	7	1				

On each ground

	O	M	R	W	Avge.	Best
Birmingham	23.4	8	76	4	19.00	4-68
Leeds	40	9	101	7	14.43	4-35
Lord's	38	16	72	2	36.00	2-28
Manchester	60	17	149	1	149.00	1-39
Nottingham	7	1	23	1	23.00	1-11
The Oval	24	4	83	2	41.50	1-4
Melbourne	+ 7	1	28	1	28.00	1-20
Totals	192.4	55	532	18	29.55	4-35
+	7	1				

Best performances

4-35	v India, Leeds	1959
4-68	v India, Birmingham	1967

How out

Caught	16
Lbw	1
Stumped	1
Total	18

ONE-DAY INTERNATIONALS
(All for England v Australia, 1972)

Full career record

M	I	NO	Runs	HS	Avge.	Ct	O	M	R	W
3	3	0	49	43	16.33	1	3	0	21	0

NOTES: Close's highest score was at Lord's.

He was run out in two of the innings and dismissed by D.K. Lillee in the other.

DOMESTIC LIMITED-OVERS MATCHES
BATTING AND FIELDING
In each season

	M	I	NO	Runs	HS	Avge.	100	50	Ct
1963	2	2	1	58	29*	58.00	–	–	–
1964	1	1	0	1	1	1.00	–	–	1
1965	4	4	1	128	79	42.66	–	1	1
1966	1	1	0	29	29	29.00	–	–	–
1967	1	1	0	1	1	1.00	–	–	1
1968	1	1	0	10	10	10.00	–	–	–
1969	12	12	0	263	96	21.92	–	2	8
1970	10	9	0	141	28	15.66	–	–	3
1971	16	15	4	467	89*	43.27	–	3	2
1972	20	20	1	484	88	25.47	–	2	8
1973	18	17	1	313	76	19.56	–	1	6
1974	24	24	0	630	131	26.25	2	–	2
1975	23	21	0	308	55	14.66	–	1	9
1976	19	18	1	391	69	23.00	–	1	8
1977	6	4	1	65	28*	21.66	–	–	2
Totals	158	150	10	3289	131	23.49	2	11	51

For each team

	M	I	NO	Runs	HS	Avge.	100	50	Ct
Yorkshire	32	31	2	631	96	21.76	–	3	14
Somerset	126	119	8	2658	131	24.03	2	8	37
Totals	158	150	10	3289	131	23.49	2	11	51

Against each opponent

	M	I	NO	Runs	HS	Avge.	100	50
Derbyshire	8	7	1	189	89*	31.50	–	1
Essex	8	8	0	128	39	16.00	–	–
Glamorgan	13	11	0	181	36	16.55	–	–
Gloucestershire	14	12	0	326	128	27.17	1	–
Hampshire	13	13	1	288	88	24.00	–	1
Kent	7	7	0	118	32	16.86	–	–
Lancashire	10	10	1	153	46	17.00	–	–
Leicestershire	10	10	1	183	34	20.33	–	–
Middlesex	10	9	1	173	59*	21.63	–	1
Northamptonshire	6	6	1	56	36*	11.20	–	–
Nottinghamshire	7	7	1	159	43	26.50	–	–
Somerset	3	3	0	70	29	23.33	–	–
Surrey	12	12	1	287	96	26.09	–	2
Sussex	9	9	0	122	31	13.55	–	–
Warwickshire	9	8	1	333	76	47.57	–	3
Worcestershire	8	8	0	221	55	27.63	–	2
Yorkshire	5	5	1	260	131	65.00	1	1
Others	6	5	0	42	21	8.40	–	–
Totals	158	150	10	3289	131	23.49	2	11

On certain grounds (qualification – four innings)

	M	I	NO	Runs	HS	Avge.	100	50
Bath	8	8	0	278	131	34.75	1	–
Bradford	5	4	0	76	25	19.00	–	–
Bristol (County Ground)	5	5	0	259	128	51.80	1	–
Bristol (Imperial Ground)	5	4	0	73	46	18.25	–	–
Canterbury	5	5	0	107	32	21.40	–	–
Edgbaston	7	7	1	287	69	47.83	–	3
Leicester	6	6	1	119	34	23.80	–	–
Lord's	9	9	1	219	59*	27.38	–	1
Old Trafford	5	5	1	89	46	22.25	–	–
Taunton	32	29	0	570	55	19.66	–	1
The Oval	4	4	0	121	96	30.25	–	1
Torquay	5	5	1	65	39	16.25	–	–
Yeovil	7	7	0	158	88	22.57	–	1
Total in Somerset	63	58	1	1265	131	22.19	1	2
Total in Yorkshire	15	14	2	288	55*	24.00	–	2
Total Other	80	78	7	1736	128	24.45	1	7
Totals	158	150	10	3289	131	23.49	2	11

NOTE: Of the five games at Torquay, only one was an away match, therefore the remaining four are included as being 'in Somerset'.

In each competition

	M	I	NO	Runs	HS	Avge.	100	50	Ct
Gillette Cup	27	26	2	567	96	23.63	–	3	11
JPL	108	104	7	2278	131	23.48	2	7	36
B & H Cup	23	20	1	444	88	23.37	–	1	4
Totals	158	150	10	3289	131	23.49	2	11	51

Centuries

131	Somerset v Yorkshire	Bath	JPL	1974
128	Somerset v Gloucestershire	Bristol (CG)	JPL	1974

Century partnerships

192	2nd	G. Boycott	Yorkshire v Surrey	Lord's	GC	1965
159	2nd	G. Boycott	Yorkshire v Surrey	The Oval	GC	1969
146	1st	G. Burgess	Somerset v Gloucestershire	Bristol	JPL	1974
111	2nd	B. Leadbeater	Yorkshire v Worcestershire	Headingley	JPL	1969
108	2nd	P.J. Robinson	Somerset v Warwickshire	Edgbaston	JPL	1973
107	4th	J.M. Parks	Somerset v Yorkshire	Bath	JPL	1974
100	3rd	G. Burgess	Somerset v Hampshire	Yeovil	BHC	1972

Bowlers with most dismissals of Close

3 R.E. East (Essex), D.M. Green (Gloucestershire), R.D. Jackman, P.I. Pocock (Surrey), M.A. Nash, D.L. Williams (Glamorgan), P.E. Russell (Derbyshire), P.J. Sainsbury (Hampshire), R.A. White (Nottinghamshire).

How out

Caught	83	59.3%
Bowled	36	25.7%
Lbw	11	7.9%
Run out	7	5.0%
Stumped	3	2.0%
Total	140	100.0%

BOWLING
In each season

	O	M	R	W	Avge.	RpO	4wi	Best
1963	30	3	102	6	17.00	3.40	1	4-60
1964	11	1	35	2	17.50	3.18	–	2-35
1965	17	6	47	2	23.50	2.76	–	1-12
1966	12	6	22	1	22.00	1.83	–	1-22
1967	2	0	8	2	4.00	4.00	–	2-8
1968	12	1	30	0	–	2.50	–	–
1969	48	11	162	7	23.14	3.38	–	3-36
1970	20	3	69	3	23.00	3.45	–	3-27
1971	55	8	206	11	18.73	3.75	–	3-17
1972	66.4	10	273	11	24.82	4.09	–	3-25
1973	96.4	5	440	19	23.16	4.55	1	4- 9
1975	3	0	21	0	–	7.00	–	–
Totals	373.2	54	1415	64	22.11	3.79	2	4- 9

For each team

	O	M	R	W	Avge.	RpO	4wi	Best
Yorkshire	152	31	475	23	20.65	3.13	1	4-60
Somerset	221.2	23	940	41	22.93	4.25	1	4-9
Totals	373.2	54	1415	64	22.11	3.79	2	4-9

Against certain opponents (qualification – five wickets)

	O	M	R	W	Avge.	RpO	4wi	Best
Derbyshire	16	2	62	6	10.33	3.88	–	3-26
Glamorgan	29	1	100	5	20.00	3.45	1	4-9
Gloucestershire	41	5	178	8	22.25	4.34	–	3-59
Surrey	20	3	50	6	8.33	2.50	–	3-27
Sussex	27	5	100	9	11.11	3.70	1	4-60
Others	240.2	38	925	30	30.83	3.85	-	3-25
Totals	373.2	54	1415	64	22.11	3.79	2	4-9

On certain grounds (qualification – five wickets)

	O	M	R	W	Avge.	RpO	4wi	Best
a) In Somerset								
Bath	23.3	5	91	7	13.00	3.87	–	3-17
Bristol (Imperial Ground)	21	1	105	7	15.00	5.00	–	3-45
Taunton	51	14	151	6	25.17	2.96	1	4- 9
Others	26.2	3	102	2	51.00	3.87	–	1-34
b) In Yorkshire								
All grounds	43	4	154	7	22.00	3.58	–	3-27

c) On other UK grounds	O	M	R	W	Avge.	RpO	4wi	Best
Lord's	45	6	161	7	23.00	3.58	–	3-36
Hove	18	2	79	5	15.80	4.39	1	4-60
Others	145.3	19	572	23	24.87	3.93	–	3-26

Summary	O	M	R	W	Avge.	RpO	4wi	Best
In Somerset	121.5	23	449	22	20.41	3.69	1	4- 9
Others	251.3	31	966	42	23.00	3.84	1	4-60
Totals	373.2	54	1415	64	22.11	3.79	2	4- 9

In each competition

	O	M	R	W	Avge.	RpO	4wi	Best
Gillette Cup	147	32	421	24	17.54	2.86	1	4-60
John Player League	167.3	16	754	34	22.18	4.50	1	4- 9
Benson & Hedges Cup	58.5	6	240	6	40.00	4.08	-	3-59
Totals	373.2	54	1415	64	22.11	3.79	2	4- 9

Four wickets in an innings

4-9	Somerset v Glamorgan	Taunton	JPL	1973
4-60	Yorkshire v Sussex	Hove	GC	1963

Batsmen most frequently dismissed

3 M.J. Procter (Gloucestershire)
2 P. Graves, A.W. Greig (Sussex), M.H. Page (Derbyshire), Sadiq Mohammad (Gloucestershire)

Most fielding dismissals off Close's bowling (all Somerset except Binks)

5 M.J. Kitchen, D.J.S. Taylor (3 ct, 2 st)
4 T.W. Cartwright, P.W. Denning, J.G. Binks (2 ct, 2 st)

How out

Caught	53	82.8%
Bowled	7	10.9%
Lbw	4	6.3%
Totals	64	100.0%

FIELDING

Players from whose bowling Close took most of his catches (all Somerset)

7 M.G. Burgess
6 I.T. Botham
4 H.R. Moseley, A.A. Jones

ALL-ROUND FEAT
A half-century and three wickets in a match
89* & 3-26	Somerset v Derbyshire	Ilkeston	JPL	1971

Match awards
96	Yorkshire v Surrey	The Oval	GC	1969
88	Somerset v Hampshire	Yeovil	BHC	1972
69	Somerset v Warwickshire	Edgbaston	GC	1976

CAPTAINCY
RECORD IN FIRST-CLASS CRICKET

	Totals				Totals as percentages		
	P	W	D	L	W	D	L
Yorkshire (County Championship)	169	65	79	25	38.5	46.7	14.8
Yorkshire (Other matches)	31	10	17	4	32.3	54.8	12.9
Somerset (County Championship)	109	34	50	25	31.2	45.9	22.9
Somerset (Other matches)	9	1	5	3	11.1	55.6	33.3
D.H. Robins' XI	12	2	7	3	16.7	58.3	25.0
Other teams	20	8	7	5	40.0	35.0	25.0
Totals	350	120	165	65	34.3	47.1	18.6

Summaries
a) by team

	Totals			Totals as percentages		
	P	W	D	L	W	D	L
Yorkshire	200	75	96	29	37.5	48.0	14.5
Somerset	118	35	55	28	29.7	46.6	23.7
Other teams	32	10	14	8	31.2	43.8	25.0

b) by match-type

	Totals			Totals as percentages		
	P	W	D	L	W	D	L
County Championship	278	99	129	50	35.6	46.4	18.0
Other matches	72	21	36	15	29.2	50.0	20.8

NOTE: Figures for 'Other teams' include one tied match in the 'Drawn' totals.

RECORD IN TEST CRICKET
Close led England in seven Tests, winning six and drawing the other – one against West
Indies (W), three each against India (W3) and Pakistan (W2 D1).

RECORD IN ONE-DAY INTERNATIONALS
Close led England in all three of the games in which he played, winning two and losing
one

RECORD IN DOMESTIC LIMITED-OVERS MATCHES

a)   For each team

	Totals				Totals as percentages		
	P	W	L	NR	W	L	NR
Yorkshire	32	17	13	2	53.1	40.6	6.3
Somerset	110	58	49	3	52.7	44.5	2.7
Totals	142	75	62	5	52.8	43.6	3.5

b)   In each competition

	Totals				Totals as percentages		
	P	W	L	NR	W	L	NR
Gillette Cup	26	15	11	0	57.7	42.3	0.0
John Player League	93	47	41	5	50.5	44.1	5.4
Benson & Hedges Cup	23	13	10	0	56.5	43.5	0.0

NOTE: The No-Result matches include one game, for Somerset in the John Player League, which was tied.

MISCELLANY
BATTING

Highest position in national averages – 25th, 1960.

Highest position in county's Championship averages:
>   Yorkshire – 2nd, 1958, 1960, 1962, 1963, 1966, 1967
>   Somerset – 1st, 1971, 1973

Highest run aggregate for county: Yorkshire – 1958, 1960
>   Somerset – 1972, 1973, 1975

Scored a century in his first first-class innings in Australia – 108* MCC v Western Australia, Perth, 1950/51

Did not score a century in the County Championship until his 136th innings – Yorkshire v Somerset, Taunton, 1955, co-incidentally this occurring in his 136th first-class match.

Holds the record career aggregate of first-class runs (34,994) not to contain a double-century (HS 198). Has also batted for the greatest number of innings without scoring a double-century – Close's 1225 innings being well ahead of Arthur Milton's 1078 (highest score 170).

Scored 1000 runs in debut season and remains the second-youngest to complete this feat after Dennis Compton.

Close and Geoff Boycott are the only two Yorkshire players to have scored over 1000 runs against each of the other (then) 16 first-class counties. Close, however, did not score all of his runs for Yorkshire.

As the following table shows, Close also features very high amongst Yorkshire's batsmen in the post-war era.

Most runs for Yorkshire in Championship by entirely post-1945 players

		Inns	NO	Runs	HS	Avge.	100
G. Boycott	1962–86	607	101	29485	260*	58.27	94
J.H. Hampshire	1961–81	654	83	19548	183*	34.23	31
D.B. Close	1949–70	683	83	18421	198	30.70	24
M.D. Moxon	1981–97	443	38	16905	274*	41.74	32
D.E.V. Padgett	1951–71	648	61	16860	146	28.72	26

BOWLING

Highest position in national averages – 49th, 1954

Highest position in county's Championship averages: Yorkshire 4th, 1954
Somerset 2nd, 1974

Highest wicket aggregate for county: Yorkshire – 1st, 1949
Somerset – 5th, 1975

One hundred wickets in debut season since 1945

		Age	Year	Wkts	Avge
C. Cook	Gloucestershire	24	1946	133	18.62
D.B. Close	Yorkshire	18	1949	113	27.87
D.L. Underwood	Kent	17	1963	101	21.12

NOTE: The feat was completed on eight occasions before 1940

FIELDING
Most catches in first-class cricket

		Catches
F.E. Woolley	1906–38	1018
W.G. Grace	1865–1908	874
G.A.R. Lock	1946–70/71	831
W.R. Hammond	1920–51	819
D.B. Close	1949–86	813

NOTE: The only other player to pass 700 catches in a post-1945 career is Arthur Milton (758).

Highest position in national 'most catches in a season' tables: 2nd – 1966; 2nd = 1971

ALL-ROUND FEATS
Close is the youngest cricketer to complete the double of 1,000 runs and 100 wickets in a season. He is also the only cricketer to complete the feat in his debut season.

30,000 runs and 1,000 wickets in first-class cricket

			Runs	Avge	Wkts	Avge
D.B. Close	Yorkshire/Somerset	1949–86	34994	33.26	1171	26.42
W.G. Grace	Gloucestershire	1865–1908	54896	39.55	2876	17.92
J.W. Hearne	Middlesex	1909–36	37252	40.98	1839	24.42
G.H. Hirst	Yorkshire	1891–1929	36323	34.13	2739	18.72
Jas. Langridge	Sussex	1924–53	31716	35.20	1530	22.56
W. Rhodes	Yorkshire	1898–1930	39802	30.82	4187	16.71

CAPTAINCY
Personal performance

	BATTING				BOWLING			
	As team member		As captain		As team member		As captain	
	Runs	Avge	Runs	Avge	Wkts	Avge	Wkts	Avge
Yorkshire	14605	31.96	8045	31.92	709	24.44	258	23.87
Somerset	1334	46.00	6233	38.24	4	22.75	70	35.64
Others	2747	35.68	1143	29.31	85	37.55	27	42.59
England (Tests)	686	26.38	201	22.33	7	42.14	11	21.54
Totals	19372	32.89	15622	33.74	805	25.97	366	27.43

England Test captains with no defeats (minimum five Tests)

			W	D	Total
F.S. Jackson	1905	Australia	2	3	5
C.B. Fry	1912	Australia (3), South Africa (3)	4	2	6
A.W. Carr	1926 (4), 1929 (2)	Australia (4), South Africa (2)	1	5	6
F.G. Mann	1948/49 (5), 1949 (2)	South Africa (5), New Zealand (2)	2	5	7
D.B. Close	1966 (1), 1967 (6)	West Indies (1), India (3), Pakistan (3)	6	1	7

NOTE: Close was the last Yorkshire captain to lead England in a Test at Headingley.

Longest-serving county captains since 1946

15 seasons	M.C. Cowdrey	Kent	1957–71
14 season	D.B. Close	Yorkshire (8) & Somerset (6)	1963–70 & 1972–77
13 seasons	K.J. Barnett	Derbyshire	1983–95
13 seasons	K.W.R. Fletcher	Essex	1974–85 & 1988

Yorkshire captains winning three consecutive Championships

Lord Hawke 1900–02   G. Wilson 1922–24   A.B. Sellers 1937–39
D.B. Close   1966–68

NOTES: Close led Yorkshire to four Championships in total, this being beaten only by Hawke (eight) and Sellers (six). Close also led the county to two Gillette Cup victories – in 1965 and 1969, these being the country's only such triumphs in the first 39 years of the competition's history. His highest Championship position with Somerset was 4th in 1977 (his final season); he took the county to runners-up spot in the John Player League in 1974 and the team also reached the semi-finals of both the Gillette Cup and Benson & Hedges Cup in the same season. Another Gillette Cup semi-final appearance was achieved in 1977.

Oldest England captains in one-day internationals

N. Gifford	v Pakistan	Sharjah	1985	44 years 361 days
D.B. Close	v Australia	Birmingham	1972	41 years 186 days

APPEARANCES AND AGE

Played in all county's first-class games in 1964 (33 for Yorkshire) and 1971 (25 for Somerset).

Played in at least one first-class match against each of the first eight touring New Zealand teams to visit England since 1945.

Close's total of 786 first-class appearances has been surpassed only by Fred Titmus (792) and Ray Illingworth (787) of players whose careers began after 1945.

Close and Titmus are the only two players to have played first-class cricket in each of five different decades since 1945.

Close made at least one appearance in first-class cricket in 30 consecutive seasons – another record for a post-1945 player and beaten by only four players before that date.

Oldest Players in First-Class Cricket in England since 1945

	Date of birth	Final match	Last day	Age
D.H. Robins	27/06/1914	D.H. Robins' XI v Indians	02/07/1971	57 years 5 days
H. Elliott	02/11/1891	Derbyshire v Warwickshire	05/08/1947	55 years 276 days
D.B. Close	24/02/1931	D.B. Close's XI v New Zealanders	02/09/1986	55 years 190 days

NOTE: Close's career lasted for 37 years and 115 days and this is the longest of any player whose career began after 1900.

Fewest days between Championship and Test Debuts by English Professionals since 1919

	Days	Matches	Championship Debut	Test Debut
A.V. Bedser	35	7	Surrey v Somerset, The Oval, 18/5/1946	v India, Lord's, 22/6/1946
D.B. Close	66	14	Yorkshire v Somerset, Wells, 18/5/1949	v New Zealand, Old Trafford, 23/7/1949
R.K.J. Dawson	158	9	Yorkshire v Leicestershire, Headingley, 29/6/2001	v India, Mohali, 3/12/2001

At 18 years and 149 days, Close remains England's youngest Test player. He is the youngest player to represent England against Australia and the youngest to play for England in Australia.

At 45 years and 140 days, Close remains England's oldest Test cricketer since 1945 except for Gubby Allen, who was 105 days older on the occasion of his last Test in West Indies in 1948.

Longest Test careers

		Debut	Last Day	Length
W. Rhodes	England	01/06/1899	12/04/1930	30 years 315 days
D.B. Close	England	23/07/1949	13/07/1976	26 years 355 days
F.E. Woolley	England	11/08/1909	22/08/1934	25 years 13 days
G.A. Headley	West Indies	11/01/1930	21/01/1954	24 years 10 days

Most Tests missed between consecutive appearances

			From	To	
104	Younis Ahmed	Pakistan	02/11/69	21/02/87	17 years 111 days
103	D. Shackleton	England	07/11/51	20/06/63	11 years 225 days
96	H.L. Jackson	England	26/07/49	06/07/61	11 years 346 days
86	P.I. Pocock	England	13/07/76	26/07/84	8 years 13 days
79	K.V. Andrew	England	01/12/54	06/06/63	8 years 187 days
74	D.B. Close	England	28/08/67	03/06/76	8 years 280 days

NOTES: The record for the longest gap in terms of time by an England player is 16 years, 315 days by G. Gunn between 1911/12 and 1929/30.

Close missed selection for 154 Tests between the first and last of his 22.

COINCIDENCES

Close's first Championship game for Yorkshire was against Somerset. His last Championship game for Yorkshire was against Somerset.

Close's first Championship century was against Somerset. He scored a century in his first match for Somerset. He also scored a century in his first match for Somerset against Yorkshire.

Close's first Test match was at Old Trafford. His last Test match was at Old Trafford.

ACKNOWLEDGEMENTS

Byron Denning, Scorer, and Andrew Hignell, Statistician, Glamorgan CCC.
Gerry Stickley, Scorer, Somerset CCC.
Peter Wynne-Thomas, Librarian, Nottinghamshire CCC.

Bibliography

John Arlott: *The Australian Challenge, 1961* (Heinemann, 1961; with Patrick Eagar: *Botham* (The Kingswood Press, 1985).

J. S. Barker: *Summer Spectacular – The West Indies in England* (Collins, 1963).

C. J. Bartlett: *Brian Close – His Record Innings by Innings* (The Association of Cricket Statisticians and Historian.

Geoffrey Boycott: *The Autobiography* (Macmillan, 1987).

Richie Benaud, *A Tale of Two Tests, 1962* (Hodder & Stoughton, 1962).

Mike Brearley: *The Art of Captaincy* (Hodder & Stoughton, 1985).

Bill Bowes: *Aussies and Ashes* (Stanley Paul, 1961)

Brian Close: *I Don't Bruise Easily* (Macdonald & Jane's, 1978).

Colin Cowdrey: *MCC – The Autobiography of a Cricketer* (Hodder & Stoughton, 1976).

David Foot: *Sunshine, Cricket and Cider – History of Somerset* (David & Charles, 1981); *Fragments of Idolatry* (Fairfield Books, 2001).

Charles Fortune: *The Australians in England, 1961* (Robert Hale, 1961).

Alan Gibson: *The Cricket Captains of England* (Pavilion Books, 1989).

Alan Hill: *A Chain of Spin Wizards* (Kennedy Brothers Publishing, 1983); *Johnny Wardle – Cricket Conjuror* (David & Charles, 1988); *Bill Edrich* (Andre Deutsch, 1994); *Peter May* (Andre Deutsch, 1996).

Derek Hodgson; *The Official History of Yorkshire County Cricket Club* (The Crowood Press, 1989).

J. M. Kilburn: *The Scarborough Cricket Festival* (Scarborough CC, 1948).

Rachel O'Connor/Geoff Cope: *Yeadon CC 125th Anniversary Brochure* (1984); *Airedale Junior Cricket League – Golden Jubilee brochure* (1939–1989).

R. A. Roberts: *The Fight for the Ashes, 1961* (George G. Harrap, 1961).

Peter Roebuck; *Tangled Up In White* (Hodder & Stoughton, 1992).
Alan Ross: *The West Indies at Lord's* (Eyre & Spottiswoode, 1963).
Peter Walker; *Cricket Conversations* (Pelham Books, 1978).

Newspaper and magazine reports from the *Yorkshire Post, Yorkshire Evening Post, Yorkshire Evening News, Scarborough Evening News, Bradford Telegraph & Argus, Daily Telegraph, Daily Express, News Chronicle, Guardian, Sunday Times, Observer, Sporting Mirror, Somerset County Gazette, Sydney Morning Herald, The Cricketer, Playfair Cricket Monthly* and various editions of *Wisden Cricketers' Almanack* and *Yorkshire CCC Year Books* have provided the nucleus of contemporary printed sources.

Index